ARCHITECTURES OF KNOWLEDGE

Architectures of Knowledge

Firms, Capabilities, and Communities

ASH AMIN AND PATRICK COHENDET

OXFORD

UNIVERSITY PRESS

OXFORD
UNIVERSITY PRESS

Great Clarendon Street, Oxford OX2 6DP

Oxford University Press is a department of the University of Oxford.
It furthers the University's objective of excellence in research, scholarship,
and education by publishing worldwide in

Oxford New York

Auckland Bangkok Buenos Aires Cape Town Chennai
Dar es Salaam Delhi Hong Kong Istanbul Karachi Kolkata
Kuala Lumpur Madrid Melbourne Mexico City Mumbai Nairobi
São Paulo Shanghai Taipei Tokyo Toronto

Oxford is a registered trade mark of Oxford University Press
in the UK and in certain other countries

Published in the United States
by Oxford University Press Inc., New York

British Library Cataloguing in Publication Data

Data available

Library of Congress Cataloging in Publication Data
Amin, Ash.
Architectures of knowledge : firms, capabilities, and communities / Ash Amin
and Patrick Cohendet.
p. cm.
Includes bibliographical references and index.
1. Knowledge management. 2. Managerial economics. 3. Economics—Sociological
aspects. 4. Economic geography. 5. Corporations. I. Cohendet, Patrick. II. Title.
HD30.2.A434 2003 306.3—dc22 2003065259

ISBN 0–19–925332–3 (hbk)
ISBN 0–19–925333–1 (pbk) *//58*

1 3 5 7 9 10 8 6 4 2

Typeset by Newgen Imaging Systems (P) Ltd, Chennai, India
Printed in Great Britain
on acid-free paper by
T. J. International Ltd., Padstow, Cornwall

For Lynne and Lucy
and our children
Usha, Sami, and Isla; Muriel and Laura
who taught us about learning through everyday enactment

Acknowledgements

We would like to thank Michel Callon, Bruce Kogut, Ray Hudson, Gernot Grabher, Patrick Llerena, and Philippe Lorino for taking the trouble to read through the whole draft manuscript and offering razor-sharp comment and suggestions for improvement. Similarly, we thank Emma Mawdsley and Colin MacFarlane for agreeing to look at the language and the flow of the text at such short notice. Then, our special gratitude to Monique Flasaquier and Niamh McElherron for helping so assiduously to put together the final typescript. We owe Anna Grandori a lot for bringing us together a few years ago through the EMOT Programme of the European Science Foundation, and also David Musson at OUP for encouraging us to work together and for seeing through this project and making it such a pleasant publishing experience. Finally, we thank Hilary Walford for copy-editing the book to such an exceptionally high standard.

Ash Amin would like to thank Nigel Thrift, a long-standing collaborator whose intellectual vitality and generosity never cease to amaze—on this occasion, through his suggestions on the value of seeing learning as an embodied and non-cognitive practice. He is also grateful to Michael Storper, Meric Gertler, Anders Malmerg, Peter Maskell, Annalee Saxenian, and Kevin Morgan, for their original work on how place matters in the innovation process, his (ex) Ph.D. students Tanya Gray and Jong-Ho Lee for constantly surprising him with new reading material. His thanks also go to the Swedish Collegium for Advanced Study in the Social Sciences in Uppsala for a Fellowship in 1999, when some of this work was initiated, but especially the Department of Geography at Durham University for study leave in 2001, when most of the research and writing for this book was done. Finally, his thanks to Peter Atkins for creating the time and space at Durham to allow him to finish the book.

Patrick Cohendet wishes to thank: Fernand Amesse and Patrick Llerena for day-to-day interactions and discussions; the 'community' of communities at BETA, Arman Avadykian, Antoine Bureth, Frederic Creplet, Olivier Dupouët, Morad Diani, Francis Kern, Christophe Lerch, Julien Pénin, and Eric Schenk, with whom he had and will continue to have long conversations discussing the fundamental concepts behind communities; Bernard Ancori, Laurent Bach, Jean Alain Héraud, Dominique Foray, Ed Steinmueller, Pierre Benoit Joly, Murat Yildizoglu, Jacques Mairesse, Frieder Mayer-Krahmer, and Francis Munier, with whom he has co-authored in recent years some of the papers that inspired parts of this book; Paul David, Franco Malerba, Robin Cowan, Richard Nelson, Sidney Winter, Giovanni Dosi, Keith Pavitt, Jean Benoit Zimmermann, and Alan Kirman, for reactions, ideas suggested during research projects, or seminars that deeply inspired the work; and Martyne Cimon for technical assistance on the book.

Contents

List of Figures

List of Boxes

Introduction

Since the early 1980s there has been intense research on innovative firms and their use of knowledge. Many insights have emerged, stressing, *inter alia*, the key role of competences and the absorptive capacities of firms, or the significance of alignment of knowledge practices and their translation in actor networks. This research has demonstrated that knowledge is not of a homogeneous nature, but is fundamentally a heterogeneous resource that must be appreciated in its different manifestations (for example, codified versus tacit, individual versus collective, specialized versus general, and so on). Out of this sensibility has grown the view that sparks of innovation emerge through the interplay of different forms of heterogeneous knowledge: their confrontation, combination, fusion, transformation. Something has to happen between at least two different forms of knowledge in order to trigger the generation of novelty.

Accordingly, in the 1980s, research on organizational learning inspired by the pioneering work of Argyris and Schön (1978) argued that the capacity to innovate depended on the ability of organizations to bridge individual and collective forms of knowledge. It claimed that new knowledge and learning were developed by individuals, while organizations played a critical role in articulating and amplifying such knowledge and learning at the collective level. In particular, it argued that innovation required specific cognitive mechanisms in order to channel individual learning to the collective level in an organization—for example, 'cognitive maps' such as organigrams.

In the 1990s a step forward was made following the work of Nonaka and Takeuchi (1995), who argued that the secret of the knowledge-creating company resided in its capacity to master the different modes of conversion of tacit and codified forms of knowledge. In their model, innovation is predicated on a continuous dialogue between tacit and codified knowledge. Nonaka and Tekeuchi's work, inspired in part by Michael Polanyi, opened a new seam of research stressing the dynamic aspect of organizational knowledge-creating processes. This seam did not reject the organizational-learning approach, but sought to integrate it in its representation of the creative company. The 'spiral model' of knowledge creation proposed by Nonaka and Takeuchi inherently combined the 'epistemological' dimension of knowledge (interaction between the tacit and codified form) and the 'ontological' dimension of knowledge (interactions between individual and collective knowledge).

Without denying the importance and salience of these two lines of research, this book argues, along with scholars who have pioneered work on learning in communities, that the time is right for research to explore the relationship between two other dimensions of knowledge in order to explain the innovative performance of firms: between knowledge that is 'possessed' (in different parts of the firm such as a functional unit, a department, a group of experts in a given domain); and knowledge that is 'practised' (processes of 'knowing'), generally within *communities* of like-minded employees in a firm. Indeed, recently, Cook and Brown (1999: 381) have suggested the true spark of innovation lies in the 'generative dance between possessed and practised knowledge'.

This book can be considered as a response to the invitation to explore this generative dance, to understand the interplay between the knowledge that firms possess in the form of established competences or stored memory and the knowing that occurs through the daily interactions and practices of distributed communities of actors. We share the view that, in this dance, movement and the rhythm are given by the 'knowing partner'—that is, by the interactions within and between communities that develop the practised knowledge. If we accept that knowledge is progressively built through the conscious and unconscious acts of social interaction, knowledge is *in primis* the preserve of those groups of actants (minds, bodies, machines, formulae, codes, and so on) that are aligned together in a joint venture and in common routines. Our focus falls on the role and importance of these communities in the generation of novelty, and on the governance challenges posed (for example, how organizations amplify the local practices of knowing and make them coherent with the accumulated knowledge of the organization).

Why, it might be asked, is it necessary to open this new avenue of research on the interplay between knowledge and knowing at this moment in time? The answer can in part be related to the dynamics of the hotly debated knowledge-based economy. It might be argued that, as the need constantly to generate new knowledge becomes a key factor in global economic competitiveness, and as the social base of education and learning increasingly widens, the traditional boundary between knowledge specialists and so-called lay groups or employees and organizations is breaking down, with knowledge becoming increasingly packaged in bundles of specialization and collaboration distributed across the social and economic spectrum (Nowotny, Scott, and Gibbons 2001). One implication is that the process of generation, accumulation, and distribution of knowledge is achieved through the functioning of communities of actors who share similar practices. If this is indeed the case, a new governance problem arises, concerning how the division of work (which distributes functions and duties between actors) and the division of knowledge (which distributes the capacity of interpretation and learning between these actors) within firms can be aligned.

It could be hypothesized, for example, that only in very stable environments, where it is proven that the most efficient organizational forms are hierarchical structures that bring together specialized units of (possessed) knowledge, does the division of work coincide with the division of knowledge. The division of work generates a division of (specialized) knowledge, and, in turn, each unit of specialized knowledge becomes the most suitable base for the division of work. But, as the competitive environment becomes more turbulent, as is the case in the contemporary economy, and as the generation of new knowledge becomes ever more pressing, the prime challenge of the firm ceases to be that of ensuring the coordination of existing bodies of knowledge. Instead, it becomes that of delicately matching the architecture of work with an always unstable architecture of knowledge that draws on the continuously changing capacity of interpretation among actors. Such an architecture of knowledge is in conflict with a division of work that tries to separate the capacities of specialized knowledge, thus posing as a central problem to firms the challenge of how the architecture of knowing can be reconciled to the architecture of possessed knowledge.

In this book, we approach these questions concerning, first, the dynamics of innovating/learning through practices of knowing, and, second, the management of the interface between transactional and knowledge imperatives, in a cross-disciplinary manner. Or, more accurately, the book represents the strange but fruitful encounter between, on the one hand, a socio-spatial theorist interested in the spatial aspects of organizational learning and convinced by the powers of knowing through the 'cognitive unconsciousness', and, on the other hand, an economist, educated in the paradigm of 'knowledge as a stock of information' (a primitive form of possessed knowledge according to Cook and Brown), but convinced that the building of competences and routines calls for a radical reconsideration of the theory of the firm. Underpinned by a strong friendship and a long record of collaboration, the dialogue was not always trouble-free between the economist who gave weight to the degree of rationality of actors and the nature of incentives offered, and the geographer who gave weight to the non-conscious and relational practices of people (and things) in day-to-day interactions. The book results from the delicate interplay between these two distant theoretical positions, which started out as two different epistemologies, but which progressively converged towards what we hope is a novel vision. This generative dance was a unique occasion to try to bring together the different streams of literature on organizational knowledge, and to explore the tensions and challenges thrown up by the confrontation.

1

Placing Knowledge

Knowledge has become the buzzword in theories of the firm and in explanations of corporate competitiveness. A polyphony of voices from various fields and disciplines (including organizational sciences, sociology of organization, social anthropology of learning, evolutionary economics, economic history, economic geography, theories of conventions, cognitive psychology, and competence- or resource-based approaches to strategy) has grown, insisting that knowledge plays a key role in the *raison d'être*, definition, functioning, and performance of firms. But, as the polyphony has got louder, so too has the desire for clarity both about the precise nature of this role, and about what firms can do to enhance knowledge-based competition. This has been fuelled by various prophecies of knowledge capitalism speculating on the centrality of 'weightless' transactions, reflexivity and education, design and creativity, ICT, learning, adaptation and organizational flexibility, and knowledge workers and entrepreneurs, in the new economy of fast, volatile, and high-value competition (Drucker 1993; Burton-Jones 1999; Leadbeater 1999).

Firms, we are told, will face mounting pressure to explore new knowledge or exploit existing knowledge, to become 'learning organizations', to maximize innovation and creativity, to become light-footed and adaptable. But how should they respond? Should they focus on core competences, develop new ones, evolve existing routines? Should they create new knowledge or apply what is already known? Should they invest in R&D, ICTs, codified knowledge, new project teams? Should they focus on tacit knowledge, embedded skills, learning in doing, and continual training? Should they concentrate on aligning and coordinating knowledge distributed around and beyond the firm in supply chains? Should they manage knowledge more centrally, or experiment with temporary coalitions, heterarchical structures, and decentralized knowledge management?

The aim of this book is certainly not to collect the new voices into an impossible compromise between conceptually and epistemologically incompatible positions in order unambiguously to answer all the above questions. Our objective, instead, is to develop a specific vision of knowledge practices in firms, by broadening the existing understanding of what people know and do in organizations (more precisely by bridging *knowledge* and *knowing* as it will be explained later in this chapter). This we do in order to arrive at a *reasonable* understanding of the mechanisms that drive the formation, accumulation, and circulation of knowledge within organizations. Our objective is, first, to clarify the theoretical debates on the production and use of knowledge in organizations, and, second, to tease out the challenges that face those managing knowledge at different levels of the organization.

To help us contextualize our vision and its specific nuances, we begin with the multitude of new voices, first underlining what they have in common and then highlighting what we consider to be the main differences among them. Behind the dissonance that underlies different schools of thought, in the new approaches to knowledge in firms, a clear convergence of view on some fundamental traits is discernible.

APPROACHES TO KNOWLEDGE

Firstly, firms are no longer viewed merely as machines of transactional efficiency, bureaucratic order, or labour exploitation. They are seen as repositories of competences, knowledge, and creativity, as sites of invention, innovation, and learning. In their seminal appeal for an organizational foundation to the theory of the firm, Kogut and Zander (1992: 383) claim:

In contrast to a perspective based on the failure to align incentives in a market as an explanation for the firm, we began with the view that firms are repositories of capabilities, as determined by the social knowledge embedded in enduring individual relationships structured by organizing principles.

Fransman (1994) has interpreted this critical change as a shift from firms conceived as pure 'processors of information' to firms conceived as 'processors of knowledge'. Viewing the firm as a processor of information has led to an understanding of the constitution and behaviour of the firm as a pure optimal reaction to external signs and factors (market prices) that are detected by the firm. The focus is on the process of allocation of resources needed to cope with such adaptation. Viewing the firm as a processor of knowledge—that is, as a locus of construction, selection, usage, and development of knowledge—leads to the recognition that cognitive mechanisms are essential, and that routines play a major role in maintaining the internal coherence of the organization. These theories focus on the processes of knowledge creation.

Secondly, different forms of knowledge have been identified. Knowledge is viewed fundamentally as a heterogeneous resource that firms value in different manifestations. The main types of knowledge distinguished in the literature are: explicit knowledge (knowledge that can be spelled out or formalized) versus tacit knowledge (knowledge that is associated with skills or know-how), and individual knowledge versus collective knowledge. But this is as far as the consensus goes, for a major source of difference between the competing approaches concerns the emphasis placed on each type of knowledge. Several approaches in economics, for instance, consider that knowledge is essentially explicit and held by individuals; while, at the other extreme (sociology of innovation, for instance), knowledge is understood as essentially tacit and of a collective nature. More recently, new dimensions in the categorization of types of knowledge have been introduced, such as 'general knowledge' versus 'specific knowledge', or 'possessed knowledge' versus 'practised knowledge'.

Thirdly, there is agreement in the literature that each type of knowledge can be associated with a distinctive aspect or imperative of learning in a firm. This has important interpretative implications, since the specific type of knowledge emphasized leads to a particular account of the learning processes at stake in the organization, and, in turn, of the most appropriate governance solutions. Thus, it is generally accepted that the 'cognitive architecture' of knowledge within the firm (the way knowledge is produced, stored, exchanged, transmitted, retrieved) strongly influences the process of organizational learning, and, in turn, the nature of the organization itself. Box 1.1 shows how, according to one account (Blackler 2002), five different types of knowledge lead to distinct forms of learning and specific types of organization.

Box 1.1. *A typology of knowledge and organizational learning*

Blackler (2002) distinguishes five types of knowledge in the literature, each suggesting a different aspect of learning in a firm:

- Literature on *embrained* knowledge, dependent on conceptual skills and cognitive abilities, which identifies the firm's 'mindset' or corporate rationality as a key influence on learning potential and adaptive capability. One example is Argyris and Schön's classic distinction (1978) between 'single-loop' learning based on a rule-following or problem-solving rationality, and 'double-loop' learning based on a rule-setting or problem-seeking rationality.
- Literature on *embodied* knowledge, which emphasizes practical thinking rooted in specific contexts, people's physical presence, sentient and sensory information, material objects, and learning in doing. Such knowledge is action oriented and is mostly tacit.
- Literature on *encultured* knowledge, emphasizing meanings and shared understandings arising from socialization and acculturation, with factors such as language, stories, sociality, and metaphors identified as mainsprings of knowledge.
- Literature on *embedded* knowledge, emphasizing the work of systemic routines, shaped by stable relationships in organizational routines, technological regimes, competence and skill parameters, and interpersonal behaviour.
- Literature on *encoded* knowledge, embedded in signs and symbols to be found in traditional forms such as books, manuals, codes of practice, and new forms such as electronically mediated information technologies.

According to Blackler, four distinct types of knowledge organization can be deduced from these varied literatures on knowledge.

(continued)

Box 1.1. *(continued)*

➤ FOCUS ON FAMILIAR PROBLEMS

1. **Knowledge-routinized organizations**

   Centrality of *embedded* knowledge routines
   - technologies, rules, and procedures
   - division of labour and control
   - skill requirements

   Governance issues
   - organizational competences and corporate strategies
   - computer-aided work systems

2. **Expert-dependent organizations**

   Centrality of *embodied* competences of key personnel
   - performance of specialist experts
   - status and power gained from professional reputation
   - key importance of training and qualifications

   Governance issues
   - nature and development of individual competences
   - computer-interface with action skills

➤ FOCUS ON NOVEL PROBLEMS

3. **Communication-intensive organizations**

   Centrality of *encultured* knowledge
   - communication and collaboration as key processes
   - empowerment through integration
   - pervasive expertise

   Governance issues
   - 'knowledge-creation', dialogue, sense making processes
   - computer-supported cooperative work systems

4. **Symbolic analyst-dependent organizations**

   Centrality of *embrained* skills of key personnel
   - entrepreneurial problem solving
   - status and power gained from creative achievements
   - symbolic manipulation as key skill

   Governance issues
   - developing symbolic analysts
   - information support and expert systems design

Source: Adapted from Blackler (2002)

Fourthly, there is growing recognition that the process of production and circulation of knowledge within the firm is a key determinant of the capability of firms to innovate (Kogut and Zander 1992, 1996; Nonaka and Takeuchi 1995; Krogh, Roos, and Kleine 1998; Choo and Bontis 2002). More precisely, there is a growing consensus that the spark of innovation is the interplay of different types of knowledge. For example, Nonaka and Takeuchi's vision (1995), is based on the idea that knowledge emerges out of a dialogue between people's tacit and explicit knowledge. They emphasize the interplay of different types of knowledge along two main dimensions: the 'epistemological dimension', centred around the critical assumption that human knowledge is created and expanded through social interaction between tacit knowledge and codified or explicit knowledge ('knowledge conversion'), and the 'ontological dimension', which is concerned with the interaction of knowledge held at different levels (individual, group, organizational, and inter-organizational).

Having outlined the new approaches, we can now summarize the fundamental differences between the different approaches concerning knowledge in firms. As we have already noted, the polyphony of voices on the role of knowledge is partly the product of differences in the literature on what counts as effective knowledge in the context of corporate learning and innovation. The varying perspectives can be grouped into three main theoretical approaches: the *strategic-management approach*, the *evolutionary-economic approach*, and the *social-anthropology-of-learning approach*. We are fully aware that reducing a multitude of nuances to three schools of thought introduces many risks of simplification and misrepresentation. However, we believe that there is some value in presenting these approaches as 'flag-bearers' of common theoretical assumptions. The three approaches can be summarized along the following lines:

- The *strategic-management approach* is typified by Prahalad and Hamel's early notion (1990) of core competences in the corporation, but also overlaps with the resource-based view (RBV) of the firm. In this approach, corporate performance is tied to corporate design. The firm's structure, procedures, and environment dictate performance, over and above the behaviour of the individuals in various roles in the organization. This stream of research privileges the governance philosophy of *management by design*— that is, managers deciding on how knowledge should be managed in the organization. They manage, under the constraint of limited attention (the rare resource), the core domain of the corporation, and try to align knowledge activities in the directions they envision. They establish an environment that encourages learning in order to reinforce and stimulate the competences accumulated.
- The *evolutionary-economics approach* is based on the seminal work of Nelson and Winter (1982). This approach views the firm as a repository of knowledge embodied in the routines of the organization. The evolutionary approach is a hybrid theory that includes the fundamental principles of any evolutionary theory—including the principle of heredity played by routines,

the principle of generation of variety, and the principle of selection—and an emphasis upon routines as the key collective organizational device for cognition. Organizational routines are considered the building blocks of the core dynamic capability that expresses the firm's ability to integrate, build, and reconfigure internal and external competences to address rapidly changing environments. In contrast to the strategic-management approach, the evolutionary approach does not privilege any particular cognitive role for the manager. Cognitive effort is considered to be shared by all members of the firm.

- The *social-anthropology-of-learning approach* is inspired by the work of Lave and Wenger (1991) and Brown and Duguid (1991). This approach centres its interest in the actual process of how knowledge is formed and made explicit through social interaction. The emphasis is on the working community as an active entity of knowing, which reveals specific forms of knowledge through its daily practices. Knowing is harnessed to the sociology of interpersonal and collective relations in firms, influenced by factors such as trust and reciprocity, corporate narratives, languages of communication, and socialization strategies. This approach favours organizing for learning *in* doing, in both an experimental and a path-dependent nature, and is based on working the social dynamics of communities and organizational cultures.

These three approaches are rooted in very different understandings of knowledge. Firstly, they vary in terms of the entity that activates, nurtures, stores, and develops knowledge. In the strategic-management approach, the focus is on managers as the sole individuals with a clear cognitive activity. In the evolutionary approach, the focus is on individuals and the way they come to collective coordination schemes (routines) through their cognitive activities. In the anthropology-of-learning approach, the focus is on community as the elementary locus of formation and generation of knowledge emerging from the daily practices of social interaction (including workers on the line who seem to have been forgotten in the literature as key agents of learning and innovation).

Secondly, they differ in their identification of the learning mechanisms at stake. In the strategic-management approach, the focus is on the ways managers can stimulate and integrate learning mechanisms in process at different levels of the firm. In the evolutionary approach, the focus is on two main learning mechanisms—searching, and trial and error—and the ways in which they interact with existing routines. In the anthropology-of-knowledge approach, the focus is on the peripherally practised learning mechanism (Lave and Wenger 1991) that aligns individuals to the functioning of a given community as a working body. The differences can extend to meanings of core concepts. For example, in the strategic-management approach, competence refers to a global strategic asset that is difficult to imitate. In the evolutionary approach, competence results from a subset of efficient routines in the firm. In the anthropology-of-knowledge approach, a given community is seen as encapsulating a competence, based on common skills, interests, or projects, and the firm's knowledge base is seen to be widely distributed amongst different communities of practice.

Thirdly, the three approaches are at odds, as already implied in Box 1.1, in their discussion of knowledge governance. In the strategic-management approach, by definition, the focus is on an existing hierarchy that permanently designs the frontiers of the firm (for example, choices of mergers, acquisitions, cooperative agreements) and establishes clear vertical devices to control and coordinate activities within the firm for both transactional and knowledge purposes. In the evolutionary approach, the management of knowledge results from the coordination of the interplay between routines and the selection mechanism of the market, affecting the balance between encouraging exploitation of existing routines and exploration of new ones. In the anthropology-of-learning approach, the imperative lies in making communities work, aligning distributed knowledge and different types of knowledge, and reconciling learning in doing with other forms of knowledge generation.

Fourthly, as a consequence, they place different emphases on incentives mechanisms to stimulate learning and innovation (that is, on mechanisms that hold the firm together and give it coherence as a knowledge entity). In the strategic-management approach, the manager is in charge of the definition and distribution of (extrinsic) incentive mechanisms such as salary bonuses or non-monetary rewards to align knowledge activities in the perspective he or she decides to promote. In the evolutionary approach, the incentives are encapsulated in the routines—'routines as truces amongst conflicts', as Nelson and Winter (1982) have emphasized, or attempts to routinize novelty. In the anthropology-of-knowledge approach, there is by definition no need for external incentives to stimulate knowledge at work. What holds the community together is respect for the social norms of the community by the members of the community, and, if incentives are used, they are in support of enculturation, not knowledge formation as an explicit goal.

Fifthly, the approaches vary in their understanding of rationality and its role in knowledge formation. While the strategic-management approach is often associated with bounded rationality (that is, constrained by the environment) and the evolutionary one with procedural rationality (that is, with powers of reflexivity), the anthropology-of-learning approach does not explicitly refer to cognitive mechanisms or, in general, embrained knowledge as a source of learning and innovation. The emphasis on embodiment, practical action, and social interaction displaces the need to explain the behaviour of individuals as the product of cognition and consciousness. Thus, if the first two approaches can be associated with an emphasis on rather high levels of rationality, the third one assumes (very) weak forms of rationality, understood as temporary coalitions of meaning and understanding that spring out of social practices of engagement.

Differences of this scale immediately suggest that any attempt to weave the three strands into a unified perspective on knowledge creation and management is fraught with difficulty, running the risk of mixing epistemological incompatibles. For example, the strategic-management approach and the evolutionary approach are associated with an 'epistemology of possession of knowledge' (Cook and Brown 1999) in that both tend to see knowledge as something people possess, while, for the anthropology-of-knowledge approach, what matters is the 'knowing' that emerges from the pragmatics of individual and group practices.[1] As Cook and Brown (1999: 381, emphasis in original) explain:

Much current work on organizational knowledge, intellectual capital, knowledge-creating organizations, knowledge work, and the like rests on a single, traditional understanding of the nature of knowledge. We called this understanding the 'epistemology of possession', since it treats knowledge as something people possess. Yet this epistemology cannot account for the *knowing* found in individual and group *practice*. Knowing as action calls for an 'epistemology of practice'. . . . We hold that knowledge is a tool for knowing, that knowing is an aspect of our interaction with the social and physical world, and that the interplay of knowledge and knowing can generate new knowledge and new ways of knowing. We believe this *generative dance* between knowledge and knowing is a powerful source of organizational innovation.

Our emphasis in this book falls on knowledge as a process and practice, rather than a possession, on the pragmatics of everyday learning in situated contexts of embodied and encultured practice. Thus, axiomatically:

1. We reject the conventional distinction between 'knowledge and learning, cognition and behaviour, the material and the mental, the social and the psychological', on the grounds that 'knowing should be studied as practice, and practice should be studied as activity that is rooted in time and culture' (Blackler 2002: 63). A reading of knowledge as the fruit of practice rejects an ontology that places knowledge in a separate realm of possession (of mental faculty, memory, text, competence, skill), to be somehow activated by another set of impulses such as learning, social interaction, application, technological instruments. Instead, the emphasis falls on knowing in the process of enactment, in which all these 'actors' are merged into one and the same ontological plane, such that no differentiation between knowledge stimulus and knowledge agent can be found. This shift in register suggests a very new departure in studies of organizational learning, from even the most influential works on knowledge in firms that purport to cover knowing as a practice. For instance, even Nonaka and Takeuchi (1995), if pushed to take the distinction between knowledge and learning to its limits, would still consider knowledge as a specific entity possessed by individuals or groups of individuals, distinguishable from the learning processes that pulsate the dynamics of knowledge.

[1] The difference, in Blackler's typology (2002), between knowledge as the product of embedded competences and embrained skills, on the one hand, and encultured routines and practices of doing and interaction, on the other hand.

2. We seek, therefore, considerably to enlarge the domain of thought that feeds into current readings on corporate knowledge and learning, to include pragmatist philosophy, which situates knowledge work in the phenomenology of material practices; cognitive psychophysiology, which situates the mind in bodily practices; work in the sociology of science, which envisages knowledge work as an unbroken continuum between scientists and their objects of knowledge and a whole series of human and non-human mediaries; and work on performativity, which explains creativity as the product of enactment, engagement, and improvisation. All these lines of thought take all types of knowledge, routine and radical, pragmatic and strategic, codified and tacit, as embodied, distributed, and transhuman, where the variation in outcome lies in the degree of combination, and in the ways in which the elements are aligned and made to speak with effect.

3. We identify *community* as the all-important site of knowledge formation; the site where hybrid knowledge inputs meaningfully interact. We share the claim by Brown and Duguid (1991: 53) that 'it is the organization's communities, at all levels, who are in contact with the environment and involved in interpretative sense making, congruence finding and adapting. It is from any site of such interactions that new insights can be co-produced.' Accordingly, we assume that the process of generating, accumulating, and distributing knowledge—both in sites of informal interaction and informally constituted units such as R & D labs—is achieved through the functioning of informal groups of people, or autonomous 'communities', acting under conditions of voluntary exchange and respect of the social norms that are defined within each group. Communities can be considered as key building blocks of the organization and management of corporate innovation and creativity.

Differences apart, we do see some merit in dialogue between the different theorizations of knowledge, between an understanding of knowledge as a possession and that of knowledge as an embodied practice. Firms do possess knowledge in the form of stored memory, codified knowledge, established competences, tacit and scripted routines, designated knowledge workers and units (for example, R & D labs), and explicit knowledge-management practices (for example, training programmes, project development teams, IT systems). They can behave and organize themselves as knowledge-possession systems, regardless of whether their effort to mobilize possessed knowledge through such initiatives as new-product development projects, retraining schemes, or knowledge-coordination efforts, proves to be effective. Firms see themselves as cognitive agents, expressive of a particular corporate rationality or mindset (for example, procedural, experimental, or reflexive), particular learning routines (for example, craft based and incremental or science based and path shaping), and particular knowledge-management repertoires (for example, new-product/process development, imitation, adaptation). They have a conduct of ownership and possession no longer confined to returns based on transactional efficiency and market power, as they become conscious of their performance as knowledge machines.

As stated above, this book takes up the challenge of explaining the interplay between knowledge and knowing, but it is important to be clear about the level at which a synthesis is sought. We do not seek a reconciliation at the level of theory, because we believe the three approaches are ontologically and epistemologically irreconcilable. What we seek, instead, is an answer to the conundrum that mechanisms and narratives of knowing and knowledge both exist within firms. For example, the work of communities always intersects or conflicts with structured schemes designed for the exchange, storage, and circulation of 'possessed' knowledge.

Thus, our interest in the problems and possibilities of interface between knowledge and knowing arises in response to a very real problem faced by firms in the generation and management of knowledge. We distinguish between different contexts of organization, identifying, at one end, those contexts in which designed forms are dominant, and, at the other end, those contexts in which the interplay between autonomous communities dominates. We examine the learning associated with different types of community and designed organization. We also highlight the difference between cognitive and non-cognitive learning and the conflict between centralized and distributed learning, and we consider the extent to which distributed practice, cognition, and design can be thought of as reconcilable tools in the manager's toolkit that can be manipulated to improve organizational performance. Finally, we consider what 'being there' means as a stimulus for learning, in the achievements both of face-to-face contact and physical proximity and of distanciated and relational proximity facilitated by various space-spanning devices.

At the heart of these issues lies the nature of the relationship between management by design and management by community. To a large extent, 'organization' can be viewed as the historical locus of managing the division of work, while communities can be seen as the building blocks of the division of knowledge. How firms can benefit from the useful knowledge held by its different distributed communities without compromising the hierarchy of the division of labour geared towards efficiency will become a key question in the future. Another challenge will be that of aligning the emergence of new communities—each with its own culture and norms—to standards at the corporate level. This book seeks to tackle various aspects of the interplay between organizations and communities, between knowledge possessed and practices of knowing, within a broadly pragmatist and non-rationalist interpretative frame.[2]

---

[2] This perspective is in line with Kogut and Zander's pioneering work (1992, 1996) on an economic conception of the firm based on social communities 'in which individual and social expertise is transformed into economically useful products and services by the application of a set of higher order organizing principles. Firms exist because they provide a social community of voluntaristic action structured by organizing principles that are not reducible to individuals' (Kogut and Zander 1992: 384).

STRUCTURE OF THE BOOK

Chapter 2 examines the reasons why knowledge is becoming more of a core element of the value-generating process in the economy, and identifies the forms of knowledge that are relevant for organizational learning. Knowledge indeed appears as a unique asset that is both an output (innovation) of the production process and an input (competence) of this process. However, this property is hidden in mainstream economics, which tends to conflate knowledge with information. We suggest that the burst of intellectual activity since the early 1990s recognizing the generative characteristics of knowledge emerged initially from the distinction made between knowledge and information. This burst abandoned the hypothesis that any form of knowledge can be made codifiable, and that human knowledge is created and expanded through conversions between tacit and codified knowledge. It also ceased to consider knowledge as centred purely on the individual, and focused instead on collective forms of knowledge formation. The chapter also emphasizes another key distinction in the literature, between treating knowledge as something people possess and appreciating the knowing found in individual and group practices. The latter perspective leads to an understanding of knowledge generation and acquisition in firms as the product of habits of everyday interaction in which thinking and acting are combined in an inseparable unity.

Chapter 3 examines the idea of the firm as a competence-builder, and explores how competences relate to organizational knowledge production. The chapter argues that the competence-based approach to the firm renounces seeing the firm as a processor of information (as in mainstream approaches, including the transaction-cost approach), to consider the firm as a processor of knowledge. This shift, we argue, necessitates a reconsideration of the classical features of the firm: its boundaries, coordinating mechanisms, incentive mechanisms, and the role of the entrepreneur. The chapter, however, also explores the complementarities between the competence-based approach and the transaction-cost approach to the firm, which, despite its limitations on the firm as a processor of knowledge, identifies inescapable cost and governance considerations. Finally, the chapter argues that, in the context of knowledge formation, the firm's central imperative is to align the functioning of communities of practice with the managerial needs to build competences.

While Chapter 3 is primarily concerned with economic theory and retains strong rationality assumptions, Chapter 4 draws on pragmatist thought to advance the idea of knowledge as a weakly cognitive practice, as the product of habits of everyday interaction in which thinking and acting are combined. In conceptualizing knowledge as an embodied social practice, the chapter questions the assumption in theories of knowledge as a possession that specific cognitive qualities are responsible for particular types of organizational learning and innovation (for example, procedural rationality for path-dependent innovation and reflexive rationality for radical innovation). It explains the generation of meaning and novelty as both intended and unintended effects, based on the deliberate and non-deliberate practices among different types of knowledge community. It makes a distinction between the knowledge practices of deliberately established epistemic communities and non-intentional knowledge work in communities of practice, but it also stresses that all communities share a common anthropology of socialization, social interaction, interest alignment, and community maintenance, which acts as a vital medium for learning.

Chapter 5 focuses on the spatial dimension of learning in firms. This dimension has been largely neglected or narrowly conceptualized in economic analysis, despite the existence of important contemporary work in economic geography on the territorial embeddedness of innovation systems. This chapter outlines the new thinking that stresses the powers of spatial proximity and territorial mooring, but it also seeks to transcend it by working with a view of space as non-contiguous and permeable, thereby allowing recognition of learning based on mobility and relational links at a distance. We do not assume that knowledge fits into neat scalar or territorial bundles. Instead, drawing especially on actor-network theory, we define spaces of knowledge as organized spaces of varying length, shape, and duration, in which knowing, depending on circumstances, can involve all manner of spatial mobilizations, including placements of task teams in neutral spaces, face-to-face encounters, global networks held together by travel and virtual communications, flows of ideas and information through the supply chain, and transcorporate thought experiments and symbolic rituals.

Chapter 6 draws on the conceptual insights developed in the book to examine the corporate governance implications of learning based on competences and communities. It focuses on the tension between the impetus in firms to manage by design (an impetus that has allowed the strategic-knowledge approach to focus on coordination mechanisms and issues of organizational design) and the impetus to manage dynamic learning by supporting community-based practices of engagement. The chapter advocates that the second mode of management, promoting dynamic learning by doing in communities, touches the very essence of the governance of organizations. It suggests that communities, as a mode of coordination in their own right, may provide specific advantages that cannot be fulfilled by management by design. The chapter also suggests, however, that coordination through communities faces other risks, such as how to link up distributed and different types of community, and those related to compatibility with organizing learning by design. This perennial tension inhibits the development of hybrid forms of management that can combine management by design and management by communities. Finally, the chapter discusses the spatial management implications of learning understood as a distributed and dispersed activity. It argues the need to rethink the widely held view that spatial clustering and local linkage are the prime means of encouraging knowledge generation and learning in firms. It emphasizes the role of devices for knowledge connectivity, alignment, and translation, capable of sustaining the firm as a heterarchy of spatial arrangements that include—increasingly as an everyday organizational arrangement—relational proximity across substantial distances.

Chapter 7 broadens the normative discussion initiated in Chapter 6, to focus on the inadequacies of traditional public policy principles and tools in grasping the challenges of knowledge formation in communities. It explores how national science and technology policies might respond to the idea of learning as a distributed, non-cognitive, practice-based phenomenon, recognizing that distributed organizational networks are both learning and governance environments in their own right. The chapter begins by reconceptualizing the role of classical instruments of public policy intervention, by focusing on the example of patents as a means of supporting the production of knowledge in expert communities. It then discusses the policy implications of focusing on the architecture of interactions between expert communities and lay communities, a key aspect of knowledge formation in the contemporary economy of complex and distributed knowledge.

It should be clear from the structure of the book that we propose a very specific theoretical and practical journey. Our starting point is the economic theory of the firm, as the base point of analysing how knowledge is produced and managed within firms. Our position is that recent breakthroughs in the economic literature have produced valuable insights on the centrality of knowledge in firms and on the associated governance challenges. But the discussion of these breakthroughs also sparks a key turning point in our journey, because we find them constrained by their interpretation of knowledge as a possession and as a product of cognitive processes. From Chapter 4 onwards, therefore, we draw on recent advances in the anthropology and sociology of learning to focus on practices of knowing within communities and distributed networks that can be considered as strings of hybrid knowledge inputs and as weakly cognitive learning environments. This step change allows us, in the final two chapters, to address the knowledge-management challenges—corporate and public policy—thrown up by mechanisms and assumptions in the real life of firms and networks of communities that belong to the two domains of knowledge possessed and knowledge practised.

The journey we have selected is a risky one, because any attempt to work with two extreme and potentially irreconcilable visions of knowledge can only be fraught with difficulty. But, the contradictions of knowledge processes themselves in firms necessitate this confrontation—both architectures of knowledge and knowledge management exist within firms, regardless of differences of worth. It is in the spirit of adventure, but with some caution, that we make this risky journey.

2

Economics of Knowledge Reconsidered

The increasing importance of knowledge in society is echoed around the world by a growing number of influential authors from various disciplines. For example, Drucker (1993) has argued that knowledge is the only meaningful resource today. For Toffler (1990), the battle for the control of knowledge ('the ultimate replacement of all other resources') and the means of communication is scaling up all over the world. Reich (1991) contends that the only true competitive advantage will reside among those who are equipped with the knowledge to identify, solve, and broker new problems. Nonaka (1994) considers the creation of knowledge as the essence of building competitive advantage by firms. According to Gibbons et al. (1994), in the domain of production of knowledge, the transformation can be considered as marking a distinct shift towards a new mode of knowledge production ('Mode 2'), which is replacing and reforming established institutions, disciplines, practices, and policies ('Mode 1').[1]

A key question is whether the increasing importance of knowledge is the result of an evolution of ideas, or the expression of a fundamental transformation in the economy, such that old theories no longer apply. Several scholars believe that there is a fundamental shift in the regime of growth, towards a new phase called the 'knowledge-based-economy' (KBE). Thus, Abramowitz and David (1996) have described the twentieth century as one characterized by increasing knowledge intensity in the production system. Their conclusions are supported by the OECD's structural analysis of industrial development. The sectors that use knowledge inputs such as R&D and skilled labour most intensively have grown most rapidly, and, in the OECD countries, the most rapidly growing sector has been the knowledge-intensive business services sector (OECD 2000). This long-term shift accelerated rapidly in the mid-1970s, with the emergence of the new information and communication technologies that offered new means to

---

[1] 'The new mode operates within a context of application in that problems are not set within a disciplinary framework. It is transdisciplinary rather than mono-or-multi disciplinary. It is carried out in non-hierarchical, heterogeneously organized forms, which are essentially transient. It is not being institutionalized primarily within university structures. It involves the close interaction of many actors throughout the process of knowledge production and this means that the process of knowledge production is becoming more socially accountable' (Gibbons et al. 1994: 3). This radical approach has been questioned by some authors (Pestre 1997), who advocate that the two modes have always coexisted in society (as, for instance, in agro-food research). However, all the authors agree at least on the fact that Mode 1 was until recently by far the dominant one, and that there is growing evidence that it is increasingly challenged by Mode 2 in many loci of knowledge production.

produce, exchange, store, and integrate knowledge. The idea of the KBE thus can be understood as the result of convergence in these two movements: increasing long-term knowledge intensity, on the one hand, and the emergence and diffusion of the new information and communication technologies, on the other hand.[2]

WHY KNOWLEDGE IS IMPORTANT IN THE ECONOMY

Whatever the reasoning behind the idea of the KBE, it forces appraisal of why knowledge *per se* is of such importance in the modern economy. The discovery is not new, and, as early as the 1940s, scholars such as Hayek[3] argued that 'the economic problem of society is not merely a problem of how to allocate given resources . . . It is a problem of the utilization of knowledge not given to anyone in its totality' (Hayek 1945: 519–20). However, it took several more decades, and in particular the seminal work of Machlup (1980), for economic theory fully to recognize knowledge as the core element in the production process. Knowledge can be considered a unique asset that appears both as an output of the production process (as analysed by the theory of innovation), and as an input of the production process (as analysed by the theory of competences). As such, it exhibits certain powerful economic properties.

As an *output*, the production of new knowledge refers to the endeavours of scientific activity (for example, publications) or technological effort (for example, patents, new products, new processes, and so on). Innovation can be regarded as the main outcome of knowledge production. It adds to existing knowledge and expresses its economic value. Interest in the knowledge production/innovation process has grown considerably since the early 1990s among economists, particularly evolutionary economists, who have analysed in depth the conditions under which new knowledge is produced, and who have underlined that the development of a new technology is fundamentally a localized, path-dependent, and interactive process.

---

[2] A full understanding of the knowledge-based economy and its consequences has to consider the two movements simultaneously. Focusing on the long-term movement alone would induce reasoning in terms of 'the growth of the service economy', while focusing alone on the new information and communication technologies would induce reasoning in terms of 'the new information society'.

[3] Hayek conceived the problem of knowledge for society in such a way that at a given moment in time each individual holds some knowledge and that there is a need to 'mobilize' socially all these forms of dispersed knowledge. He drew attention to the importance of implicit, context-specific knowledge (knowledge of the particular circumstances of time and place) compared to the knowledge of general rules (what he called scientific knowledge). 'The peculiar character of the problems of a rational economic order is determined precisely by the fact that the knowledge of the circumstances we must make use of never exists in concentrated or integrated form, but solely as the dispersed bits of incomplete and frequently contradictory knowledge which all the separate individuals possess' (Hayek 1945: 519).

The production of knowledge is cumulative and integrative. Today's advances lay the foundation for succeeding rounds of progress. Scotchmer (1991) compares the cumulative effective of inventive activity to standing on the shoulders of giants, from where one can see further. The cumulative characteristic of knowledge implies path dependence and the progressive creation of barriers, as established participants in given technologies accumulate a differential advantage over potential entrants. Synthesis is generated through convergence or integration between previously independent pieces of knowledge. Thus, for many industries advances take place across generations; new products or processes are not radical departures from existing modes, but build on and extend the knowledge and technology used in the production of the products and processes they supersede. This gives rise to successive improvements, defining a trajectory. Accordingly, the process of knowledge generation produces positive learning externalities. The generation of a new piece of knowledge increases the probability of creating useful new products, processes, and ideas arising from novel and unanticipated combinations. As Machlup (1980: 167) summarizes, 'the more that is invented, the easier it becomes to invent still more'.

The accumulation of knowledge as an *input* allows recognition of *competences*. Competences express the ways through which knowledge is elicited, used, and applied to specific contexts and domains by learning agents engaged in the innovation process. As Malerba and Orsenigo (2000) observe, the notion of competences aims at capturing the ways in which agents structure their knowledge and manage their interactions between differentiated fragments of dispersed knowledge. Thus, economic units organize themselves intentionally to enhance learning in order to lay the foundation for further rounds of progress.

Acknowledging the critical role of knowledge in the economy has been hampered by orthodox economics, which treats knowledge as a by-product of the more central information-processing process. In mainstream economics, as a result of the focus on 'how much and what kind of information agents have about the world they operate and how powerful is their ability to process the information' (OECD 2000: 3), knowledge has been reduced to a specific step in a linear process of transformation of information (knowledge as a stock resulting from the accumulation of the flux of information). Thus, in traditional economics, the vision of knowledge as an input or as an output of the production process has been hidden implicitly or deliberately behind the information veil.

In the domain of production of knowledge, Arrow (1962*a*) and Nelson (1959) examined the characteristic of knowledge-reduced-to-information as a public good. For Arrow, the process of invention was broadly the production of knowledge that can be assimilated to information. He raised the problem of appropriability by showing that it is difficult or even impossible to create a market for knowledge once it is produced, making it hard for producers of knowledge-reduced-to-information to appropriate the benefits that flow from it. 'There is a fundamental paradox in the determination of demand for information; its value for the purchaser is not known until he has the information, but then he has in effect acquired it without cost' (Arrow 1962*a*: 610). The complexity of knowledge is clearly reduced to an information-codified form, a simplification that has inspired public intervention in the domain of R&D for decades.

In the traditional schema, the notion of competence (knowledge as an input) hardly matters. Economic agents are supposed to have given endowments in resources, they absorb external knowledge at no cost, and they do not exhibit learning capabilities.[4] The use of knowledge-reduced-to-information in the production process does not change the agents' representation of the world or their strategic position in the competitive arena. From this perspective it is impossible to grasp the interactive nature of the innovation process, which implies that agents increase their competences while engaging in the innovation process.

OVERCOMING FOUR OBSTACLES TO A FULLER ACCOUNT OF KNOWLEDGE IN ORGANIZATIONS

Placing knowledge at the centre, with the aim of fully recognizing its unique properties as an input and output of the production process, is a task that requires the entrenched theoretical barriers of traditional economics to be overcome.[5] Such a recognition has been growing progressively in the social sciences by surmounting the following four theoretical obstacles:

1. the vision of knowledge as a simple stock resulting from the accumulation of information in a linear process;
2. the hypothesis that any form of knowledge can be made codifiable;
3. the vision that knowledge is limited to individuals;
4. the idea that knowledge is limited to something that people 'possess'.

The burst of intellectual activity that has accompanied the recognition of the centrality of knowledge in the production process can be grouped around efforts to tackle these four obstacles.[6] The reconceptualization is still in progress, and it is clear from the discussion that we examine below that significant advance has already been made.

Surmounting the Vision of Knowledge as a Simple Stock Resulting from the Accumulation of Information

Mainstream economics allows knowledge to be considered as a stock accumulated from interaction with an information flux.[7] This vision of knowledge is in

---

[4] An exception is 'learning by doing' (Arrow 1962*b*), but this category of learning is not considered deliberate or contributory to modifying the cognitive capabilities of agents.

[5] Particularly in economics, where the analysis of knowledge is made more difficult because it implies a significant reconsideration of the 'code-book' of the discipline.

[6] Beyond these challenges, we will see that there is clearly a price to pay: a departure from the traditional vision must take into account weaker degrees of rationality.

[7] This section draws from Ancori, Bureth, and Cohendet (2000).

Figure 2.1. *The 'linear process' of knowledge formation*

Source: Ancori, Bureth, and Cohendet (2000: 262)

line with a rationalist epistemology.[8] This definition of knowledge as 'justified true belief' supposes a split between the knower and the known. In the rationalist vision of knowledge, there is thus no connection between knowledge and action. The result is a 'spectator' theory of knowledge that separates theory and practice. To a large extent, the traditional vision of economics is based on such a position, which accepts the separation of economic knowledge from the economic subject. In this rationalist vision, individual beliefs are given (Walliser 1998) and remain unchanged through the process of quest for the 'truth'. Agents have fixed cognitive features, because there is no room in this approach for any learning by the agent that would shape progressively his or her set of beliefs from the experience gained in the search for knowledge.

The rationalist quest for knowledge can be described as a linear process of transformation (Winkin (1996) labels this 'telegraphic' communication): data are turned into structured pieces of information, information contributes to increasing the stock of knowledge, and knowledge is converted to 'wisdom' or 'meta-knowledge', which encompasses beliefs and judgements (see Fig. 2.1). This vision emphasizes information processing as a critical step in the formation of knowledge for a given cognitive entity. The more efficient the channels to process data and information, the more freely information can circulate, and the more efficient the process of formation of knowledge, seen as the ability to examine and assess different combinations of information.

To a large extent, most of the economic uses of the concept of knowledge are based on such an interpretation. However, a growing number of voices now argue that this vision is too simplistic and call for a change of paradigm. One of the most significant attempts to go beyond this restricted version of the relationship between information and knowledge has come from Machlup (1980), based on Boulding's famous assertion (1955: 103–4):

We cannot regard knowledge as simply the accumulation of information in a stockpile, even though all the messages that are received by the brain may leave some sort of deposit here. Knowledge must itself be regarded as a structure, a very complex and quite loose pattern with its parts connected in various ways by ties of varying degrees of strength. Messages are continually shot into this structure; some of them pass right through its

---

[8] Rationalism assumes the existence of an a priori knowable external reality that is true at all times and in all places. Knowledge cannot be gained from sensory experience. Absolute truth is deduced from rational reasoning grounded in axioms (which can be assimilated to a 'quest for the truth'). Thus knowledge can be attained deductively, for example, by employing mental constructs such as concepts, laws, and theories.

interstices without effecting any perceptible change in it. Sometimes messages 'stick' to the structure and become part of it. . . . Occasionally, however, a message which is inconsistent with the basic pattern of the mental structure, but which is of such nature that it cannot be disbelieved hits the structure, which is then forced to undergo a complete reorganization.

There is in general no direct relationship between information and know-ledge: a given piece of information may be added to the existing stock of know-ledge, but it may well leave it unchanged or contribute to its complete reorganization. Everything depends on the cognitive capacities of agents and on their abilities to proceed to learning processes. It is generally impossible to deduce without ambiguity any knowledge from the set of information held by a given agent. If, then, we consider two or more agents receiving the same set of information, they will in general react and assimilate it differently, simply because their cognitive capabilities are different.

Thus, according to Machlup, information is fragmented and transitory, whereas knowledge is structured, coherent, and of enduring significance. Further, information is acquired by being gathered, whereas knowledge can be acquired by thinking and doing. Any kind of experience, accidental impression, or observation, and even an 'inner' experience, can initiate cognitive processes leading to changes in a person's knowledge. Such differences underline the need to develop a distinction between knowledge and information that is not restricted to a simple stock or flux distinction, and also a framework that explic-itly acknowledges the cognitive capabilities of individuals. This can be done in part by abandoning the vision of a purely linear process in the formation of knowledge, and in recognizing that knowledge does not only result from a one-way cumulative process (from information to knowledge), but requires continuous feedback loops between the different main components involved (data, knowledge, wisdom). Figure 2.2 expresses this interactive vision of the knowledge-formation process.

Such a conception of the process of knowledge formation requires explicit recognition of the cognitive features of the individual (that is, abandoning the rationalistic hypothesis of the separation between the knower and the known), and in particular of the role played by those cognitive mechanisms—memory, pattern recognition, perception, communicative skills—at the interface between experience and practice, on the one hand, and beliefs and judgements, on the other hand (Ancori 1992).

Surmounting the Hypothesis that Any Form of Knowledge Can Be Made Codifiable

As we have seen above, by accepting the Cartesian view that separates economic knowledge from the economic subject, economists have implicitly acknowledged the assimilation of knowledge with information. However, there is another way in which knowledge and information have been tightly coupled by the economics

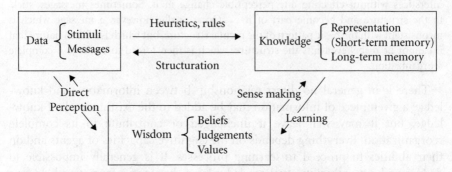

Figure 2.2. *The interactive system of knowledge formation and the different processes at stake*

Note: The first component, 'data', can be distinguished in terms of 'stimulus' in the case of an emission of data from nature, and 'message' in the case of an emission of data from a human source.

The second component, 'knowledge', results from a specific structuration of data that depends on the 'world view' of the cognitive entity. There is a need here to distinguish short-term memory ('representation') and long-term memory. If both representation (as short-term memory) and long-term memory knowledge result from cognitive structuration by the agent, representation is contextual and temporary, and has to do with the mental attitudes in a given context such as 'how to listen to this conversation, how to solve this problem, etc.', which presumes a short-term reaction, which long-term memory knowledge corresponds to more long-term 'sedimentation'.

The third component, the 'world view' of the cognitive entity, corresponds to its wisdom, which includes beliefs, judgements, and values. These are meta-categories that determine the nature of the rules and the direction of the learning processes to be followed by the agent.

Source: Adapted from Ancori, Bureth, and Cohendet (2000: 263)

mainstream—namely, through the deliberate *conversion* of knowledge to information. The claim is that, in order to be treated as an economic good, knowledge must be put into a form that allows it to circulate, to be exchanged, or to be engaged in commercial transactions. This is how the *codification* of knowledge is conceptualized. It is through this form that mainstream economists generally measure and assess objectively, or at least 'comfortably', knowledge. Codification allows them to treat knowledge-reduced-to-information according to the standard tools of economics: 'Information is knowledge reduced to messages that can be transmitted to decision agents. We can take the standard information-theoretic view that such messages have information content when receipt of them causes some action' (Dasgupta and David 1994: 493). This approach makes it incumbent for knowledge to become an object with discernible and measurable characteristics.

Without question, codification of knowledge thus defined can be related to the tremendous increase of all forms of knowledge production, in particular the digital revolution, which has drastically modified the ways of doing research, conceiving new products or processes, processing standard products, and shaping consumption norms. The fall in the cost of telecommunication has facilitated the diffusion of codified knowledge. Through systems such as the Internet, any piece of codified knowledge has many more potential users. Codified knowledge can now be transmitted over long distances and within complex networks, at a highly reduced cost and at high speed. These changes have clearly increased the potential value of codified knowledge.

But there are strong risks associated with assuming that all knowledge can be codified as information, that 'tacit knowledge' is an economic residual of knowledge, that it too can (at some cost) be codified. The assumption that codified knowledge can substitute tacit knowledge has been widely criticized, on the grounds that codified knowledge requires tacit knowledge in order to be useful. These criticisms view codified and tacit knowledge as essentially complementary to each other. The debate on this central question deserves some attention, starting with the nature of the process of codification.

The codification of knowledge is a process that aims at converting knowledge into messages. These messages can then be processed as information that will serve to 'reconstitute' knowledge at a later time, in a different place, or by a different group of individuals. The scope in this process of transformation of knowledge is to facilitate the treatment of knowledge as an economic good, which can be exchanged, especially through market transactions.[9]

The process of codifying knowledge, however, is much more complex than is assumed in mainstream economics. It entails three distinct but related steps: creating models, creating languages, and creating messages (see Box 2.1 for examples). Each of these aspects has its own costs, and at each level, as the process unfolds, typically, new knowledge is created. The first two steps generally involve high fixed costs. Indeed, they require time and effort to implement standards of reference (numerical, symbolic, geometrical languages, and taxonomies of many kinds), standards of performance, a vocabulary of precisely defined and commonly understood terms, and a grammar to stabilize the language. Once these steps have been achieved, a 'codebook' becomes available, and only then can the third step start, allowing agents to carry out knowledge operations at low marginal costs, since messages are reproducible.[10]

---

[9] The treatment of knowledge as a commodity is sometimes called the 'commodification of knowledge'. A confusion to be avoided is the assumption that codification of knowledge will automatically allow the commodification of knowledge. Codification obviously facilitates the exchange of knowledge, but, in many situations, knowledge can be transferred without codification (for instance, by recreating the learning context, as in the case of the driving lessons). Conversely, the codification of knowledge does not necessarily ensure its commodification, because it may leave the knowledge highly specific (a difficult mathematical theorem, an industrial operating procedure). Furthermore, if the codes are kept secret—and this can be done on purpose or not—codification may even impede the commodification of knowledge.

[10] As noticed by Steinmueller (2000), this simplified vision of the process of codifying knowledge as a three-step process, does not encompass all the cognitive issues associated with the codification process. In particular, there may be problems in aligning cognitive understanding with the language by which models and messages are constructed.

Box 2.1. *Examples of codification of knowledge in industrial organization*

For Cowan and Foray (1997) the process of codification entails three aspects: creating models, creating languages, and creating messages. One example is provided by the history of industrial organization, which has experienced three main waves of codification since the early nineteenth century: the development of engineering drawings in the nineteenth century, to codify physical objects; the Taylorist project of codifying human work during most of the twentieth century; and the ISO standard as a process of standardizing quality procedures in the organization at the end of the twentieth century. Each of these codification stages (which had a dramatic impact on the nature of industrial organization at that time) appears to have followed the three steps outlined by Cowan and Foray.

1. Engineering drawings

Monge's model of descriptive geometry was developed at the end of the eighteenth century by the French mathematician. It then took several decades for the *language* (angle projection) of multiview orthographic projection to be completely set up as a standard. Once these two steps were taken, the transfer of knowledge (in the form of *messages*) from engineers to mechanics became feasible at low cost. In fact, as Belofsky (1991, cited in Cowan and Foray 1997) notes, two 'dialects' that became two standards emerged: the first angle and the third angle. Each of these languages, was developed in a specific geographical zone (Europe, America) and took about 100 years from 1795 to 1895 to become completely fixed as standards.

2. The Taylorist project of codifying human work

The Taylorist process of rationalization of work can be seen as an intense process of codification of human work. In the codification of gestural knowledge, for example, a model to break up elementary movements was developed by Gilbreth (a disciple of Taylor). The elementary micro-movements were called 'therbligs' (seventeen therbligs were identified). As Cowan and Foray (1997: 607) note, 'this led to an "alphabet" in which any micro-movement was codifiable in symbolic terms. Gilbreth tried then to codify any action: for instance signing a letter is a process characterized by nine therbligs. It is clear that this particular process of codification required the creation of a language, the creation of a model and the action of codification *per se*.' Then, messages could be exchanged within the organization in terms of prescriptions of work tasks, coded procedures, and so on.

3. The ISO standard as a process of standardizing quality procedures in the organization

The ISO 9000 is a series of five related standards about quality management and quality assurance, elaborated over many years by the International Standards Organization, and used for the first time in 1987. As Bénézech et al. (2001) argue, the ISO 9000 standards constitute a 'codebook' (resulting from building a specific model aimed at coding collective procedures of work) used by firms to provide messages regarding useful knowledge about quality management principles and respect for procedures. The codebook includes three types of documents: (1) the quality manual (which covers the quality policy planned by the top management; (2) the manual of procedures (which defines and describes the production processes and the role of each of the actors involved); and (3) the operational instructions and registration documents.

As already emphasized, knowledge is simultaneously an input and an output of the codification process. Thus, some knowledge is needed to codify knowledge, and, furthermore, knowledge is needed to exploit a given piece of codified knowledge. This recursive and dynamic structure of knowledge has two consequences. One is that knowledge cannot be regarded as mere stock resulting from an accumulation of information. The second is that knowledge cannot be considered separately either from its holder(s), or from its time/space location. Both consequences reveal the importance of the (individual and collective) cognitive processes through which knowledge is converted, combined, stored, retrieved, exchanged, and interpreted.

The codification process alters the relationship between the *codified* and the *tacit* form of knowledge. Codified knowledge is necessarily explicit, formal, or systematic, and can be expressed in words and numbers, scientific procedures, or universal principles. This codified category of knowledge is easy to transfer, store, recall, and valorize. On the other hand, tacit knowledge is extremely difficult to transfer. The main forms of tacit knowledge are know-how (gathered from the accumulation of practice), mastery of a language (gathered from the accumulation of the ability to communicate), and 'representations of the world' (gathered from the accumulation of wisdom).[11] All these forms result from complex learning processes that require considerable amounts of time and practice to be translated from an 'emitter' to a 'receiver'. However, in contrast to codified knowledge, tacit knowledge allows people to solve specific problems, even when there is no explicit understanding of the reasons behind these problems or optimal rational methods for their solution. Skills or know-how are associated with the use of implicit routines or procedural rules that can be shared via learning, imitation, and practical examples, rather than via explanations, manuals, and repeated practices. However, in order to be effective, tacit knowledge must be permanently activated, otherwise, after a time, knowledge will be forgotten and lost.[12]

Among the tacit forms of knowledge, some fundamentally cannot be *articulated*, which means that it would 'cost' too much, at a current state of knowledge, to try and articulate these pieces of knowledge.[13] Cowan, David, and Foray (2000) have argued that this category of knowledge is infra-marginal. Very little knowledge is inherently tacit and impossible to codify. Most tacit knowledge is just *unarticulated*, and the process of codification can be viewed as an attempt to transform, at a finite cost, unarticulated pieces of knowledge into codified ones. However,

---

[11] Many economic decisionmakers can barely formalize the representations they use in the decision-making process: not just because they cannot explicitly describe the mental images they use, but also because it is impossible explicitly to retrieve all the bodies of knowledge from which representations are derived.

[12] This is another incentive to codify knowledge, and, furthermore, to codify carefully how to use the code.

[13] For example, some of the (tacit) know-how of glass-blowers is still considered as inarticulable.

reducing the process of codification to the mere conversion of tacit knowledge into a codified form, where the new codified knowledge simply substitutes part of the tacit form, is to oversimplify the complex nature of the process and leads to misleading interpretations.

Nonaka and Takeuchi (1995) have shown that the codification process is a complex conversion process, in which the codified and the tacit forms are not substitutes, but complements. In most contexts, agents need at least the tacit knowledge involved in mastering a language so that codified knowledge can be reconstituted as operational and generative. In addition, as more knowledge gets codified, the nature of the tacit form also generally changes, since the process of codification is a process of knowledge creation that alters both the codified and the tacit forms of knowledge.[14] As new knowledge is codified, new concepts and terminology will inevitably be introduced, and so the codification of knowledge inherently involves the further creation of knowledge.

The combination and the composition of tacit and codified knowledge depend strongly on the *context* within which agents or organizations manipulate knowledge. This means in particular that there are contexts in which agents will be willing to invest more in codification, and other contexts in which they would rather use and reinforce their tacit knowledge. Thus, the ability of a cognitive agent to exploit different categories of knowledge matters. On the one side, the existence of given tacit forms of knowledge (beliefs, languages, know-how), of accumulated learning and habits, and of norms will shape the ways codified knowledge is produced. On the other side, the way codified knowledge is produced (the nature of the codes, the types of organization, the nature of physical carriers of knowledge) will also shape the ways learning processes are directed, focused, and assimilated. The context-dependent nature of knowledge clearly suggests that tacit knowledge also refers to knowledge that is not mobilized (at least consciously) when conducting some activities in a given context. To this extent, some codified knowledge can be made tacit by an agent who places part of her knowledge in a zone of 'subsidiary awareness, whereas some other part is put under her focal awareness' (Polanyi 1962: 55).

The context-dependent nature of the codification process is particularly important when considering the type of tacit knowledge that is the focus of the codification effort. The nature and cost of the codification process are not the same if the aim is to codify a belief, a representation of the world, or a specific know-how, or to master a given language. Cowan (2001) has shown that, in the case of expert systems, different types of know-how (for example, artisanal,

---

[14] As Cowan (2001: 1370) underlines, in the case of the design of expert systems: 'the act of codifying is not merely translating the expert's knowledge out of his [*sic*] head and onto "paper", but is typically an act of *knowledge creation*'. As suggested by Gernot Grabher (personal communication), a better way to qualify the process of codification would be to view it as a creative/destructive process, where attempts to embed the 'creative process' in a more scientifically oriented approach could also block or neutralize creative potential.

strategic, creative) lend themselves with different degrees of compliance to codification.[15]

In emphasizing the importance of context in the analysis of the relationships between tacit and codified knowledge, Polanyi (1962) argued that what matters is the *degree of attention* of the cognitive agent.[16] In a modern economy, the rapidity of knowledge production and codification, and the low and decreasing costs of storing codified knowledge, make the question of the degree of attention more and more acute (as we shall see in the building of competences by firms). It is attention rather than information that is becoming a rare resource, as screening and selection of information become important functions. Information abundance is making it more difficult for agents to discriminate between information that is important to store and memorize, and information that can simply be 'put into the basket'.[17] The more knowledge is stored and made available in codified form, the more important becomes knowledge management. To use Lundvall's taxonomy, when the knowledge we seek to understand is tacit, 'know-who' becomes extremely important, because of the need to know who holds the tacit form of knowledge that is sought and also how to interact with them, which is an important aspect of the 'know-who'. In contrast, when it is stored in codified form, 'know-where' becomes important, because of the need to know where to find the codified forms of knowledge. This may require a new skill to be cultivated, such as how to find things using, for example, search tools on the web.

Surmounting the Vision that Knowledge is Limited to Individuals

If traditional economics has inherited a cultural predilection for privileging codified knowledge over tacit knowledge, it also tends to privilege individual

---

[15] 'Relatively linear direct processes with a known and fixed goal, like those pursued by the artisan, can be easily codified into a list of instructions or decision rules which can be implemented by a machine. Activities that involve significant amount of pattern recognition, generalisation and use of analogy are more difficult. . . . Forming strategies, trading different, conflicting, goals off against each other is harder yet' (Cowan 2001: 1370–1).

[16] We can refer here to the famous analogy to craftsmanship drawn by Polanyi (1962: 55; emphasis in original): 'When we use a hammer to drive in a nail, we attend to both nail and hammer, *but in a different way*. We *watch* the effect of our strokes on the nail and try to wield the hammer so as to hit the nail most effectively. When we bring down the hammer we do not feel its handle has struck our palm but its head has struck the nail. Yet in a sense we are certainly alert to the feelings in our palm and the fingers that hold the hammer. They guide us in handling it effectively, and the degree of attention that we give to the nail is given to the same extent but in a different way to these feelings. The difference may be stated by saying that the latter are not like the nails, object of our attention, but instruments of it. They are not watched in themselves; we watch something else while keeping intensely aware of them. I have a *subsidiary awareness* of the feeling in the palm of my hand which is merged into my *focal awareness* of my driving in the nail.'

[17] The advent of the Web is allowing people to store too much, and put too little in the basket. The same is true for most people when they look at their old email—we retain much more than is necessary.

26 *Economics of Knowledge Reconsidered*

knowledge over collective knowledge. Simon (1991: 125) asserts that 'all learning takes place inside individual human heads'. In the traditional perspective, the work done by a group of people is not epistemologically distinct from that done by a 'representative' individual in it. The Cartesian individual is the primary wielder and repository of what is known. However, this view is now widely questioned by those scholars who argue that the process of knowledge formation has a strong collective dimension that is epistemologically distinct from the individual dimension. The formation and use of knowledge depend on the nature of the organization and other collective assets.

Considering knowledge as a collective process raises a number of new issues, in particular the need to understand how knowledge can be transmitted from the level of the organization to an individual, and vice versa. The building of 'common knowledge', and the need to set collective rules and languages to facilitate the formation of knowledge, and the need to 'mobilize socially the dispersed forms of individual knowledge' (Hayek 1945) all underline that knowledge results from a collective social process. Social processes contribute to shaping the way knowledge is produced and circulates. In explicitly introducing several agents in the formation, circulation, and exchange of knowledge, we can pinpoint the need for interaction and communication between the agents. In this framework (see Fig. 2.3 in the case of two individuals) some specific issues arise such as the need to build a common classification and categorization of messages, a common language, a common knowledge, a collective learning, and a common shared vision.

The central concept in the economic literature on the formation of collective knowledge is the notion of *routines*. A useful definition of routines is offered by Cohen et al. (1996: 683): 'A routine is an executable capability for repeated performance in some context that has been learned by an organization in response to selective pressures.' A significant body of work (in particular, March and

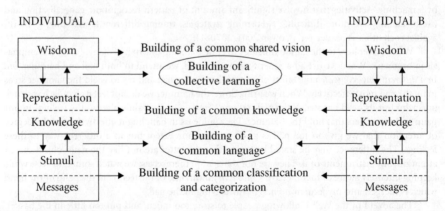

Figure 2.3. *Interactions between agents in the formation of knowledge*
Source: Adapted from Ancori, Bureth, and Cohendet (2000: 265)

Simon 1958; Nelson and Winter 1982) has explored the intrinsic properties of routines. In organization science the concept of routines is central to explain the functioning and properties of organizational learning (routines as an elementary 'coordination scheme'). In evolutionary economics the concept of routines plays a central role on the interface between the process of generation of diversity and the process of natural selection (routine as the 'gene' that stores a piece of collective knowledge of the organization), and leads to the building of the competence-based approach of the firm (as we will see in Chapter 3). From these different approaches, we can summarize the following ways in which routines contribute to knowledge formation in organizations:

1. As a capability, in the sense that routine is a capacity to generate (collective) action, to 'guide or direct an unfolding action sequence, that has been stored in some localized or distributed form' (Cohen et al. 1996: 683). Routines guarantee the regularity and predictability of individual behaviour necessary for collective action. This property can be linked to the characteristic of routine as organizational memory and expresses the cognitive and coordination dimension of the routine. As Paoli and Principe (2001: 12) argue, 'routines embody the successful solutions to problems solved by the organization in the past. They are retrieved and executed whenever the organization faces a problem resembling one already solved.' Thus, memories of an organization stored in routines carry much of the knowledge (both tacit and that which can be articulated) needed to perform activities based on repertoires of knowledge. However, for members of an organization, the required knowledge is much more than knowing that 'there is much more to "knowing one's job" in an organization than merely having the appropriate routines in repertoire. There is also the matter of knowing what routines to perform. For the individual member, this entails the ability to receive and interpret a stream of incoming messages from other members and from the environment' (Nelson and Winter 1982: 100). Routines can thus be considered as memory about what to do and how (that is, which coordinated sequences of actions to undertake).

2. As a cognitive device, routines economize on the scarce or bounded information processing and decision-making capacity of agents (March and Olsen 1976; Simon 1997). Thus routines as attention-focusing mechanisms economize on scarce cognitive resources in order to 'free-up higher degrees of awareness, mental deliberation and decision making for the more complex decision' (Hodgson 1997: 667). As Becker (1999: 62) notes, 'to focus attention means to reduce the space of events that managers should scan in order to avoid bad surprises and take advantage of the good ones . . . This is achieved by perceiving as noise and ignoring what does not receive attention. . . . Thus focusing has two sides: it has as much the meaning of *leaving something out of the window* as it does have the meaning *of being aware of something,* or *drawing attention to something.'* Such focusing, in being not only spontaneous but also intentional, opens the door to a specific role for managerial capabilities (and especially 'dynamic capabilities' (Teece and Pisano 1994)).

3. Routines are essentially context dependent. The execution of a routine is only possible in a given context that provides the locus of attention for collective action. The 'context' includes the physical state of equipment, external memories, and the work environment. And, as Nelson and Winter (1982: 105) emphasize, most importantly, 'the context of the information possessed by an individual is established by the information possessed by all other members'. Thus, the context is generative because the 'creation of shared languages and shared meanings stems from the interaction of organizational members. The relationship among organizational members is quintessential for the development and consequential execution of organizational patterned activities that embody the memory of the organization. The organizational context is both prone to active individual's mnemonic processes, and more importantly activate organizational mnemonic processes' (Paoli and Principe 2001: 12).

4. As a capability, routines may be altered in the future by a wide variety of learning processes. Learning implies a modification of routines, even if these are usually hard to change and are responsible for inflexibility and inertia in organizational behaviour (Nelson and Winter 1982: 400; Langlois and Robertson 1995). Routines change with experience through two main mechanisms. The first is trial-and-error experimentation (Cyert and March 1963). The second mechanism is organizational search: 'An organization draws from a pool of alternative routines, adopting better ones when they are discovered. Since the rate of discovery is a function both of the pool and of the intensity and direction of search, it depends on the history of success and failure of the organization' (Radner 1986: 19). According to March (1988: 3), the importance of search is related to bounded rationality: 'Since only a few alternatives, consequences, and goals can be considered simultaneously, actions are determined less by choices among alternatives than by decisions with respect to search.' However, as now commonly understood (Nelson and Winter 1982; Dosi and Egidi 1991; Dosi et al. 1999; Grandori and Kogut 2002), innovative activities involve a process of learning that is quite different from Bayesian probability updating and regression estimation. It is a process that requires agents to build new representations of the environment they operate in (and that remains largely unknown) and to develop new skills that enable them both to explore and to exploit a world of ever-expanding opportunities. Such representations are embedded in the routines that characterize the organization. Creating an appropriate environment for learning is a fundamental factor in the long-term performance of firms.

5. Various processes of selection act as filters of evolution of routines. When an existing routine is successful in business terms, replication is likely to be desired, but, when a routine leads to failure, Nelson and Winter (1982: 121) describe the possibility of its 'contraction'. In a model of economic selection based on routines, many factors (the market, amongst other selection mechanisms) are involved in determining the consequences of sustained adversity on

the persistence or change of routines. Most of the selection mechanisms mentioned in the existing literature are external to the organization, and could thus be compared to 'natural selection mechanisms' finding an appropriate role in the evolution of the routines of a firm. Finally, inaction can lead to the elimination of routines. As Nelson and Winter argue, memory loss (due, for instance, to personnel turnover) can accelerate the decay of a routine.

The concept of routine is a rich and powerful tool to capture and analyse the notion of collective knowledge. However, its actual use has been made difficult by claims on it by different theoretical schools with radically different perspectives on routines. First, in the tradition that derives from the earlier works of Simon, routine is considered as the main analytical tool for understanding information processing in organizational-learning approaches (March and Simon 1958; Argyris and Schön 1978). Routine is the key tool in reducing the information-processing burden when complex problems have to be simplified. This vision neglects the potential for creating knowledge at the organizational level. As Nonaka and Takeuchi (1995: 38) argue:

For Simon, implicit knowledge is nothing more than noise, and the logical content of human reasoning and decision making is far more important than such things as value and meaning. Nor did he pay sufficient attention to the role of ambiguity or diversity that resides in a problem, or to the importance of the redundancy of information in the organization. . . . In addition, Simon viewed the organization as passive. He argued that the organization reacts to the environment mainly by adjusting the information-processing structure. What he missed was the proactive aspect of the organization's action on the environment. The organization acting on the environment not only performs effective information processing but also creates information and knowledge by itself.

Secondly, in an evolutionary framework based upon Nelson and Winter's pioneering work, a view of routines as genes of the organization paved the way for the neo-Schumpeterian approach of the economy (Dosi 1988; Dosi and Metcalfe 1991; Nelson 1994*b*). In this fundamentally dynamic approach, the routine is the elementary building block of the 'competence-based' approach to the firm, in an ambitious attempt to restore a theory of the firm based on the production side as an alternative to the dominant transaction-cost approach (Prahalad and Hamel 1990; Kogut and Zander 1992, 1996; Dosi and Marengo 1994; Teece and Pisano 1994; Langlois and Foss 1996). For Nelson and Winter (1982: 128), 'the behaviour of firms can be explained by the routines that they employ. Knowledge of the routines is the heart of understanding behaviour. Modelling the firm means modelling the routines and how they change over time.'

Our view, as we shall argue in Chapter 3, is that only the second approach to routines is useful for theorizing the collective formation of knowledge. Here, we need to finish the discussion on what we consider as the main barriers to overcome in order to situate knowledge at the core of the production process.

Surmounting the Idea that Knowledge is Limited to Something that People 'Possess'

The mainstream in economic analysis considers knowledge to be a specific abstract entity formed in the minds of individuals or encapsulated in the collective routines of groups. In other words, people are seen to 'possess' knowledge. The formation of new knowledge, and the exchange and exploitation of existing knowledge, are viewed as processes triggered by learning mechanisms that are seen to be distinct from the possessed forms of knowledge. If we relax this classical separation, there is room explicitly to introduce the role and importance of learning processes related to experience, along the lines of the pioneering thinking of the pragmatist William James in the 1950s. James proposed that we should consider the building of knowledge as an interactive relationship between 'knowledge about' (*wissen* in German, *savoir* in French) and 'knowledge of acquaintance' (*kennen* in German, *connaître* in French). Action through experience provides immediate knowledge of 'acquaintance', while knowledge 'about' is the result of systematic thought that eliminates the subjective and contextual contingencies. This distinction has social and organizational implications: knowledge of 'acquaintance' needs essentially to be gathered and integrated, while knowledge 'about' needs essentially to be diffused. This distinction is of considerable importance in understanding the nature of knowledge; thus, for example, cognitive anthropologists have recently demonstrated the significance of situated skills and pragmatic knowledge. These new approaches reveal that the circumstances of action shape even the most abstractly represented tasks, they demonstrate that practices are distributed socially and technologically, and they emphasize the collective, situated, and tentative nature of knowing.

Thus, as Cook and Brown (1999) have argued, while the traditional understanding of the nature of knowledge relies on 'the epistemology of possession', knowing as action calls for 'an epistemology of practice'. 'Recast in this way, knowing in all its forms is analysed as a phenomenon that is (a) manifest in systems of language, technology, collaboration, and control (i.e. it is mediated); (b) located in time and space and specific to particular contexts (i.e. it is situated); (c) constructed and constantly developing (i.e. it is provisional); and (d) purposive and object oriented (i.e. it is pragmatic)' (Blackler, 2002: 58). This line of thinking tends to suggest, as we will argue in Chapter 4, that the proper unit of analysis for knowledge formation in terms of knowing found in practice should be neither individuals nor organizations, but socially distributed activity systems, such as communities (Engestrom 1993).[18] Within a given community, collective action is driven by the conception that members have of the object of their activity. Language plays a key role for the creation and coherence of the community. It enables collective interpretations, signals group membership, and helps the enactment of practical actions.

[18] Blackler (2002) claims that the recent developments on knowing have their origin in the ideas of the 'activity theory' elaborated by the Russian psychologist Vygotsky in the 1920s. According to Vygotsky (1962), it is not the consciousness of humans that determines their social being, but social experiences that shape their consciousness.

THE QUESTION OF RATIONALITY

The above discussion has highlighted the barriers that need to be overcome in order to place knowledge at the centre of the analysis of the production of economic value. It suggests a re-theorization of organizations in order to grasp the main characteristics of productive knowledge. However, beyond the different lines that have been opened to recentre knowledge, the fundamental issue of *rationality* has to be tackled in order successfully to address the theoretical challenges at stake. As the different barriers that have been examined are surmounted, it is clear that the 'price to pay' for a better theorization of knowledge is to renounce assumptions of high levels of rationality.

The modern dominant approaches to organizations, in particular transaction cost economics (TCE), rely on the hypothesis of bounded rationality: the ability of agents to process information is constrained by their limited cognitive capacity. As Foss (2001) argues, however, the acknowledgement of bounded rationality, though expressive of a lesser degree of rationality than that at the pure substantive level, still expresses a high level of rationality. Goals and procedural clarity are both high, and choice is guided by a performance program. As Simon (1991) himself has argued, under conditions of bounded rationality, the decision maker still follows (as in a universe of perfect rationality) the logic of consequence that 'human behaviour is intendedly rational, but only limitedly so'. Thus, an organization facing a complex environment should design itself in a way that minimizes the need for information distribution among existing bodies of specialized knowledge in order to reduce the information load on them. Lorenz (2001: 311) has observed that 'consistent with the information processing view of individual cognition, problem-solving in the behavioural theory of the firm is analysed in terms of internal search processes designed to select an appropriate program for the organization's existing repertory'. The firm is viewed as a 'repertory of programs', and the perspective renders an allocative vision of the coordination of existing knowledge between the different units of the organization. In a context of bounded rationality, organizations are conceived of as institutional devices that are designed to cope with market failures. Within organizations, hierarchies have authority to create and coordinate the horizontal and vertical division of work based on existing bodies of specialized knowledge.

However, the assumption of bounded rationality cannot cope with the fundamentally dynamic and praxis-based process of creation and circulation of new knowledge. First, this is because the cognitive capabilities of agents are supposed to be fixed and unchanging through time by the experience accumulated by agents. There is no place for observing an actual learning process in such a framework. Secondly, if the coordination of vertical and horizontal activities might be efficient in a static environment, it can lead to radical difficulties in an innovative environment. As Marengo (1994) has shown, horizontal coordination through an ever-increasing specialization of tasks could hamper the efforts of hierarchical coordination to foster the creation of knowledge through contact between independent units. Conversely, if vertical coordination facilitates communication from the hierarchy to the different units of the organization, it is inefficient to coordinate non-routinized tasks, because, as shown by Adler (2001: 216), 'lower levels lack both the knowledge to create new knowledge and the incentives to transmit new ideas upwards'.

In TCE, which is the dominant approach to the organization within a frame of bounded rationality, a direct consequence of the limited rationality of agents is the incompleteness of contracts, which leads to the possibility of opportunistic behaviour. In the relationships that agents have, the agents cannot predict in advance the set of situations that will influence the result of their transaction. This is the reason why agents, when choosing an appropriate structure of governance, will pay specific attention to the *ex-post* outcome of a given contractual relation. The main objective of the structure of governance is to constrain the unproductive, rent-seeking, behaviour that imperfect information permits. The purpose of hierarchy is to design incentive schemes that align the behaviour of members of the organization to the objective of the hierarchy.

When it is the production and exchange of knowledge (not reduced to information) that is at stake, incentive schemes in accordance with the TCE approach have severe limitations. In the production of knowledge, agents have cognitive capabilities that are changing through time. At a given moment in time they might be rationality bounded, but this is not what matters: what is central is the process through which agents learn, memorize their experience, and orient their searching capabilities to gain more knowledge. As March and Simon (1993) have stressed, the main constraint in such a process is the limited attention or capability to focus. A given agent must choose some domain of the knowledge space where he or she will concentrate his or her cognitive attention (by memorizing, cumulating, and eventually participating in this domain to the creation of new knowledge), while being satisfied with just 'being informed' on the rest of the knowledge space.

Thus, we hypothesize that, in distinguishing knowledge from information, the dynamics of knowledge can be observed in a context not of (strong) static bounded rationality, but of (weak) dynamic procedural rationality. When knowledge generation and diffusion are at stake, the 'logic of consequence' of the static world applies far less. As Fransman (1995: 3) has argued, the decision-maker then faces 'interpretive ambiguity':

Such ambiguity exists when the decision-maker's information set is capable of sustaining contradictory inferences regarding the courses of action that are available and/or consequences of these alternatives. The significance of interpretive ambiguity is that under such conditions, the logic of consequences necessarily breaks down for the simple reason that the decision-maker has no way of making calculations regarding alternative actions and/or consequences. . . . In the face of interpretive ambiguity, the world appears to be fuzzy with a consequent lack of clarity regarding alternatives and consequences. Under these conditions, the difficulty arises from the breakdown of the logic of consequence rather than from constraints on the information-handling abilities of the decision maker.

The process of production and development of new knowledge works with such an 'interpretive ambiguity', that weaker degrees of rationality have to be considered. We will in particular emphasize in this book that, in such conditions, firms build competences that serve the function of creating order out of chaos and of imposing a degree of clarity in a fuzzy world.

To move the argument on, when working analytically at the level of situated learning in communities, the need to relax assumptions of rationality is even more important (see Chapter 4). Situated learning involves very weak levels of rationality ('unconscious cognition'), where respect for the social norms of the group and the practices of engagement are a more important guide to behaviour than a rational decision-making context (that would imply strongly conscious cognition and rational ordering to identify alternatives, project the probabilities and outcomes of alternatives, and evaluate outcomes according to known preferences). However, if the functioning of communities actually 'economizes' on cognition, it would be misleading not to consider some key cognitive activities at stake such as the elaboration of a common language and a collective representation of the community, although how far these activities can be put down to the effort of rationality remains debatable. In using the terms 'strong' and 'weak' rationality in this book, we are fully aware that there is a risk of thinking purely in terms of different 'degrees' of (the same) rationality. One alternative is the Habermasian distinction between strategic/instrumental and communicative rationality,[19] although even this dualism does not fully recognize the powers of non-cognitive processes such as bodily knowledge.

CONCLUSION

The traditional approaches of knowledge 'reduced to information' fail to grasp some of the fundamental distinctions that characterize an in-depth analysis of knowledge: the distinction between codified and tacit knowledge, the distinction between individual and group knowledge, the distinction between 'possessed' knowledge and knowing. These traditional approaches treat all knowledge as essentially the same, as if codified and tacit knowledge, or collective and individual knowledge, abstract and practical knowledge were just variations of a unique kind of knowledge, which is mostly conceived in terms of individual/codified forms of knowledge.

The interest of some recent approaches to knowledge in organizations is precisely to recognize and theorize the fundamental characteristics of knowledge work. Nonaka and Takeuchi (1995) have suggested that we should consider all the four basic types of knowledge (codified/individual; codified/collective; tacit/individual; tacit/collective) as epistemologically different and as of equal importance (see Box 2.2). This typology has led Nonaka and Takeuchi to formulate the key hypothesis that the potential of a given organization to innovate is associated with the mastering of the 'modes of conversion of knowledge'. An effective circulation and distribution of knowledge expressed in any of the

---

[19] As suggested to us by Gernot Grabher.

basic forms is thus a prerequisite for being an innovative organization. In turn, Brown and Duguid (1991) and Lave and Wenger (1991), among others, have opened new avenues of research by highlighting the distinction between abstract knowledge and practical knowledge.

The traditional approaches of knowledge assume strong levels of rationality (including the levels of static bounded rationality) in a context of allocation of resources. However, understanding how new knowledge can be generated, assimilated, and transferred requires a different theoretical perspective that appreciates the knowledge work of weaker levels of rationality. One of the main questions at stake is how firms, as the central entity of the economy in charge of the

---

Box 2.2. *A typology of knowledge*

Looking across the numerous definitions of and approaches to knowledge currently circulating, we can synthesize the typology as shown in Fig. 2.4. The quadrants should be read as 'ideal types', since every real firm is a mixture of different types. Spender (1997: 52) acknowledges that 'the weakness of the matrix is that it tells us little about how these various types of knowledge interact and thus little about how the firm becomes a context especially favourable to the interaction of knowledge creation and knowledge application processes'.

	Individual	Social (or) collective
Explicit	Conscious (Spender)	Objectified (Spender)
(or codified)	Embrained (Blackler)	Encoded (Blackler)
	Know-what (Lundvall)	Know-why (Lundvall)
Tacit	Automatic (Spender)	Collective (Spender)
	Embrained (Blackler)	Embedded/encultured
	Know-what (Lundvall)	(Blackler)
		Know-who (Lundvall)

Figure 2.4. *Typologies of knowledge from Spender's matrix*
Source: Adapted from Spender (1997)

Objectified knowledge (arithmetic, logic, physics laws, and so on), as shown in the top-right quadrant, is explicit, codifiable, transmittable without bias through language, generic. It refers to knowledge that constantly evolves through the pursuit of science, and that serves as a platform to investigate new empirical phenomena. Blackler refers to this category of knowledge as 'encoded' knowledge. In Lundvall and Johnson's typology, objectified knowledge corresponds essentially to the 'know-why' (referring to scientific knowledge of principles and laws of motion in nature, in the human mind and in society).

Collective knowledge (routines, rules of conduct, and so on), as shown in the bottom-right quadrant, is tacitly shared knowledge that guides individual as well as collective action. This form of knowledge is created by convention through the collective use in language and action. Blacker distinguishes at this level two categories of collective knowledge: 'embedded knowledge', which resides in systemic routines, and 'encultured knowledge', which results from the process of acquiring shared understanding. There is no clear match at this level with the Lundvall and Johnson typology, since their conception of know-how essentially refers to individuals (see automatic knowledge). But we certainly could incorporate as a subcategory 'know-who' (referring to specific and selective social relations).

Conscious knowledge as shown in the top-left quadrant is constituted by the formal knowledge possessed by individuals. Such knowledge is held by professionals (physicians, lawyers, economists) who know the ways to perform and use formal methods and are certified in doing so. Blackler refers to this type of knowledge as 'embrained knowledge', which is constituted by conceptual skills and cognitive abilities. In the Lundvall and Johnson typology, conscious knowledge corresponds to the 'know-what' (referring to knowledge 'about' facts, and knowledge 'that').

Automatic knowledge, as shown in the bottom-left quadrant, is the personal tacit and non-conscious knowledge that allows the individual to understand and develop explicit knowledge. This refers to the tacit form of knowledge developed by Polanyi. This form of knowledge is gained through learning. Blackler refers to this type of knowledge as 'embodied knowledge'. In Lundvall and Johnson's typology, automatic knowledge corresponds to 'know-how', or knowledge of acquaintance (referring to skills).

acquisition, production, assimilation, and diffusion of knowledge, build their own competence and process knowledge.

The next chapter analyses the theoretical conditions under which the firm can be viewed as a generator of resources, defined as distinctive knowledge and organizational routines. It discusses a key problem faced by firms—namely, the governance problem of reconciling creation and allocation of resources. We propose learning in communities as part of the solution, on the basis that they help to generate meaningful links in daily practices across the distributed mechanisms of governance in a firm.

3

The Firm as a Locus of Competence Building

The recent development of the competence-based approach to the firm (Prahalad and Hamel 1990; Kogut and Zander 1992; Dosi and Marengo 1994; Teece and Pisano 1994) has opened some promising avenues of research for the economics of organization. The essential characteristic of this competence approach is that the firm is conceived of as 'a processor of knowledge', as a locus of setting-up, construction, selection, usage, and development of knowledge. The competence-based approach relies on a completely different point of view from the traditional theories. It is more sensitive to the sharing and distribution of knowledge than it is to the distribution of information. It is not so much the saturation of its abilities to deal with information, which concerns the firm, as the risk of becoming too confined by inefficient routines. In fact, considering the firm as a processor of knowledge leads to the recognition that cognitive mechanisms are essential, and that routines play a major role in keeping the internal coherence of the organization. The focus of the theory thus falls clearly on the process of creation of resources. This perspective on the firm has been taken forward by, amongst others, Cyert and March (1963); Cohen, March, and Olsen (1972); Loasby (1976, 1983); Eliasson (1990); Cohen (1991); Dosi and Marengo (1994); Marengo (1994, 1996).

We consider that these new approaches to the firm (rooted in evolutionary economics, and organizational science/sociology) support a growing tendency to express the firm fundamentally as a processor of knowledge. However, at the moment, the ambition of these new approaches faces three main limitations, which are addressed in turn in this chapter.

1. The existence of two alternative visions of the firm (the firm as a processor of information versus the firm as a processor of knowledge) raises a fundamental question. Does the competence-based approach bring a complementary or competing view when compared with the traditional theories of the firm, in particular the dominant transaction-based approach? As Langlois and Foss (1996: 10–11) note, we are confronted with the choice between, on the one hand, a traditional contractual approach based on transaction, where 'firms and other institutions are alternative bundles of contracts understood as mechanisms for creating and realigning incentives', and, on the other hand, 'a qualitative

coordination—that is, helping cooperating parties to align not their incentives but their knowledge and expectations'.

The first purpose of this chapter is to argue that the two main approaches can be reconciled by assuming that they are complementary for understanding the functioning of the firm. Our hypothesis is that firms simultaneously manage competences and transactions, but they do so according to a specific order of priorities. First, firms choose the domain of their core competences,[1] the governance of which is specifically devoted to knowledge coordination. Secondly, they organize the process of current allocation of resources and adaptation to the environment. This suggests two governance mechanisms have to be considered by the firm: the mechanism for governing competences, which is defined by the need to coordinate knowledge; and the mechanism for governing transactions, which relies on the need to manage transactions. This implies a dual structure of governance, one for governing the domain of the core activities of the firm, the other to govern the remaining activities (the 'non-core' domain). This immediately raises the problem of the coherence of the firm, related to how two different mechanisms of governance can coexist.

2. The risk of dissonance between the theories that we have grouped so far under the umbrella of competence-based theories of the firm is growing. Since the 1990s a significant number of different (sometimes diverging) approaches have emerged. Each focuses on a specific aspect of the firm viewed as a processor of knowledge. For example, terms such as 'competences', 'core competences', 'capabilities', 'dynamic capabilities', 'resource-based', 'strategic assets', are currently used without a clear delineation between them. The second objective of this chapter is thus to propose a synthesis of these new approaches of the firm, especially the strategic-management approach and the evolutionary approach, by acknowledging, beyond their main differences, certain complementarities between them.

3. Despite their diversity, the new theories do not capture all the fundamental aspects of competences and knowledge formation and exchange. As indicated in the Preface to this book, these theories fail to capture the essence of the knowledge held in the daily practices of 'knowing' in communities dispersed across and beyond the firm. In the conclusion of the chapter, we start to address the challenges raised by taking into account the dynamic of practices, which are then taken up more fully in subsequent chapters.

[1] As Hamel and Heene (1994) underline, core competences are not restricted at all to a technological domain. They distinguish in fact three main types of core competences: core competences based on 'functionality' (e.g. as miniaturization was for Sony), core competences based on a mastering of a sequence of the process of production (e.g. logistics for Fedex), core competence based on the access to the market (e.g. EdF, the French electricity company, has accumulated unique knowledge of the way to interact with municipalities).

THE FIRM AS A PROCESSOR OF INFORMATION OR KNOWLEDGE?

The Firm as a Processor of Information

Traditional theories of the firm share some basic common features.[2] They understand the behaviour of the firm in terms of an optimal, information-processing response to signals from the external environment, provided that the technical conditions (as expressed by the production function) remain unchanged.[3] The neoclassical theories of the firm, in particular principal/agent theory, have reduced coordination principles to bilateral contracts that are meant to achieve coordination through appropriate incentive schemes that align self-interested individual action with common organizational goals. An important consequence of this approach is the absence in it of any serious treatment of the production process as a collective activity. The transaction-cost approach, despite its different core assumptions and its specific focus on the boundaries of the firm, comes to a similar fundamental conclusion: the firm can be seen as a 'nexus' of contracts. Its very *raison d'être* is to correct market failures, when information processing of market mechanisms becomes too costly. Transaction-cost theory supports the principal/agent vision that information is imperfect and that the existence of potential asymmetries of information authorizes unproductive rent-seeking behaviour. The firm is thus conceived of as a governance structure to solve the problem of misaligned incentives resulting from imperfect information.[4]

The emphasis on adaptation to imperfect information signals from the environment does not imply that the contractual approach is unable to incorporate some cognitive dimensions of economic agents and their abilities to experience learning processes. The transaction-cost approach is based on the hypothesis of bounded rationality that admits the existence of cognitive constraints on individuals and the key learning processes such as learning by doing. However, the scope of such recognition is narrow, for the simple reason that the cognitive capabilities of agents are taken as given. Agents are not seen to change their representation of the world through time, differ in their perception of the environment, or pay

---

[2] The following sections result from extended discussions that Patrick Cohendet had with Fernand Amesse and Patrick Werena. We are grateful to them for their comments.

[3] As Fransman (1994) argues, the main traditional theories of the firm—neoclassical, theory of teams (Alchian and Demsetz), agency theory, Coasian theory, Simonian vision of the firm, transaction-cost theory—share a common vision of treating the firm as a processor of information (even if the information-related problem varies from one theory to another), and lead to a final contractual vision of the firm.

[4] According to Williamson (1975: 257), 'hierarchy extends the bounds of rationality by allowing specialization in decision making and savings in communication; curbs opportunism by allowing incentive and control techniques; "absorbs" uncertainty and allows independent units to adapt to contingencies; resolves small-numbers indeterminacies by fiat; and reduces information gaps between exchange agents by allowing audits and other checks'.

attention to common sets of rules, codes, and languages within the organization. In the same vein, the traditional approaches acknowledge the significance of knowledge, but here, too, the conception of knowledge is limited. Knowledge is seen as a mere stock resulting from the process of accumulation/disinvestment of information considered as a flux. As we have seen in Chapter 2, this is a restricted conception of knowledge-reduced-to-information (or 'tight-coupling' between information and knowledge, as Fransman (1994) suggests) that assumes there is no cognitive mechanism at stake. Thus, the assumption is that knowledge can be managed in much the same way as information is managed.

The Firm as a Processor of Knowledge

A significant body of research located in different disciplines (economic history, industrial organization, sociology of organization, evolutionary theory, management science, and so on) has grown seriously to question the traditional contractarian vision of the firm (Penrose 1959; Richardson 1960, 1972; Chandler 1962, 1992; Nelson and Winter 1982; March and Simon 1993). This body converges around the common axiom that competences are the key to understanding the organization of firms, their diversity, and their persistence (Dosi and Marengo 1994). It views the firm as a social institution, the main characteristic of which is to know (well) how to do certain things, based on competences or coherent sets of routines used in an efficient way. Some competences are seen as strategic ('core competences', according to Teece (1988)), constituting the main sources of competitiveness, the results of a selection process both within and external to the firm. The management, construction, and combination of these competences are seen to be critical in understanding the limits as well as the coordination and incentive structure of the firm.

In this approach, the firm is conceived of as an institution where competences are continuously built, shaped, maintained, and protected. This is a cumulative and strategic process that relies intensively on the management of knowledge. The competence-based approach essentially focuses on the ways, for a given firm, knowledge is acquired, produced, absorbed, memorized, shared, and transferred. This has some important consequences, in particular for the coordination of the firm. First, knowledge of complex production processes is necessarily distributed (see Hayek 1937) and cannot be fully grasped and controlled by a single individual. Thus, a primary role of organization becomes that of coordinating this dispersed knowledge. Secondly, coordination in this case generally involves the creation of commonly shared bodies of knowledge: sets of facts, notions, 'models of the world', rules, and procedures that are—at least partly—known to all the members of the organization involved in a given interaction. Thus, in contrast to the traditional theories of organization (that implicitly suppose that all these mechanisms for the coordination of actions are already in place), the competence-based approach focuses on how the coordination of dispersed knowledge and the building of commonly shared bodies of knowledge are actually constructed within the firm. The successful circulation of knowledge within an organization supposes the capability to transfer knowledge from individuals to a collective body (a team for instance) and vice versa. This requires the firm to provide appropriate contexts of learning: on the one side, to amplify the knowledge created or possessed by individuals and crystallize it at the group level through dialogue, discussion, experience sharing, and observation, and, on the other side, to favour teaching and socializing activities.

Although transaction costs have their importance in a knowledge-based economy, coordination by hierarchy is unable to manage the complex processes of production, validation, and diffusion of knowledge, which often occur through long-term constructions. As Langlois (1993: 9) notes, transaction costs in the Coasian sense are essentially costs of a short-term nature, which means not taking into account the automatic resolution of uncertainties and conflicts through the daily routines of production: 'in a (hypothetical) long-run world in which change has ceased, routine (or, rather, routines in the sense of Nelson and Winter (1982)) attenuate any problem of writing repeated contracts; plasticity vanishes; and various external social institutions arise to mitigate any residual tendency to opportunism or moral hazard' (Langlois 1993: 9). Langlois concludes that the problem of opportunism due to moral hazard thus fades away in the long term, such that the existence of the business is not solely due to the costs of short-term transaction: 'perhaps we ought to look not at transaction costs *per se* but at their source: change and uncertainty. As may perhaps be obvious, but as I will argue anyway, change and uncertainty arguably offer us explanations for the existence of firms that go beyond traditional transaction-cost explanations' (Langlois 1993: 10). Hierarchies are limited in compensating for market failures.

The Question of Incentives

In any theory of the firm, the question of incentives is a critical one, to ensure that individuals act in line with the global objectives and vision of the firm. Aligning the incentives of individuals is thus stressed as the main item in the governance of the firm. The nature of incentives determines what 'holds' the firm together as a coherent entity. In the two main approaches to the firm that we are analysing, it appears that the purpose and role of incentives differ dramatically.

In a context of information processing, the central question of incentives is dominated by the existence of asymmetries of information. These result from opportunistic behaviour by agents that are reluctant to reveal all the information they have, or reveal it with bias or by cheating. The risk of opportunism[5] directly influences the transaction costs, which in turn lead to the determination of an adequate structure of governance to align incentives.[6]

---

[5] The two main risks of opportunism are 'adverse selection' (individuals may cheat before signing a contract), or 'moral hazard' (individuals may cheat after signing a contract).

[6] For example, some traditional incentives are the unit-based bonuses in a Taylorian work situation, or stock options in some modern companies.

In a context of management of knowledge, asymmetries of information are still valid, but their interpretation calls for different types of governance mechanisms. First, the nature of asymmetries differs. As Bessy and Brousseau (1998: 460) observe:

Regarding its value, knowledge is a highly uncertain resource when it is transferred between two economic units. This is partly due to the well-known information asymmetry about quality inherent in every market transfer of information (Arrow 1962*b*). But it is also due to the radical uncertainty over the potential use of knowledge. Two different phenomena are in question: (1) the receiving party can use knowledge in ways that are not easily observable by the prior holder. This is typically a moral hazard problem (*hidden action*), but in a specific informational context where it is impossible to build *ex ante* incentive schemes or (infallible) supervision mechanisms because all the potential usage of knowledge cannot be anticipated and made observable, and (2) knowledge is itself an input in the process of knowledge creation. The unit that benefits from a transfer can be conducive to the creation of new knowledge, that will increase the value of the initial knowledge. The question is then how to remunerate each party for its contribution to the knowledge creation process. Again, due to the uncertainty of such a process, it is very difficult to solve it *ex ante* by an optimal incentive scheme.

Secondly, contrary to the static context of allocation of resources, in a dynamic process of knowledge creation and distribution, the fact that agents have diverging preferences, diverging intentions, or diverging capacities could in certain circumstances be considered as beneficial (Schelling 1978; M. D. Cohen 1984; Loasby 1989). Thus, not only do asymmetries of knowledge not coincide with asymmetries of information, but their existence calls for qualitatively different forms of governance.

Ambiguity, persistent information and knowledge asymmetries, and unresolved conflict are all phenomena that indeed short-term efficiency but are vital elements for long-term learning. A world where all incentives are perfectly aligned and information asymmetries and conflicts are optimally resolved by appropriate contractual arrangements is indeed a world where the organization has lost all opportunities for learning. Some persistent imperfection in the alignment of information and incentives is the main driving force behind the organizational learning process.

Thus, the central question that remains is what kind of incentive mechanisms are most effective in promoting which kind of learning (Cohendet et al. 1998). An interesting answer is provided by Coriat and Dosi (1998), for whom the incentive mechanisms needed in a dynamic context are embodied in the routines of the firm. Following Nelson and Winter (1982), they suggest a dual account of the role of routines: as problem-solving repeated actions and as mechanisms of governance and control ('routines as truces among conflicting interests'). It also might help to differentiate between types of routines and rules. For example, Favereau's work (1993, 1995) on salary rules distinguishes between two types of rules and routines: one that corresponds to rules that are very precise, leaving no room for interpretation, and another that entails 'interpretive ambiguity' (Fransman 1994)—in fact, the emergence of learning processes.

In short, in a context of circulation and creation of knowledge, the potential existence of asymmetries of information certainly matters, but is not the primary reason to define and implement incentive schemes and other governing mechanisms. The latter should be shaped in order to align dispersed bodies of knowledge within the organization and to respect a satisfactory balance between the exploration and exploitation of knowledge.

Towards a 'Dual' Firm

We are thus confronted with two visions of the firm that differ on the formalization and representation of knowledge. The risk of these two visions diverging is high, ruling out dialogue between the vision of the firm based on the allocation of resources, and the vision of the firm based on the creation of resources. Even though we fully reject the hypothesis of tight-coupling between information and knowledge, and we accept the presence of interpretative ambiguity that leads to a 'loose-coupling' between information and knowledge, we believe that there is scope for some compromise[7] between the two theoretical approaches to the firm.

At the root of the compromise, it seems that the nature of the relationships between the firm and its competitors and suppliers is accurately expressed by the emphasis of traditional approaches on transactional mechanisms. The degree of opportunism, the frequency of transactions, the degree of uncertainty, and the degree of specificity of assets help determine the nature of the contractual relationships between the firm and external organizations. In such a context, it is important to note that the firm has no preferred activities; each activity is given the same weight and is maintained within the firm or externalized according to transaction-cost criteria.

In the context of a knowledge-based economy, our view is that the core statement of the modern theory of the firm is that the firm must be seen *in primis* as a processor of knowledge, and not just as a mere information-processing device. The focus of attention is the key limiting factor[8] in a knowledge-intensive dynamic perspective. Activities do not have the same weight. Firms are able to rank their activities according to an index of growing distance from the 'Core activity' (the activity receiving the highest focus of attention from the firm).

---

[7] Many authors have investigated this key issue of relationships between transactions and competences (e.g. Loasby 1996). In a recent contribution, Williamson (1999: 49) too pays attention to this issue: 'Given that both governance and competence are bounded rationality constructs and hold that organization matters, both share a lot of common grounds. Governance is more microanalytic (the transaction is the unit of analysis) and adopts an economizing approach to assessing comparative economic organization, whereas competence is more composite (the routine is the unit of analysis) and is more concerned with processes (especially learning) and the lessons for strategy. Healthy tensions are posed between them. Both are needed in our efforts to understand complex economic phenomena as we build towards a science of organization.'

[8] As we have seen in Chapter 2, following Simon (1982), it is attention rather than information that is becoming a rare resource, as screening and selection of information become important functions.

More precisely, we hypothesize that firms fix their attention first on a closed sub-set of activities that define the domain of competences, and then rank other activities (the 'peripheral domain') along a decreasing index of attention from the domain of competence.

Such an order implies that the firm manages *competences and transactions simultaneously, but it does so according to a specific lexicographic order of priorities.* As Langlois and Foss (1996: 31) claim, 'as firms move increasingly from their core businesses, they confront increasing adverse selection and moral hazard, since management becomes increasingly unable to efficiently monitor employees or to evaluate their human capital. Agency costs rise correspondingly, producing the net profitability disadvantage associated with further integration . . . .' In other words, in the domain of competences, low-opportunism conditions prevail and allow more valuable knowledge to be applied to the firm's activities. In the peripheral domain, meanwhile, the risk of opportunism is high and leads to the situation described by the classical transactional approach. Consequently, the 'design' of the firm involves the following steps.

Firstly, the firm focuses its limited attention and chooses the domain of its com-petences, the governance of which is specifically devoted to knowledge coordina-tion. Within its set of competences, the firm functions as a knowledge processor giving full priority to the creation of resources. The firm's domain of competences is not considered to be tradable on the market: activities belonging to the domain of competences are 'disconnected' from the make-or-buy trade-off suggested by transaction-cost theory.[9] More precisely, two subsets can be distinguished in this domain: (1) the zone of *core competences* where the firm aims at being ahead of the competition and decides to derive competitive advantage; (2) the zone of *competences* that encompasses the activities that the firm 'knows well how to perform', but that are not necessary for competitive advantage over others.

Secondly, along with choosing the domain and direction of creative resources for the long term,[10] firms organize in the peripheral domain the ongoing alloca-tion of resources and adaptation to the environment. This requires governance mechanisms that are well analysed by the transaction-cost approach.[11] These

[9] The size of the set of core competences is very limited, for managing core competences is by definition very costly: it requires specific sunk costs, forging and managing alliances and other types of cooperation with institutions that have complementary forms of knowledge, accessing and absorbing the most recent scientific results related to the domain of core competences, and so on. For this reason companies generally choose only few core competences to develop, extend, and protect over the long run. For instance, Sony vies for command in one core competence: *miniatur-ization*; Benetton has two core competences, *Design* and *Marketing*, and so on. (Prahalad and Hamel (1990) note that, in general, it is rare for a company to possess more than five core competences.)

[10] So far, we are still adhering to the hypothesis that a firm has a single decision centre and is pop-ulated by the rational agent.

[11] This hypothesis implies that there are two main governance mechanisms to be considered by the firm: the mechanism for governing competences, defined by the need to coordinate knowledge, and the mechanism for governing transactions, reliant on the need to manage transactions (see also Amin and Cohendet 1999). The organization of the firm requires a dual governance structure, the one to govern the domain of the firm's core activities, the other to govern the remaining activities (the peripheral domain).

activities are necessary to support core activities, and they generally correspond to the larger number of activities and employment positions in the firm. These activities do not require by definition a strong commitment in terms of knowledge management. The firm just needs to 'be informed' of best practice among other firms and of organizations that can offer equivalent support services, and, if it appears that these activities are too costly to be run within the firm compared to market mechanisms (according to transaction-costs criteria), they will be outsourced.

Representing the 'Dual Firm'

The expression 'dual firm' is employed to claim that firms tend first to focus their attention on their domain of competences and then to select the activities according to traditional transactional criteria. However, this expression serves primarily for pedagogical purposes. In reality, the choices belong to a continuum of activities that can be ranked form the core (as indicated in Fig. 3.1). Considering the ranking of activities from the core, one can distinguish three main zones. Each zone is characterized by a given set of relationships (in particular contractual forms) between the firm and external organizations, by some dominant modes of institutional design, and by some main directions of exchange of knowledge.

Zone 1 is the core itself. For a given firm, in terms of exchange of knowledge, this zone is characterized by 'partners' or 'quasi-integrated' suppliers that produce high-value components or systems that are highly strategic. They could be wholly owned suppliers or partly owned affiliate suppliers in which the firm holds an equity stake and they typically transfer personnel to work on a

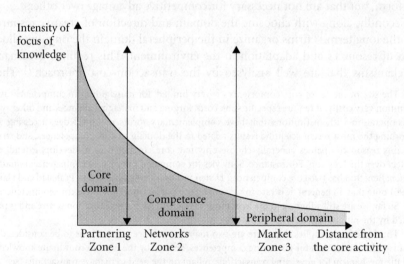

Figure 3.1. *Ranking of the firm's activities from the core competences*

Source: Amesse and Cohendet (2001: 1469)

part-time or full-time basis. These suppliers participate fully or partially in long-term strategic plans, capital investments and capacity planning, and personnel transfers. The formal duration of the typical contract is long term, and most of the contracts are renewed automatically. Moreover, the suppliers tend to take part in building the firm's knowledge base and benefit from the absorptive capacities accumulated by the firm. But it is also important for a firm to enhance the absorptive capacities of the suppliers themselves. The firm provides assistance to its suppliers not only in the areas of quality, cost reduction, factory layout, and inventory management, but also in terms of increasing technological competences and research facilities. What is essentially transferred in this zone are creative ideas through multiple functional interfaces (manufacturing to manufacturing, engineering to engineering, and so on). Such a perspective requires permanent benchmarking of capabilities within the group of partners, substantial investment in inter-firm knowledge-sharing routines, and regular socialization. Still in this zone, the relationship with competitors is highly unstable and conflicting, and generally leads to acquisitions or mergers.

In Zone 2 the firm holds significant pieces of knowledge, but needs to access complementary forms of knowledge held by other firms to be able to develop and use the knowledge efficiently. This zone is characterized by 'networks'. In terms of knowledge transfer, what is at stake in this zone is the mutual exchange of complementary forms of knowledge. Networks precisely offer a way to share and exchange knowledge complementarities. What differentiates a given economic agent, such as a firm, from another is its specific body of tacit knowledge. Through networks, agents can organize an efficient circulation of codified knowledge through a structure that renders compatible different segments of specific tacit forms of knowledge. Agents agree to increase their specialization in a given tacit form of knowledge, because they are confident that the other agents will increase their specialization in complementary forms. This arrangement reduces the risks of overspecialization, and relies intensively on building mutual trust in the production of knowledge. The degree of trust also influences the choice between specialization and cooperation in the production of knowledge:

Trust is a tacit agreement in which rather than systematically seeking out the best opportunity at every instant, each agent takes a longer perspective to the transactions, as long as his traditional partner does not go beyond some mutually accepted norm. Sharing the risks of specialization is an aspect of co-operation that manifests an important trust mechanism in network functioning. Specialization is a risky business. One may sacrifice the 'horizontal' ability to satisfy various demands in order to gain 'vertical' efficiency in an effort to increase profitability. Any specializing firm accepts this risk, network or not. A risk-sharing mechanism is essential because, while aggregate profits for participating firms may indeed be superior to the situation where firms are less specialized, the distribution of profits may be very hazardous. To make specialization worthwhile, the dichotomous (win–lose) individual outcome must be smoothed somehow by a cooperative principle of risk sharing. (Zuscovitch 1998: 256)

Trust is relevant with regard to the reliability of other specialized producers of complementary knowledge.[12] From such a perspective, there is less worry about excessive uncontrolled spillovers and risks of excessive imitation, precisely because of significant transaction costs. Imitation is very costly, and loose cooperation in informal networks, allowing a certain control over spillovers between agents, can be an efficient form of collaboration that ensures compatibility of their mutual interactions. Therefore, one of the key issues that determines the functioning of innovative networks is the constant trade-off by agents involved in these networks between the delimitation of property rights, on the one hand, and the determination of rights of access to complementary forms of knowledge, on the other.

Zone 3 is the peripheral zone where the firm holds no specific advantage in terms of knowledge and where the risks for it in terms of asymmetries of information are very high. This is a 'quasi-market' zone, where the degree of supplier–buyer interdependence is generally low. Products are standardized and require few interactions with other inputs. Contracts are arm's length, and their duration depends on the classical transactional parameters. For a given firm, in terms of supplier management practices, this zone requires minimal assistance to suppliers, with single functional interfaces (sales to purchasing, for instance), and the practice of price benchmarking. In terms of knowledge transfer (usually technology transfer), what is at stake in this zone is the exchange of an artefact, rather than innovative ideas or new tacit knowledge.

Conceiving of the firm as a locus of competence building must give full priority to the fact that *in primis* the firm is a processor of knowledge, as Kogut and Zander (1992: 390) have argued for some time:

While the boundaries of the firm are, unquestionably, influenced by transactional dilemmas, the question of capabilities points the analysis to understanding why organizations differ in their performance. The decision which capabilities to maintain and develop is influenced by the current knowledge of the firm and the expectation of the economic gain form exploring the opportunities in new technologies and organizing principle as platforms into future market developments. We propose that firms maintain those capabilities in-house that are expected to lead to recombination of economic values.

Thus, drawing on the theoretical considerations above, it is possible to reinterpret and revisit the key concepts of the traditional theories of the firm, and in particular the question of transactions. Indeed, starting first with the classical conceptualization based on processing information and then trying to fit in knowledge considerations leads to a theoretical dead end. An example of such a

---

[12] The institutionalization of incentives as validation processes (peer-referring processes, for instance) in some communities may vary widely. The choice for agent A to specialize in one domain of knowledge (and to agree to bear the sunk costs) in cooperation with others agents that agree to specialize in turn in the complementary types of knowledge that are necessary for A (while A's knowledge would be considered complementary by the other agents) seems to be one of the main lines of research to understand the management of knowledge by organizations.

theoretical impassse is given by Marengo (1994) in discussing the limits of the well-known multidivisional ('M-form') and functional ('U-form') forms. He notes that these traditional forms are conceived of in such a manner as to solve information problems (information overload by managers, in particular) and that they are not appropriate for creating knowledge. On the U-form, thus, he notes:

It can be argued that the U-form centralizes competences in interfunctional coordination and decentralizes instead to functional departments competences in many strategic issues concerning products and diversification. With the growing multiplicity of products the functional structure does not seem that of information overload, but that of mismatch between competences and tasks. Chief executives are unable to do their job effectively, not because they are burdened by excess information, but rather because the organizational structure does not enable them to develop the necessary competences. Chief executives should respond to environmental changes, but when such changes push towards product diversification, many of the competences that are necessary to promote and manage diversity remain, in the U-form, at the level of functional departments.   (Marengo 1994)

In fact, in the classical cases of theorizing M- and U-forms, priority has been given to information processing and not to knowledge processing by the firm—that is, to the process of allocation of resources and not to the process of creation of resources. What is assumed in a dynamic perspective centred around core competences is precisely the reverse hypothesis: priority is given to the process of knowledge creation, and then, bounded by this priority, attention is given to the mechanisms of allocation of resources (see Box 3.1 for an example). This, however, returns to the problem of the internal coherence of the firm.

Box 3.1. *Managing competences: the Nortel case*

To support our theoretical analysis, we use as an illustration the case of Nortel Networks in the 1990s. During this decade, Nortel, a strong contender in the 1980s in the digital switch market, became a dominant firm in the new Internet and optical network market. However, since the beginning of the new century what seemed to be a success story has been mitigated by Nortel's severe losses in the financial markets. At the beginning of the 1990s, the firm suddenly moved towards a new model of technology management (going 'from vertical integration to virtual integration', according to senior management) that can be interpreted along the theoretical lines developed in this chapter. When Jean Monty became president in 1992, he adopted a long-term vision of Nortel focused on building selected core competences, which included a major new focus on opto-electronics. This core domain determined which companies should be acquired to reinforce the company's core knowledge, and explained the nature of the strategic alliances and technological networks in which Nortel was involved.

The following main aspects stand out about Nortel's strategy after 1992:

- At the beginning of the 1990s, Nortel's only core technological competence was digital switches. Since this technology was becoming mature, it was inevitable that Nortel's competitive gap with followers would be sharply reduced in that area.

(continued)

Box 3.1. *(continued)*

- Monty decided to increase significantly the amount spent on R & D (from 11 to 16 per cent of sales for a given period), but he brought forward a new vision of knowledge management. At the same time as implementing a severe programme of cost reduction involving plant closures and lay-offs, he drew on the company's experience (mainly by capitalizing on Nortel's Fiberworld experience) to build a new core competence in opto-electronics. Meanwhile, in order to afford this new strategy, Nortel started selling peripheral units, such as STC Submarine Systems, in 1994. The whole value-added chain began to be reshuffled from a knowledge-based perspective.

- At the same time, Nortel began a process of shaping the next generation of core competences by investing in integrated networking solutions and paving the way for a core competence in Internet protocol systems. It is remarkable to see how this strategy began with Nortel's involvement in loose networks with other companies that had expertise in that field.

Then in 1997 Monty's successor, John Roth, extended the core competency in the Internet protocol network (end-to-end broadband solutions).

- When Roth became Nortel's president in 1997, the process accelerated with dramatic acquisitions. In 1998 Northern Telecom changed its name and became Nortel Networks, with the clear mission (the 'webtone vision') of becoming a world leader in Internet network systems. In 1998 its first and most significant acquisition was Bay Networks ($9.1 billion), then Nortel acquired numerous start-ups (many with no sales), carefully selected in terms of knowledge complementarity with the new core domain. In two years, Nortel bought sixteen enterprises at a total cost of $22 billion. These acquisitions were conceived of as a means of absorbing outside technologies and research capabilities to enhance Nortel's lead in opto-electronics.

- It should be emphasized that the process of acquisitions and alliances implemented by Nortel obeys specific conditions, in order for Nortel to maintain and reinforce its internal core knowledge: when a new company is acquired, Nortel assigns carefully trained employees to the newly acquired unit to facilitate integration. For example, when describing what followed the acquisition of Bay Networks, MacDonald (2000) explains: 'Little was left to chance. . . . Integration teams were created, which got groups of Bay and Nortel employees focused on solving the adjustment problems. Another measure was the establishment of an immediate and continuous flow of communication between the two types of organizations so that employees at all levels would be kept informed and rumours could be dispelled' (p. 193). MacDonald underlines this claim by quoting Roth himself: 'I saw inside Bay a lot of practices that had been brought in from Intel . . . And these practices were closer to the mark than what we had been doing. So we took these practices and put them across the corporation, like bonus treatments, and how we rewarded people and how we measure our progress in R & D' (p. 193). Meanwhile, Nortel's internal R & D structure was modified to absorb technologies and knowledge from the acquired unit more quickly. Research centres were reorganized along 'business lines', each offering solutions to a well-identified group of 'customers' (carriers, wireless, and so on). Each business line

has considerable autonomy, to absorb as quickly as possible the knowledge possessed by a new unit entering the group.
- In its move towards a new vision, Nortel is experiencing a major shift in the way
  it organizes production. Initially, Nortel was an equipment manufacturer, producing high-quality, reliable components and systems. With its new core competence,
  it is becoming a 'virtual' integrator that delegates to carefully selected partners the
  tasks required to produce physical systems and components. Nortel is selling
  plants and operations to selected suppliers linked to Nortel under long-term contracts. Here again, the need to absorb, circulate, and diffuse as quickly as possible
  the new knowledge acquired and produced has been the main trigger of change.

The heavy losses of Nortel in financial markets since the late 1990s, does not seem
to be leading to a radical reconsideration of Nortel's strategy. However, these events
underline that the building of competences is a risky business that takes time, and
that acquisitions of firms on financial markets do not lead automatically to an acquisition of new knowledge held by the acquired companies.
  The evolution of Nortel's strategy after 1990 to manage core competences are
illustrated in Fig. 3.2.

Source: Amesse and Cohendet (2001); see also Amesse, Séguin-Dulude, and Stanley (1994)

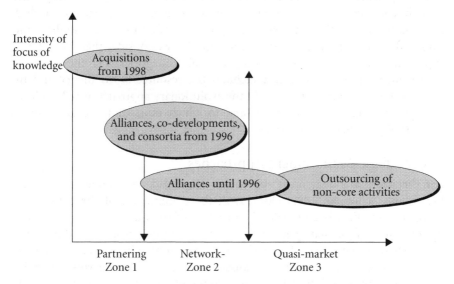

Figure 3.2. *Managing core competences at Nortel, 1990–2000*
Source: Amesse and Cohendet (2001: 1472)

Thus far, we have proposed a theoretical vision of the firm conceived as a processor of knowledge, in which the classical transactional arguments are still present
but their force is secondary when compared to the strength of knowledge considerations and focus. This could be interpreted as a step to explore the

interaction between 'non-opportunism-based' knowledge considerations and opportunism-related factors in the choice of organizational modes. The present knowledge-based approach also may be extended to organizational entities and to more complicated or hybrid modes, such as multilevel corporations, alliances, joint ventures, and legal partnerships' (Conner and Prahalad 2002: 119).

However, the conditions that are required to 'hold' the firm as a coherent entity have not yet been examined. In particular, it has been explicitly assumed so far that the firm can be considered as a unique cognitive entity, represented by a manager acting with procedural rationality. This hypothesis was made for reasons of simplicity, but it has to be acknowledged that, on this fundamental issue, there are conflicting voices within the competence-based approach. At this particular stage of the argument, we need to separate the set of new theories of the firm that we have grouped under the umbrella of 'competence-based' theories into distinct subsets that suggest different ways of building appropriate governance mechanisms in the knowledge processing firm.

THE DIFFERENT SUBSETS OF THE 'COMPETENCE-BASED' THEORY OF THE FIRM

The competence-based approach to the firm is not a homogeneous approach. It can be considered as the meeting point of heterogeneous approaches that share a common denial of the firm viewed as a processor of information, but that come from different streams of thought. Schematically, we consider that the different approaches can be regrouped into two main categories: (1) the strategic-management approaches (which includes the resource-based theory and the core-competence approach), and (2) the evolutionary approach (which includes the dynamic-capabilities approach and to which most of the organizational learning approaches can be related).

The Strategic-Management Approaches

For the *strategic-management* approaches (Prahalad and Hamel 1990; Stalk, Evans, and Schulman 1992; Doz 1996), the delimitation of the competence domain of the firm is essentially the privilege of the manager, who designs an *ex ante* vision of the management of knowledge within a firm. According to this approach, managers are in charge of defining the frontier between the domain of competence and the domain of transaction. They thus endeavour to design specific incentives to align the behaviour of members of the firm to the vision of the firm they wish to promote. Both the resource-based view of the firm and the strategic-competence-based approach to the firm emphasize behavioural concepts of strategy by focusing on *how* a firm chooses to compete rather than on *where* it chooses to compete, but each also exhibits some distinctive features.

The resource-based view of the firm (Wernerfelt 1984; Barney 1991), inspired by Edith Penrose's work in industrial economics distinguishing tangible resources from the services these resources provide, aims at explaining and predicting why some firms are able to establish positions of sustainable competitive advantage and earn superior returns. A firm's resource at a given moment of time can be defined as those assets (tangible and intangible) that are tied semi-permanently to the firm (Caves 1980). The firm is viewed as a bundle of idiosyncratic resources. The resources that lead to competitive advantage (for example, brand names, in-house knowledge of technology, employment of skilled personnel, trade contracts, machinery, efficient procedures, and so on) must, by definition, be scarce, valuable, and reasonably durable (Barney 1991), and unlikely to be available from others (Rumelt 1987). The claim that resources (that are difficult to imitate and only imperfectly substitutable) create sustainable advantages challenges the standard micro-economic argument that firm differences should erode over time owing to imitative mechanisms.

Despite its significant insights, the resource-based theory of the firm still faces several limitations. The main criticism concerns its tautological argumentation: 'At its worst, the resource-based view is circular. Successful firms are successful because they have unique resources. They should nurture these resources to be successful' (Porter 1994: 145). Then, as Krogh and Grand (2002: 168) note, 'while the resource-based view uses equilibrium arguments from industrial organizations to analyse rent creation, when identifying sources of abnormal returns and competitive success from an economic perspective, it relies on process arguments to understand inimitability, based on such concepts as emergence, path dependence, and learning'. Another strong criticism concerns the static vision of the resource-based theory, which we will return to later in this section.

The strategic-competence-based approach relies on strategic-management concepts suggested by Prahalad and Hamel (1990: 82) and centres around 'collective learning of the organization, especially how to coordinate diverse production skills, and integrate multiple skills of technology'. It centres on the view of the firm as a social institution, the main characteristic of which is to know (well) how to do certain things. Competences are coherent sets of capabilities used in an efficient way. Some of the competences are strategic ('core competences' according to Prahalad and Hamel 1990)) and constitute the main sources of the competitiveness of a firm ('what a firm does well and better than the others'). They are the products of a selection process both internal and external to the firm.

How these competences are constructed, combined, protected, and managed is critical for understanding the boundaries of the firm as well as the coordination and incentive structure of the firm. Core competences are firms, specific skills and cognitive traits directed towards the attainment of the highest possible levels of customer satisfaction vis-à-vis competitors. Core competences may be leveraged directly to satisfy customer needs or indirectly to develop a range of core products or core services. Firms with core competences have to build appropriate cognitive traits, which include: (1) recipes and organizational routines for approaching ill-structured problems; (2) shared value systems that direct action in unique situations, (3) tacit understanding of the direction of technology, organization dynamic, and product market.

The focus of the competence-based approach is on 'the effects caused by a competence' (Drejer and Riis 1999: 632), rather than on its structural characteristics. For Prahalad and Hamel, as well as for most of the authors of this stream of research, top managers play a key role in identifying, developing, and reinforcing core competences. 'Because capabilities are cross functional, the change process can't be left to middle managers. It requires the hands-on guidance of the CEO and the active involvement of top line managers' (Stalk, Evans, and Schulman 1992). Thus, one of the limits of the strategic-competence-based approach is its strong dependence on the 'perfect' vision of the manager. In addition, Probst, Büchel, and Raub (1998: 243) consider that the competence-based approach does 'not provide an explanation about how resources such as organizational knowledge develop over time'.[13] These criticisms are partially overcome in the evolutionary approach of the firm.

Evolutionary Competence-Based Theories

For *evolutionary competence-based* theories (Dosi and Marengo 1994; Teece, Pisano, and Schuen 1997), the determination of a competence domain and a peripheral domain within the firm is essentially the result of the process of evolution of routines. Knowledge is stored in routines, seen as the regular and predictable behavioural pattern of the firm, and innovation is an inherently unpredictable mutation of routines that cannot be guided by the vision of a sole manager. As Krogh and Grand (2002: 170) argue:

Whereas the resource-based view sees strategy as having a strong intentional element (Barney 1986, 1991; Porter 1991; Hamel and Prahalad 1993, 1994), evolutionary theories are traditionally more pessimistic about the possibilities of significant, managerially led, proactive change (see also Witt 1994). The question of intentionality becomes particularly salient when considering how a firm sets out to build a given set of capabilities. . . . As a consequence, a theory of knowledge creation, in order to be practically useful as well as to become a real theoretical contribution, has to reintegrate managerial discretion into its theory of strategic behaviour and return appropriation.

Along the same lines, Langlois (1994: 8) has added:

Knowledge in an organization is not something that resides in the head of managers; rather, the organization's knowledge is nothing other than its complex of routines, including routines for coordination among routines and routines for changing or creating routines. This repertoire of routines is what defines the conditional states of readiness on which messages from the environment operate. To put it another way, the complex of routines that make up an organization not only determines what an organization can do

---

[13] Probst, Büchel, and Raub try to provide a partial corrective by mobilizing metaphors from evolutionary economics (e.g. imitation, selection, variety, replication, etc.). For example, they relate changes in organizational knowledge to the cumulative effects of individual and group learning: when such learning becomes routinized and synthesized through agent interaction and shared beliefs over time, the organizational knowledge set can be said to be transformed. Thus, replication at one level becomes a precondition for innovation at another level.

well but also conditions how the organization will interpret messages; how information from the environment will alter the organization's existing repertoire of routines. That is to say, the organization's routines are in a broad sense its cognitive apparatus, its 'map'. They determine what information the organization recognizes as meaningful, and they strongly influence how the organization learns and how it perceives opportunities.

In this vision, knowledge is not mobilized in separate domains of the firm, and the formation of a domain of competence is simply the '*ex-post* result' of a continuous process of evolution of routines. There are two approaches that have developed this vision of knowledge: the dynamic-capabilities approach and the organizational-learning approaches.

The dynamic-capabilities approach—centred around routines—stresses the firm's ability to integrate, build, and reconfigure internal and external competences to address rapidly changing environments. 'Dynamic capabilities thus reflect an organization's ability to achieve new and innovative forms of competitive advantage given path dependencies and market positions' (Teece et al. 1997: 516). The capabilities of the firm rest on processes (organizational and managerial, integration, learning, reconfiguration, and transformation), positions (in business assets, difficult to trade assets, and assets complementary to them such as reputation assets), and paths (path dependency, technological opportunities). However, distinctive organizational capabilities can provide competitive advantage and generate rents only if they are based on a collection of routines, skills, and complementary assets that are difficult to imitate. As Nelson (1991: 68) emphasizes:

Successful firms can be understood in terms of a hierarchy of practised organizational routines, which define lower-order organizational skills and how these skills are coordinated, and higher order of decision procedures for choosing what is to be done at lower level. The notion of organizational routines is a key building block under our concept of core organizational capabilities. At any time, the practised routines that have to be built into an organization define a set of things the organization is capable of doing confidently. If the lower-order routines for doing various tasks are absent, or if they exist but there is no practical higher-order routine for invoking them in the particular combination needed to accomplish a particular job, then the capability to do that job lies outside the organization's extant core capabilities.

The organizational-learning approaches, following the seminal work of Argyris and Schön (1978), emphasize the need for organizations to change continuously. They focus on two kinds of learning activities: obtaining know-how in order to solve specific problems based upon existing premises ('single-loop learning'); and establishing new premises (paradigms, mental models, and so on) to override the existing ones ('double-loop learning'). By recognizing that organizational learning is a process of adaptive change that is influenced by past experience, and based on developing or modifying routines, these approaches share some strong features with the evolutionary approach.

Like the evolutionary approach, they are cautious about the role played by the manager in the design of the organization, even though scholars such as Nonaka and Takeuchi argue that the Argyris and Schön vision still requires a manager or at least someone having the knowledge of when and how to put the double loop into practice.[14] Among the theorists of organizational learning who are clearly sceptical about the leading role of managers in organizational learning, a recent influential voice is that of Senge. Senge, in defining the 'learning organization' as 'a place where people are continually discovering how they create their reality. And how they can change it' (1990: 12–13), sees only an indirect role for managers in the design of the organizations. For him, managers should limit their intervention to: (1) stimulating the adoption of 'system thinking'; (2) encouraging personal mastery of their own lives; (3) bringing prevailing 'mental models' to the surface and challenging them; (4) building a share 'vision'; and (5) facilitating 'team learning'.

Towards a Synthesis of the Competence-Based Approaches of the Firm

The different subsets of the competence-based approach that have been examined might be seen as different theoretical vantage points to look at the formation and use of knowledge assets by the firm. However, a logical question that follows is whether there is a fruitful way of putting these different theoretical pieces together.[15] An interesting perspective on the interaction between these approaches is offered by Ciborra and Andreu (2002), through the model of the 'learning ladder' (Fig. 3.3). They link the generation and transfer of knowledge to a variety of internal learning processes within a given organization. According to them, 'core capabilities develop through a series of transformations, by which standard resources available in open markets (where all firms can acquire them),

---

[14] Nonaka and Takeuchi (1995: 45–6) argue, 'it has been widely assumed implicitly or explicitly that double-loop learning—the questioning and rebuilding of existing perspectives, interpretation frameworks, or decision premises—can be very difficult for organizations to implement by themselves. In order to overcome this difficulty, the learning theorists argue that some kind of artificial intervention, such as the use of an organizational development program is required. The limitation of this argument is that someone inside or outside an organization "objectively" knows the right time and method for putting the double-loop learning into practice.'

[15] There are several examples in the recent literature that implicitly or explicitly integrate the different approaches that have been detailed. One example is Leonard-Barton's analysis (1995) of the core technological capabilities that provide a competitive edge for Chapparal. She identifies at least four dimensions:

- dynamic knowledge reservoirs (or competences): (1) employee knowledge and skills; (2) physical technical system;
- knowledge control and channelling mechanisms: (3) managerial systems; (4) values and norms.

She also considers that the 'critical knowledge building activities' (dynamic capabilities) are: (1) cross functional expertise to solve operating problems, (2) integrate new tools and methodology, (3) experiment, (4) import knowledge (benchmark).

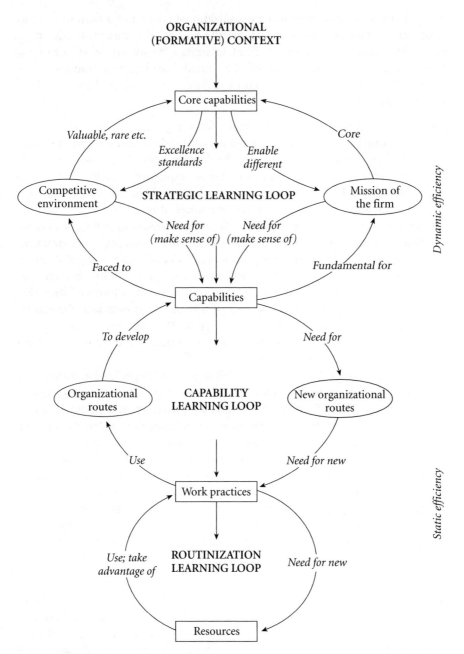

Figure 3.3. *Learning in the capabilities and core capabilities development processes*
Source: Ciborra and Andreu (2002: 578, fig 32.1)

are used and combined within the organizational context of a firm to produce capabilities, which in turn can become the source of competitive advantage, especially if they are rare and difficult to imitate or substitute' (Ciborra and Andreu 2002: 576). The stages of the varied learning and transformation processes through which the firm's core capabilities are generated are considered to be the following:

- *Stage 1: A routinization learning loop.*   This stage implies two different kinds of learning processes: mastering the use of standard resources and products (the efficient work practices), and the development of new work practices. Work practices resulting from this stage are expressed in codified or operative forms (such as the usage of a spreadsheet). This loop routinizes work practices, and indirectly routines, in the usage of resources.
- *Stage 2: A capability learning loop.*   This stage correspond to a transformation that 'abstracts' and 'constructs' capabilities from existing work practices. It involves combining emerging work practices and organizational routines. In this process, the emergent capabilities (which are more abstract than work practices, 'skills without a place') are described in terms of *what* they do and *how* they do, but lack 'a sense of *why* they exist or at least the reasons for their existence are seldom challenged. The *why* appears with more clarity as they involve into *core* capabilities through a third learning loop' (Ciborra and Andreu 2002: 557).
- *Stage 3: A strategic learning loop.*   This stage is the upper level of transformation, where capabilities can evolve into 'core capabilities' (core competences, according to the definition that we have adopted), which differentiate a firm strategically (in turn, core capabilities can reshape the context itself). 'This loop gives meaning to capabilities in the context of the firm's competitive environment and business mission, thus allowing the selection and elicitation of core capabilities' (Ciborra and Andreu 2002: 578). The competitive environment of the firm will thus reveal progressively the capabilities that have strategic potential, as it reveals also the role and scope of capabilities (the sense of *why* a given capability is important). The authors add that the firm's business mission is also relevant for identifying the core capabilities because it sets priorities in the alignment between them and the current mission.

Ciborra and Andreu's framework helps to bridge the theoretical gap between the different streams of the competence approach to the firm. In a first step, resources and other strategic assets (examined by the resource-based theory) result from cumulative knowledge and former efforts to build capabilities through the progressive transformation into work practice. Then, the dynamic capabilities (stressed by the evolutionary approach) express the unique ability of firms to organize learning and integrate routines and work practices in order to sustain and reinforce the strategic domain of core competences of the firm (analysed by the strategic-competence approach). This domain is progressively shaped by two selection mechanisms acting together: the environment that faces the firm (the external factor of selection), and the 'business mission' (the internal factor of selection).

A recent typology proposed by Kusonoki, Nonaka, and Nagata (1998) offers a complementary way of looking at the interactions between the different theoretical positions on the formation and use of competences. According to the authors, the organizational capability related to knowledge creation can be categorized in three types:

- knowledge base (distinctive individual units of knowledge, functional knowledge, elemental technologies, info-processing devices, patents);
- knowledge frames (capture linkages of individual units of knowledge and their priorities);
- knowledge dynamics (interaction between knowledge base and knowledge frames).

We believe that the resource-based theory deals with the first category (knowledge base), the competence approach deals with the second category (knowledge frames), while the dynamic-capability approach deals with the third category (knowledge dynamics). Each approach brings a specific insight on the organization of knowledge in the competence approach of the firm (see Fig. 3.4).

While the respective domains of each of the approaches and the nature of their interactions can be clarified, a lingering point of friction or conflict between the strategic competence approach and the evolutionary approach concerns the understanding of how selection mechanisms operate on routines/capabilities to shape the core competences of the firm. In the strategic-competence approach, it is the manager's vision that shapes the domain of core competences; while in the evolutionary approach the driving force remains the external environment of the firm. Even though authors such as Andreu and Ciborra observe that both mechanisms

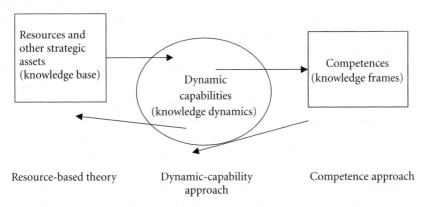

Figure 3.4. *The respective roles and domains of the theoretical subsets of the competence-based approach of the firm*

operate on routines and dynamic capabilities to shape the core competences of the firm, the relative importance of each basic mechanism and its potential interplay with the other one remains an unexplored issue.

Governance Mechanisms in the Knowledge-Based Firm Reconsidered

We thus need to return to the problem of governance mechanisms in the knowledge-based ('dual') firm. Our hypothesis is that both the strategic-competence and evolutionary approaches yield a specific conception of the governance mechanisms of the firm.

In the *managerial vision of competences*, the consequence of the lexicographic choice (first the focus on core activities, then managing the periphery) of the manager is that the firm needs to define two distinct structures of governance to manage the different domains. The first is a structure of governance to manage the domain of competences in order to align dispersed knowledge and expectations. Within this 'core' structure, some contractual schemes may be implemented (for example, stock options, or specific rewards for inventors within the organization), but they are not essential when compared with the priority given to the stimulation of collective learning processes. The second is a structure of governance conceived along transaction-costs criteria to manage the periphery. In this structure of governance, classical contractual schemes are dominant to ensure the information processing that is central to the functioning of the periphery.

On the basis of this double emphasis on, first, the generation of knowledge and, second the cognitive set-up of the firm, we would argue that a key governance challenge for firms is to reconcile organizational arrangements for transactional efficiency with those for sustaining learning. This is much the same as the exploration–exploitation trade-off signalled by James March (1991) to mark the dilemma faced by firms in balancing the short-term exploitation of existing competences and the long-term exploration of new competence.

Thus, in the 'learning domain', organizational and management practices must facilitate the creation and circulation of knowledge as well as strengthen recursive decision making. The challenge is to build trust, long-term commitments, and knowledge externalities, to encourage experimentalism, variety, and creative friction, to mobilize memory, retain slack, and forget old routines, and to facilitate the conversion of knowledge (between tacit and explicit, between individual and collective, between local and global). All these goals tend to privilege decentred management, distributed capability, and, to a degree, organizational 'excess' in the form of slack and redundancy (Nohria and Ghoshal 1997). In contrast, the transactional domain (for example, securing supply, achieving scale economies, make–buy trade-offs) demands the efficient allocation of resources, largely through substantive or procedural responses to the environment. Here, as ever, the governance choice is between hierarchy and market, dedicated to cost efficiency in dealing with transactions largely of a contractual nature. Organizational excess here is simply a waste of resources.

The *evolutionary vision of competences* avoids the risk associated with the strategic-management approach (rooted in its identification of two distinct operational domains and governance imperatives) of presenting the firm as a static and neatly divided entity in which management has (or should have) a panopticon understanding of what needs to be done. The evolutionary understanding of the formation of competences avoids this risk by framing the firm as a set of overlapping routines, processes, and practices, involving regular interchange between procedural and recursive behaviour and governance solutions emerging from the practices themselves. What is crucial in this understanding is that the rules of the game are not taken as exogenously given (in particular by a hierarchy) but emerging and evolving in the very process of interaction within the firm.

As we have already observed, Nelson and Winter (1982) were the first to introduce the idea that, in addition to the cognitive dimension, routines incorporate a motivational dimension. This key step for building a theory of the firm that considers routines as governance or control mechanisms has yet to be fully elaborated. Only Coriat and Dosi (1998) can be credited for clearly acknowledging that routines may be considered as 'a locus of conflict, governance, and a way of codifying micro-economic incentives and constraints'.[16] This claim needs to be better understood and further developed in the theory of the firm. The idea that routines embody mechanisms of governance and authority for collective behaviour in a context of employees potentially striving towards their own interests is indispensable in elaborating the competence-based approach to the firm. The establishment of a routine within an organization, its evolution, the testing of its problem-solving capacities, its reinforcement, or its rejection, forges a direct link with the nature of control and incentive mechanisms, the conflict-solving mechanisms, and the sharing mechanisms of the relational quasi-rent that govern relationships between individuals whose interests are not necessarily convergent.

The evolutionary approach, thus, carries the important idea that routines may encapsulate micro-governance mechanisms. However, it has not gone beyond this idea, partly because it has yet to explore the *localized dimension* of routines in the organization. Our thesis is that routines experienced and located in a functional group, in a project team, in a network of partners, in a social community, are all different in terms of their power of replication, degree of inertia, and potential for search. The nature of the activities concerned (production, research development, finance, and so on), and the goals and motivations of the potential users and developers of the routines, shape the dimensions and adaptive potential of emerging and practised routines. Some of these located routines— especially the work of communities, as we argue in the next two chapters—are strong micro-governance mechanisms.

---

[16] The authors analyse this assumption by studying the archetypal forms of organization such as Taylorism, Fordism, and Ohnism.

CONCLUSION: RESTORING THE MISSING
LINK—THE ROLE OF PRACTICES

We have argued thus far that a competence- or resource-based perspective of the firm—as opposed to a contract- or transaction-based perspective—opens up considerably the scope for exploring how firms learn and adapt in complex and changing business environments. The acquisition and renewal of knowledge—both tacit and codified—are crucial for survival, cannot be taken as pre-given, and occur at a variety of levels through a variety of means. For such reasons, the firm has to be seen as much more than an allocating mechanism. It is primarily a generator of resources, defined as distinctive knowledge and organizational routines, locked in core competences or capabilities, which are its strategic assets to the degree that they are valuable, rare, inimitable, and non-substitutable. As such, they are the staple sources of competitive advantage.

Viewing the firm as a processor of knowledge, we have tried as a first step to reconcile the specific problem of management of knowledge within the firm, with the traditional problem of allocating resources based on the transaction-cost approach. At the very least, this allows the approaches to be put into their right place. For example, as Milgrom and Roberts (1988: 450) note, 'the incentive-based transaction cost theory has been made to carry too much of the weight of explanation in the theory of organizations. We expect competing and complementary theories to emerge, theories that are founded on economizing on bounded rationality and pay more attention to changing technology and to evolutionary considerations.'

We have thus claimed that a key governance challenge for firms is to reconcile organizational arrangements for transactional efficiency with those for sustaining learning. We have also argued that the cognitive set-up of firms—more specifically their organizational 'rationality'—is crucial for framing expectations and outcomes. Thus, substantive rationality, based upon the principle of rule-following behaviour, is efficient for decision making in stable and simple-response situations (for example, mass production for planned markets), but inappropriate for a continually changing environment. In contrast, a procedural rationality favours learning through continual adjustment as agents modify their behaviour to external circumstances, but is ill equipped for strategic action in the context of radical change. In practice, individual firms are required to draw on these rationalities selectively depending on the nature of the task in hand, but they still tend to settle around one or a combination as the dominant cognitive set-up, which is precisely why we can claim an important linkage between firm rationality and learning potential.

But the theorization of learning needs to go further. The limitations of the competence-based approaches, despite our attempts at synthesis and integration, necessitate fuller recognition of an intermediate level between the analysis of the behaviour of individuals and the behaviour of the whole organization. We have acknowledged the role of permanent interaction between the individual level and the organization level in the design of the routines. However, we consider that these interactions are shaped and determined at an intermediate level: the level of 'communities' (from those sharing a functional specialization such as finance, mechanical engineering, to those defined either by the production of new knowledge or by a common interest for a given practice). In the chapters that follow, we argue that ongoing practices of learning rooted in communities are closer to reality than any idea of learning based on cognitive rationalities.

4

Practices of Knowing

Our aim in this chapter is to edge the knowledge-based perspective in a new direction, towards an understanding of knowledge generation and acquisition in firms as a weakly cognitive practice, or, more accurately, as the product of habits of everyday interaction in which thinking and acting are combined in inseparable unity, as are different types of knowledge, tacit and codified, mental, manual, and technological. Following on from Chapter 3, the competence-based approach (in both its evolutionary and its strategic-competence versions) deals with possessed knowledge and not with processes of knowing, with the consequence that an entire domain of knowledge production is neglected. In seeking to conceptualize knowledge formation as an embodied and material practice, we question the emphasis on rationality in the competence-based approach and the assumption that specific cognitive qualities are responsible for particular types of organizational learning and innovation (for example, procedural rationality for path-dependent or incremental innovation, and reflexive rationality for radical innovation; or tacit knowledge for non-imitable learning, and codified knowledge for more standardized learning).

We draw on an epistemology of pragmatic knowledge, and the supposition that meaning and novelty are generated through a combination of deliberate and non-deliberate practices of social engagement located in different types of community within and across organizations. Drawing on the fine-grained social anthropology of knowledge work in organizations, we argue that these communities are responsible for generating both routine and strategic learning, through practices of socialization, interaction, interest alignment, knowledge translation, and community maintenance—practices in which knowing is as much a matter of embodied behaviour as it is of rational decisions.

THE EMBODIED MIND

There is a long tradition of thought, currently highlighted in writing on the 'knowledge economy', that assumes that practical knowledge can be separated from intellectual knowledge, as each form is understood to draw on a distinctive set of attributes and capabilities. Thus, for example, the knowledge of artisans or of manual and technical workers has been seen to be of an applied nature, rooted in practical experience and know-how, technical mastery and grounded skills, while that of scientists or of research and development workers is considered to be of an intellectual nature, rooted in the powers of reason, logic, cognition, formal education, and mental work in general. Just this kind of distinction has supported the myth that the era of manual dexterity and grounded knowledge that characterized much of the twentieth century is giving way to a new era centred upon the necessity for intellectual reflexivity in both strategic and everyday work. Intellectual capability and dexterity in handling information, securing new knowledge, and mobilizing creativity are expected from managers, scientists, and information professionals, as well as from technical, manual, and service workers. Intellectual work has been elevated to the apex of the knowledge hierarchy, which, in turn, is thought to be thoroughly infused with mental labour. Informed by such thinking, futurologists and policy-makers have managed to drum up an urgency for science, information technology, academic qualifications, and knowledge work defined as a mental/intellectual activity, which, in turn, is disputed from time to time by commentators claiming the continued relevance of manual work, practical knowledge, and tacit knowledge located in application and experience.

This dualism, and all the consequences that follow from it, are questionable. For example, the long-standing assumption that the division of knowledge (scientists and designers, on the one side, and workers, on the other side) is a sub-set of the division of work has been put into question by the idea of the knowledge-based economy, which suggests that it is from the division of knowledge that the division of work now derives. Indeed, there exists a long tradition of thought that has never accepted the mainstream distinction between practical/particular knowledge and intellectual/universal knowledge (see Nonaka and Takeuchi 1995: ch. 2, for their attempt to reconceptualize knowledge work in firms through early Japanese Buddhist philosophy of knowledge based on the continuity between mind and body). The basis of the rejection lies in claims concerning the inseparability of the two forms of knowledge, or, more accurately, the practical and embodied nature of intellectual knowledge, and the weakly cognitive or embodied/neurological dimensions of mental reasoning and reflexivity. For example, early in the twentieth century the pragmatist philosopher John Dewey (1916/1997) gave three reasons for recognizing the continuity between mind and body. First, drawing on advances in physiology and psychology at the time, he noted the connection of mental activity with that of the nervous system, arguing further that, if 'in fact the nervous system is only a specialized mechanism for keeping all bodily activities working together' (p. 208), the 'brain is essentially an organ for effecting the reciprocal adjustment to each other of the stimuli received from the environment and responses directed upon it' (p. 209). Knowledge, therefore, is neurologically and organically conditioned, and, most importantly, the product of ongoing adjustment to maintain the continuity of activity:

The continuity of the work of the carpenter distinguishes it from a routine repetition of identically the same motion, and from a random activity where there is nothing cumulative. What makes it continuous, consecutive, or concentrated is that each earlier act prepares the way for later acts, while these take account of or reckon with the results already attained—the basis of all responsibility. (p. 209)

Secondly, Dewey drew on evolutionary biology to claim that 'its effect upon the theory of knowing is to displace the notion that it is the activity of a mere onlooker or spectator of the world'. Instead for Dewey, 'the living creature is a part of the world, sharing its vicissitudes and fortunes, and making itself secure in its precarious dependence only as it intellectually identifies itself with the things about it . . . and shapes its own activities accordingly' (p. 210). Thus, 'knowledge is a mode of participation, valuable in the degree in which it is effective' (p. 210). Following from this emphasis on knowing through engagement, Dewey's third insight was that knowledge is acquired experimentally and iteratively, and that experiment is the way of 'making sure that it *is* knowledge' (p. 210). This, on the one hand, 'means that we have no right to call anything knowledge except where our activity has actually produced certain physical changes in things' and, on the other hand, 'the experimental method of thinking signifies that thinking is of avail; that it is of avail in just the degree in which the anticipation of future consequences is made on the basis of thorough observation of present conditions' (p. 210).

The idea of knowledge as an embodied practice was later pursued by Michael Polanyi (1967), albeit in reference only to individuals rather than in any collective form: 'By elucidating the way our bodily processes participate in our perceptions we will throw light on the bodily roots of all thought, including man's highest creative powers' (p. 15). Polanyi made his case by unbundling the ontology of tacit knowing ('a way to know more than we can tell' (p. 18)), which he described as 'an act of knowing based on indwelling' (p. 124). For Polanyi, 'such an act relies on interiorizing particulars to which we are not attending and which, therefore, we may not be able to specify, and relies further on our attending from these unspecifiable particulars to a comprehensive entity connecting them in a way we cannot define' (p. 124). Polanyi's account of the ontology of tacit knowledge is similar to Dewey's, who interestingly saw also intellectual and scientific knowledge or the powers of reason and logic working in much the same way.

Through advances in certain strands of cognitive psychology over the last half century, we now know why all forms of knowledge can be seen as embodied, contextual, and evolutionary, as intimated by Dewey and Polanyi. In developmental psychology, for instance, the pioneering work of Jean Piaget with children showed that 'intelligence is internalized action and speech, and that both knowledge and meaning are context dependent' (Nooteboom 2000*a*: 2). Extending this analogy to all stages and all social contexts of learning, it could be argued that we know and understand through the practice of acting (for example, through speech acts and embodied behaviour), rather than in advance of these acts. These practices of action are context dependent. 'Ecologies of mind' (Bateson 1972) are inseparable from the practices in which they are located, which is precisely what allows us to claim different anthropologies of knowing from different cultural systems of meaning, from the conventions and semantic codes of Balinese artists and New Age communities, to those of globe-trotting business executives and Outer Hebridean schoolchildren.

Cognitive 'indwelling' also has a literal sense, as shown by research in cognitive psychophysiology, which weaves cognition strongly into sensory and bodily functions, explaining that neural processes develop, and are 'enacted', through the latter (Maturana and Varela 1980). Lakoff and Johnson (1999), in their path-breaking book *Philosophy in the Flesh*, surmise from the observation that 95 per cent of all thought is unconscious that 'all of our knowledge and beliefs are framed in terms of a conceptual system that resides mostly in the cognitive unconscious' (p. 13), which functions like a 'hidden hand':

Reason is not disembodied, as the tradition [e.g. faculty psychology] has largely held, but arises from the nature of our brains, bodies, and bodily experience. . . . The same neural and cognitive mechanisms that allow us to perceive and move around create our conceptual systems and modes of reason. Thus, to understand reason we must understand the details of our visual system, our motor system, and the general mechanisms of neural binding. In summary, reason is not, in any way, a transcendent feature of the universe or of disembodied mind. Instead, it is shaped crucially by the remarkable details of the neural structures of our brains, and by the specifics of our everyday functioning in the world. (p. 4)

This is an account of cognition as 'enacted action', where 'cognitive structures emerge from recurrent patterns of sensorimotor activity' (Varela 1999: 16). Varela, for example, cites research that shows that basic levels of categorization such as table, chair, dog, cat, fork, knife are psychologically fundamental in shaping perception, categorization, and interpretation, and that categorization at this level depends, 'not on how things are arranged in some pre-given world, but rather on the sensorimotor structure of our bodies and the kinds of perceptually guided interactions this structure makes possible' (p. 17). Another example cited by Varela regarding the powers of sensory perception is an experiment of 'seeing with the skin', involving use of a video camera by blind persons that stimulated the skin by electronically activated vibration. Images formed with the camera were translated into tactile sensations. Varela reports that, if subjects remained motionless, the images projected on the skin had no 'visual' content. But if subjects directed the camera by moving parts of their body for a few hours, remarkably, the 'tactile sensations became visual perceptions, the pattern of vibration on the skin were not felt but seen as images projected into the space being explored by the bodily directed "gaze" of the video camera. Thus in order to experience "real objects out there", it was enough for the person to actively direct the camera' (p. 14), an 'excellent example of the perceiver-dependent nature of what otherwise seems an internal representation of a perceiver-independent word of features' (p. 14).

The computation that occurs in the brain, thus, is not, 'as a once dominant viewpoint had it, the operation of logic machines that process symbols' (Turner 2001: 122), but a giant processing exercise of sensory impulses along parallel neural pathways aided by a broad-based learning algorithm, rather than by detailed rules. Turner explains:

The inputs are not symbolic, but simply impulses originating from various sensory sources, which are distributed through the brain in pathways made of 'connections' that are formed statistically, by the association of impulses of one kind with impulses of another kind. These are modelled mathematically as 'weightings' of the impulses, which travel from 'node' or pathway link to 'node' and which modify the link by passing through it, just as a person walking in the forest makes a path, increasing the likelihood of future impulses of a similar kind being distributed in a similar way. The changes in the likelihoods are 'learning'.   (pp. 122–3)

The implication is that the production of these paths in its own right is learning: often-used paths allow a reduction of complexity through the use of 'gestalt'— that is, cognitive frames resulting from usage.[1] Learning, thus, starts from a state in which some learning has already occurred. It is activated and directed by the history of the embodied mind, it is the product of statistical connections in complex computational nets, and it is dependent upon the nature of the sensory impulses that are received. This is precisely why the paths can also hinder unlearning and the exploration of novel learning.

SOCIAL EMBEDDING AND ACTOR NETWORKS

It would be incomplete to stop at an explanation of human learning as the product of a 'conceptual system that resides mostly in the cognitive unconscious' (Lakoff and Johnson 1999: 13), despite the considerable gains made in revealing the fiction of rule-based and reason-driven cognition. Individual and collective learning is also the product of social practices that are not simply the sum of a multitude of individual neural nets. Communities in their specific social settings characterized by conventions of meaning and communication and the cultures of action and interpretation that are the product of *social* organization and interaction act as learning environments in their own right. While their dynamics too, as we argue below, generate knowledge as an embodied, iterative, relational, and practical act, this is not the product of the 'conscious unconscious' of neural computation, but of the 'conscious unconscious' of the embedded social conventions and social iterations in each setting.

Collins (2001a) has argued that even after conceding as much as possible of the tacit element of tacit knowledge to neural nets, 'there is still some left which the working sociologist cannot dispense with' (p. 108). This is the knowledge that comes from social embedding. As an illustration, Collins returns to Polanyi's famous example of bike riding as the product of tacit knowledge (plus its explicit cognition through codified routines), arguing that much of what Polanyi discussed—and which could potentially be theorized using the language of neural nets—is limited to the physics of bike balancing. Collins argues that another aspect of the tacit knowledge of bike riding is riding in traffic, where the actions of the rider, such as crossing in front of an oncoming car, are the product of visual communication between the rider and others, informal local traffic conventions, the relative status of bikes and cars in different countries, and a whole

---

[1] We are grateful to Gernot Grabher for this insight.

series of other contextual social codes and norms. 'This aspect of bike-riding requires embedding in the social milieu from the beginning to the end' (p. 116), and the learning that goes on is the product of such embedding.

Collins's argument can be pushed further, towards a recognition of the influence of social practices in intentional actor networks on learning and knowledge formation. This has been one of the pioneering insights of the literature on the sociology of scientific knowledge—based on detailed studies of scientific and other knowledge communities—that has grown in influence since the 1980s. Philosophically, this literature shares with pragmatism the assumption that everyday activity is the powerful source of socialization, which, in turn, is the stimulus and carrier of cognitive activity. 'Social practice proponents argue that knowledge-in-practice, constituted in the settings of practice, is the locus of the most powerful knowledgeability of people in the lived-in world' (Lave 1988: 15). While part of the argument here is about the powers of social context, embodiment, and knowing through acting, it is also about the significance of knowing through the hermeneutics of social interaction and enrolment. Such knowledge-in-practice is as much a hallmark of uses of and inventions with arithmetic in after-school settings and supermarkets (Lave 1988), as it is of the 'high' knowledge that is generated by scientists in different laboratory settings.

There are many reasons for linking knowledge to social connectivity. We can mention five here (mostly all drawn from the sociology of laboratory life). Firstly, knowledge is not simply communicated between actors (human and machinic), but is generated through *communication*—speech acts, conversations, bodily gestures, glances, expressions, data exchanges, machine-to-machine interactions, are the relational iterations through which we know, understand, and learn. Without them, we have neither the means to express what we know, nor the means to know through what we express. The interlocutor, so vital for the completion of the knowledge circuit, becomes absent.

Secondly, *sociality*, from casual conversations to orchestrated social occasions such as conferences and formal dinners, counts as an important knowledge practice. It cements the trust and mutuality for tacit knowledge to be circulated, it can reinforce group feelings and identities necessary for shared knowledge conventions, it provides the serendipity for new knowledge encounters, and it allows ideas and routines to be tracked and modified. Importantly, its ambient vitality can actually stimulate and shape thinking, even when it consciously jars. Reflecting on his own irritation and boredom at a set-piece, rambling international conference of scientists, Rabinow (1996: 13–14) reinterprets the event as a knowledge event through the work done in conversations, meeting old acquaintances, gossip, and the like.

I propose that a primary site of thinking is friendship (*philia*). . . . It is sometimes forgotten that mutual advantage needs to be identified and negotiated as much as anything else. Hence, professional self-interest, the accumulation of symbolic capital and the like, is more than a question of predefined roles or 'objective interests' or even dispositions, although those dimensions constitute the preconditions for utility/philia. . . . Conventions are among the biggest sector of the American economy. The face-to-face encounters, repeated with some regularity over time, while hard to justify in quantifiable economic terms, clearly continued to be valued, probably for reasons that could not be explicitly defended by corporations and universities, but which do, indeed, have some value in the terms we have been using.

While conventions may be dominant in the USA, elsewhere the organized sociality comes in different forms, perhaps as associations in France, professional bodies in Germany, clubs in the UK.

Thirdly, novelty is the product of *connections*, as Callon (1999*a*: 2) explains:

Innovation is by definition an emergent phenomenon based on gradually putting into place interactions that link agents, knowledges, and goods that were previously unconnected, and that are slowly put in a relationship of interdependence: the network, in its formal dimension, is a powerful tool for making these connections, and for describing the forms that they take. What marks innovation is the alchemy of combining heterogeneous ingredients: it is a process that crosses institutions, forging complex and unusual relations between different spheres of activity, and drawing, in turn, on interpersonal relations, the market, law, science, and technology.   (translation from original in French)

An example of such alchemy is the role of patients' associations in advancing medical knowledge. Callon has shown that, in areas of medicine such as the treatment of rare genetic diseases that are poorly understood by medical and pharmaceu-tical institutions, lay associations have forced the pace and direction of research and remedy by engaging in a:

primitive accumulation of knowledge: researching and identifying diseases; organising and effectively participating in the collection of DNA; producing films or compiling photo albums designed to be effective observation tools for monitoring and comparing clinical developments of the disease and establishing the effects of certain treatment; recording testimonies which transmit live experiences; and carrying out surveys among patients, which sometimes go as far as the publication of articles in academic journals.   (Callon 1999*b*: 90)

In the area of muscular dystrophy, such lay knowledge in France, enshrined in the power of the French Muscular Dystrophy Association, has produced pioneering advances in understanding and treatment through research commissioned by the Association, the availability of a historical record of evidence, patient experience and lay knowledge, the constant interactions between patients, doctors, and biologists, power play between the lay organizations and public bodies, and other aspects of what has become a model of hybrid and collective learning (Rabeharisoa and Callon, forthcoming). At the centre lies the task of enrolment and translation, through work on common semantics and other forms of cognitive alignment by a given community to convince and hold other communities in the network.

Fourthly, it is usually through *visualization* of the elements of myriad interactions that characterize a given social ensemble, involving intricate links between humans and non-humans (for example, machines, chemicals, paper, tools), that knowledge paths are cognized and given effective power and influence. Without the complex interactive ontology of social phenomena, the need for cognitive signs would disappear, but then so would the basis of empirical knowledge. Latour (1986*a*: 3–4), again with laboratory science in mind, clarifies:

I was struck, in a study of a biology laboratory, by the way in which many aspects of laboratory practice could be ordered by looking not at the scientists' brains (I was forbidden access!), at the cognitive structures (nothing special), nor at the paradigms (the same for thirty years), but at the transformation of rats and chemicals into paper. . . . Focusing on the literature, and on the way in which anything and everything was transformed into inscriptions was not my bias, as I first thought, but was for what the laboratory was made. Instruments, for instance, were of various types, ages, and degrees of sophistication. Some were pieces of furniture, others filled large rooms, employed many technicians and took many weeks to run. But their end result, no matter the field, was always a small window through which one could read a very few signs from a rather poor repertoire (diagrams, blots, bands, columns). All these inscriptions, as I called them, were combinable, superimposable and could, with only a minimum of cleaning up, be integrated as figures in the text of the articles people were writing. Many of the intellectual feats I was asked to admire could be rephrased as soon as this activity of paper writing and inscription became the focus for analysis.

The inscriptions, in the form of working signs and finished papers, are an important means by which new knowledge is acknowledged and ordered, but also extended beyond the laboratory as an 'immutable mobile' and a visible object that commands the attention of others and becomes their frame of reference too. They are a key device to ensure communication and commonality in complex knowledge networks, and, for this, should be recognized as crucially important everyday governance mechanisms to ensure effective interaction between diverse and distributed knowledge communities in a given organizational setting (see Chapter 6).

Fifthly, thus, it is the *ordering and alignment* of the ensemble of relations that make up a community of interest that generate knowledge in an intelligible and usable form—tacit and codified. It is the manipulation of social relations in service of a given project that counts. As Knorr Cetina (1999: 29) explains:

The social is not merely 'also there' in science. Rather, it is capitalized upon and upgraded to become an instrument of scientific work. Laboratory processes align natural orders with social orders by creating reconfigured, workable objects in relation to agents of a given time and place. But laboratories also install reconfigured scientists who become workable (feasible) in relation to these objects. . . . In the laboratory, scientists are methods of inquiry; they are part of a field's research strategy and a technical device in the production of knowledge.

This is an interesting, situational and non-humanist twist to the meaning of social interactions and their role in knowledge practices. Knorr Cetina again (1999: 32): 'By the time the reconfigurations of self-other-things that constitute laboratories have taken place, we are confronted with a newly emerging order that is neither social nor natural—an order whose components have mixed genealogies and continue to change shape as laboratory work continues.'

The above are some of the ways in which social embedding and social connectivity instantiate knowledge. Like the neural processes that unite body and mind in individuals, they constitute a field of social practices in which the everyday cannot be dissociated from the extraordinary, in which thinking cannot be broken down to different cognitive realms or separated from an ensemble of sensory, emotive, ethical, bodily, and object-mediated practices, and in which discovery is a matter of connecting dispersed bits and pieces and making the connections visible and count as generalized truths—one reason why the categorization and classification of information is such a powerful knowledge device (see Bowker and Star 1999).

ORGANIZATIONAL LEARNING

An emphasis on the 'cognitive unconscious' and on social practices as the spark for knowledge acquisition has profound implications for the theorization of innova-tion and learning in business organizations. We have already mentioned how it pushes the economics-centred theoretical approaches considered in Chapters 2 and 3 away from knowledge as a possession to knowledge as a practice. However, through the ever-expanding literature on organizational learning, much of it based in business studies, we can interpret the emphasis on practice as signalling another shift. This is the contestation of models of formal, rule-based, and hierarchical innovation by models of interactive and heterarchical learning (Starkey 1996; Nowotny, Scott, and Gibbons 2001).

Innovation is no longer seen as the privilege of detached R&D labs and senior management, passing blueprints and rules of conduct down the corporate hierarchy to a compliant workforce fixed to standard routines. Instead, innovation, learning, and creativity are increasingly seen as key assets for corporate survival, based on the distribution of competences and authority in small teams across the organization, as well as the mobilization of individual and social potential and commitment. Distributed competences, rule-free and flat organization, social capital, employee autonomy, information sharing, connectivity, results orientation, flexibility and adaptability, continuous learning, and visionary leadership have become the new watchwords of knowledge-based success. Much of this new rhetoric is hype in the service of legitimating a new brand of business and concealing its power inequalities, but it does signal an entirely new way of conceptualizing knowledge production.

To illustrate the kinds of connection being made with knowledge creation, we can pick up on a recent account of one of these watchwords—social capital:

Social capital bridges the space between people. Its characteristic elements and indicators include high levels of trust, robust personal networks and vibrant communities, shared understandings, and a sense of equitable participation in a joint enterprise—all things that draw individuals together into a group. This kind of connection supports collaboration, commitment, ready access to knowledge and talent, and coherent organizational behaviour.   (Cohen and Prusak 2001: 4)

Similarly, Nahapiet and Goshal (2002) discuss organizational knowledge and knowing in terms of the relations between intellectual capital, which they define as the reservoir of different types of knowledge possessed by organizations, and social capital, defined as the assets gained from social interaction. This turn in the business literature resonates with the ontology of individual and social knowledge that we have outlined above, although the case is rarely made along the lines we have suggested, partly because of lack of interest in the ontology of cognition. One consequence, it seems to us, is that the anthropomorphic dimensions of knowing and learning continue to be overemphasized (for example, even Nonaka and Takeuchi (1995), who recognize embodiment, interaction, and practised routines, have little to say about non-humans as active knowledge actants). The work of such knowledge mediaries (for example, diagrams, maps, codes, communications infrastructures) that cannot be reduced to human relations remains largely unrecognized in the business literature.[2]

As Pickering (1993: 104) notes, 'one very distinctive feature of modern technoscience is . . . its capacity to unleash upon the world new and nonhuman actors' (cited in Shapin 1995: 313). This alone should force recognition of the non-human actors involved in organizational learning. For example, the typical brainstorming session to resolve a problem or to launch a new idea gathers more than the people in that room and their human knowledge attributes or their bodily expressions such as gestures, quizzical looks, raised arms, seating postures, raised eyebrows, smiles, grimaces, and so on. The exchange of information and the new knowledge produced are also the work of jottings in the notepad, words prioritized on the flipchart, notes brought to the meeting, text messages, live Internet and other virtual exchanges, and an array of real-time computer-aided knowledge exercises such as scenario building or data analysis. These are not simple aids to what remains a human knowledge practice, but part of the knowledge chain, in the form of knowing objects and mechanical know-how.

This is most evident (even if rarely recognized) in laboratory science. Knorr Cetina (1999) has shown in her innovative anthropology of laboratory epistemic cultures that this is as much a feature of the active role of chemicals, cultures, instruments, samples, microscopic patterns, and data displays in experimental work done in molecular biology as it is a feature of the 'inner life' of complex, high-energy detectors in particle physics experiments that depend on machine-to-machine knowledge transactions. For example, the high energy detector that lies at the centre of experiments in particle physics

has an internal life of its own: it exhibits an internal dynamic not completely under the experiment's control. In this sense, the detector is like a *complex organism*, whose physiology

[2] This may well explain the current overplay of social connectivity rooted in trust, face-to-face encounter, social bonding, group identification, talk and storytelling, and joint projects (Bennis and Biederman 1997; Cohen and Prusak 2001). Social practices are read as human practices, rather than as a recursive continuum of mind–body–object practices in specific organizational settings (e.g. the life of different laboratories).

is ruled by its own laws and which has its own powers, capabilities, and tendencies to react. [The] responses of this organism are not self-evident. They must be monitored and measured, so that with sufficient observation, hard work, and familiarity (achieved through a joint biography with the detector), they may be 'understood.' . . . Thus, the organism remains a kind of being rather than a thing, with essential components functioning like organs to maintain responses of the whole.   (Knorr-Cetina 1999: 121, emphasis in original)

Both the rise of complex 'thinking' machines (see Cowan 2001) and the age-long codification and technological embodiment of knowledge persuade some to call into question the idea that organizational learning can be reduced to the work of knowing human subjects.

Another consequence of the neglect of cognitive processes in the recent turn towards interactive and heterarchical[3] learning in organizational literature is the continuing tendency hierarchically to differentiate cerebral knowledge and to distinguish the latter from practical/embodied knowledge. In part, this relates to the strong legacy of rationality-based models of cognition in organization science, leading to explanations of corporate knowledge in terms of the 'mental models' of individuals and collectives. For example, the distinction between single- and double-loop learning has become commonplace in work on organizational learning and is frequently invoked to explain the difference between businesses (or sections within businesses) capable of path-dependent innovations and those that generate novelty of a path-breaking nature. As we have seen in Chapter 3, this distinction is based on Argyris and Schön's pioneering differentiation (1978) of single-loop learning, defined as the changes in subjective theories or mental models within an existing paradigm (thus allowing better exploitation of existing know-how and expertise), from double-loop learning, defined as reflection upon what has been learnt and deliberate questioning of core assumptions, leading to exploration beyond the paradigm.

The different learning outcomes are seen to be the product of different rationalities or cognitive capabilities (for example, a rule-following or procedural rationality is seen to allow routine-based or environmentally conditioned knowledge steps, while a strategic or reflexive rationality is seen to facilitate experimental knowledge and leaps in thinking that exceed the constraints of context). For example, Hayes and Allison (1998) have related learning repertoires to 'cognitive style', or 'a person's preferred way of gathering, processing, and evaluating information' (p. 848). They have identified twenty-two different dimensions of cognitive style, based on variations in intuition, analysis, perception, memory, thought, and other mental faculties. On this basis, they can claim, for example, that 'people who occupy senior positions in many occupations and organizations

---

[3] We use the term heterarchical to indicate processes of learning that are distributed and that derive their benefits from heterogeneity and the retention of redundancy and slack in the selection environment. Knowledge inputs, thus, are neither hierarchically organized nor selected on the basis of immediate needs.

tend to share a cognitive style that differs from that which characterizes members at lower levels' (p. 851). Through organization, a collective mental model is formed along similar lines: organization 'stores the knowledge that is accumulated over time from the learning of its members in the form of an organizational code of received truth' (p. 853). In this way, particular forms of corporate mindset with distinctive learning potentials are established.

Even if it were possible to reduce knowledge acquisition to particular mental dispositions and cognitive styles, is it useful to see the corporate mindset or cognitive style as the sum of individual rationality? According to Popper and Lipshitz (1998), organizational learning is not an extension of individual learning, because organizations and their members lack the typical means for undertaking cognition as a mental act. They suggest, instead, that organizational learning is the product of purposeful collective structures and cultures, rather than the work of particular cognitive dispositions at group or individual level. They emphasize the role of 'Organizational Learning Mechanisms', defined as 'institutionalized structural and procedural arrangements that allow organizations systematically to collect, analyse, store, disseminate, and use information relevant to the performance of the organization and its members' (p. 168). Typical examples include structured evaluations of actions taken in order to learn from them, or scenario building in strategic planning units. In turn, they argue that effective organizational learning depends upon establishing an appropriate corporate culture, based on values that have little to do with the psychologies of single- or double-loop learning. For them, organizational learning is promoted through a culture of 'inquiry, openness, and trust' (p. 170), supported by continuous learning at the apex, the availability of full and verifiable information, transparency, and accountability. Whether it is these values that promote learning is clearly a matter of debate (for example, there can be a thin line between opportunism and trust (see P. Adler 2001)), but the point to note here is that organizational learning is an instituted process that is not reducible to agent rationalities (Tracey, Clark, and Lawton Smith 2002).

Indeed, a new body of research is emerging on the fine-grained social anthropology of knowledge creation within organizations, one that resonates with the practice-based ontology of knowing we have outlined above. Work on both incremental and radical innovation in firms, at odds with notions of innovation as a science-based, mental, or top-down activity, is revealing that knowing and learning occur through the daily interactions and practices of distributed communities of human and non-human actors. Brown and Duguid (1991: 53), who have years of senior-level involvement in the research divisions of major US technology-based corporations, have come to the conclusion, for example, that:

Alternative worldviews . . . do not lie in the laboratory or strategic planning office alone, condemning everyone else in the organization to a unitary culture. Alternatives are inevitably distributed throughout all the different communities that make up the organization. For it is the organization's communities, at all levels, who are in contact with the environment and involved in interpretative sense making, congruence finding, and adapting. It is from any site of such interactions that new insights can be co-produced. If an organizational core overlooks or curtails the enacting in its midst by ignoring or disrupting its communities-of-practice, it threatens its survival in two ways. It will not only threaten to destroy the very working and learning practices by which it, knowingly or unknowingly, survives. It will also cut itself off from a major source of potential innovation that inevitably arises in the course of the working and learning.

The rest of the chapter explores the dynamics and implications of learning through the practices of different kinds of community, practices often gathered around the collective 'cognitive unconscious'.

Learning in Communities

In and across organizations, there are many different kinds of communities, which vary in remit, organization, and membership (Cohendet, Creplet, and Dupouët 2000). Firms can be seen as constellations of diverse communities of learning—sites where knowledges are formed, practised, and altered (Liedtka 1999). These communities might be found in traditional work divisions and departments, but they also cut across functional divisions, spill over into after-work or project-based teams, and straddle networks of cross-corporate and professional ties. For example, within firms, classical communities include *functional groups* of employees who share a particular specialization corresponding to the hierarchical division of labour (for example, marketing or accounting). They also include *teams* of employees with heterogeneous skills and qualifications, often coordinated by team leaders and put together to achieve a particular goal in a given period of time. Some of these communities emerge spontaneously from the hierarchical structures of the firm (some workshop staff may constitute a community of practice overlapping with the functional division of operations in the firm), while some communities may result from an adherence to a common passion of very dispersed individuals within the firm (for instance, a community of practice of people interested in computing in a given organization will not in general overlap with the staff of the computer department, but may comprise agents of the firm working in different positions, departments and even locations of the firm).[4]

Such communities, bound by relations of common interest, purpose, or passion, and held together by routines and varying degrees of mutuality, are now being considered as key sites of knowledge formation and exchange, and learning. Communities thus defined (with no implicit reference to moral worth or homogeneity of membership) embody the pragmatic, situated, interactive, and enacted knowledge routines that have been outlined above. These are characteristics that, as we have seen, cannot be captured by individual-centred or classical organization-centred approaches. Instead, they do seem to fit with the workings of project- or task-focused groupings caught up in daily processes of interaction

---

[4] Such a type of community may also include members from outside the firm.

and practices of knowing through the combination of conscious and unconscious rhythms of work. Two types of community in particular have received
special attention in the literature as important sites of knowledge formation.
These are *epistemic communities* and *communities of practice*. They are singled
out as different from task groups, project teams, and functional units
on the grounds that, while the latter are still organized along lines of hierarchal
lexicon of instruction and order, the former are largely autonomous and left to
their own community routines, which act as the main organizing principle.

Epistemic communities

Epistemic communities, a term first introduced by Knorr Cetina (1981), are
involved in the deliberate production of knowledge and may include employees
in an R&D unit, international groups of scientists, or task forces set up to launch
new advertising campaigns. They comprise 'agents who work on a mutually
recognized subset of knowledge issues, and who at the very least accept some
commonly procedural authority as essential to the success of their collective
building activities' (Cowan, David, and Foray 2000). The existence of procedural
authority such as a professional code of conduct aids in the resolution of potential disputes and provides a reference point for recognizing completion at various stages of the process of making knowledge explicit. In these communities the
knowledge base from which the agents work can often be highly codified (for
example, scientific manuals, laboratory classifications, digitized computation),
but 'paradoxically, its existence and contents are matters left tacit among the
group unless some dispute or memory problem arises' (Cowan, David, and Foray
2000: 234). What characterizes the knowledge activities within these communities is that they are deliberately focused on the production of new knowledge,
with little a priori reference to the different contexts in which the new knowledge
produced will be used.

  Epistemic communities are structured around a goal to be reached and a
procedural authority endowed internally or externally to fulfil that goal. Within
an epistemic community, agents are bound together by their commitment to
enhance a particular set of knowledge. The recruitment rule is thus defined with
regard to the contribution an agent makes to fulfil this goal. Notions of autonomy and identity are thus weaker than in the case of communities of practice
(see below), thus favouring group creativity (Leonard-Barton 1995): being in a
community increases the ability to seize future opportunities. This form of
organization spawns knowledge creation by favouring the synergy of individual
varieties. Individuals accumulate knowledge according to their own experiences,
while validation is made according to the procedural authority: what is evaluated
is the contribution of the agent to the cognitive goal with regard to the criteria
set by the procedural authority. Because of the heterogeneity of the agents, and
the desire for knowledge creation for its own sake, a priority of epistemic
communities is to create a 'codebook' of conventions and practices, since
deeply shared values are absent. Hence, knowledge circulating within epistemic

communities is explicit (but not necessarily codified since it remains mainly internal to the community (Baumard 1999)).

Communities of practice

The concept of communities of practice has been introduced by Lave and Wenger (1991), to note groups of persons engaged in the same practice, and communicating regularly with one another about their activities. Communities of practice can be seen as a means to enhance individual competences, and are oriented towards their members (Lave and Wenger 1991; Brown and Duguid 1991). This goal is reached through the construction, the exchange, and the sharing of a common repertoire of resources (Wenger 1998). Communities of practice (for example, repair engineers or insurance claims processors) are bound by common skills and tend to learn as a by-product of working together, as Wenger and Snyder (2000: 139) explain:

they're groups of people informally bound together by shared expertize and passion for a joint enterprize—engineers engaged in deep-water drilling, for example, consultants who specialize in strategic marketing, or frontline managers in charge of check processing at a large commercial bank. Some communities of practice meet regularly—for lunch on Thursdays, say. Others are connected primarily by e-mail networks. A community of practice may or may not have an explicit agenda on a given week, and even if it does, it may not follow the agenda closely. Inevitably people in communities of practice share their experiences and knowledge in free-flowing, creative ways that foster new approaches to problems.

A community of practice—drawing on interaction and participation to act, interpret, innovate, and communicate—acts as 'a locally negotiated regime of competence' (Wenger 1998: 137).

Wenger (1998) and Brown and Duguid (1991, 1998) state that self-organization is an essential characteristic of communities of practice. Self-organization is the ability of a system to acquire new properties by organizing itself or by modifying its own organization by itself (Lesourne 1991). It confers to the system an adaptive ability to evolve without any constraint of authority or determined goal. The system is autonomous and creates a sort of 'organizational closure' in the terminology of the theory of self-organization. More precisely, autonomy and identity of communities, the key characteristics of self-organization, allow the collective acquisition and processing of stimuli from the environment (Dibiaggio 1998; Wenger 1998).

Self-identity is also visible in the mutual commitment of the community, built around activities commonly understood and continually renegotiated by its members. A community's member contributes with his or her experience and, in turn, relies on the knowledge capitalized by the community to carry out his or her activity. These processes can take the shape of stories that members tell when they gather, to develop a jargon understandable by the members only. In turn, Lave and Wenger (1991) interpret the practice of community as the vector of learning. The evaluation of an individual is made by the community of practice as a system and is focused both on the values adopted by the individual and on the progress made in his or her practice, the two being co-constitutive. The privileged knowledge is thus essentially the collective know-how that is tacit and socially localized.

In the literature that has grown to recognize learning in communities, the distinction between epistemic communities and communities of practice tends to be based on a linear representation of the process of knowledge transformation. This process is viewed as evolving from separate departments in charge of producing new (deliberate) knowledge or handling and distributing information to the other departments that assimilate and use this new knowledge to improve their current activities. These departments can also produce new knowledge from their routine activities, but this is a non-deliberate form of knowledge production that emerges as a by-product of learning by using or learning by doing.

Even in accounts that recognize the circularity of knowledge transfers and relationships between communities, separate knowledge practices tend to be ascribed to different sites or moments in the knowledge chain. Nonaka's four-step model of knowledge generation in an organization (1994) is a classic example. The first step—presumably a central feature of communities of practice—is the sharing of tacit knowledge through socialization. The second step is the conversion of tacit to explicit knowledge through articulation, while the third is the standardization of new explicit knowledge by combining it with other explicit knowledge. Both steps are presumably a core aspect of epistemic communities. Nonaka's final step is internalization, or the conversion of explicit knowledge to tacit knowledge through familiarization and usage (presumably another strength of communities of practice). Though Nonaka does not use the language of communities, he is in no doubt that the tacit/explicit distinction has meaningful implications for the type of knowledge produced and its significance for the firm. In addition, he is clear about the intermediate role played by 'groups' in between the level of individual and the organization (which could be read as 'communities') in the knowledge-creating process (Nonaka and Takeuchi 1995: ch. 3).

We will argue, in contrast, that, while the separations between deliberate and non-deliberate forms of knowledge and that between tacit and codified knowledge are useful analytically as a means of dissecting a complex knowledge process, it would be an error to assume that these separations hold in reality. While epistemic communities may be established explicitly as knowledge communities, the sociology of their knowledge practices is not radically different from that of communities of practice. We would, thus, go further than the currently fashionable claim that the rise of the knowledge economy is encouraging convergence on the grounds that the essence of successful innovation and learning lies in the ways these two types of communities deliberately interact and jointly organize the production and circulation of knowledge. A recent OECD report (2000), for example, claims that the emergence of new forms of learning such as 'experimental learning' makes the differentiation between 'on-line' and 'off-line' learning activities less and less relevant. For Lundvall, experimental learning may start 'on-line'—that is, during the process of producing a good— but usually includes deliberate experimentation during the production process:

By doing so, one creates new options and variety. This form of learning is based on a stra- tegy whereby experimentation allows for collecting data, on the basis of which the best strategy for future activities is chosen. For example, a professor can undertake pedagogical experiments; the craftsman can seek new solutions to a problem even during the fabrica- tion process. The possibility of moving this type of learning in many activities represents an important transition in the historical emergence of the knowledge-based economy. In effect, as long as an activity remains fundamentally based on learning processes that are routine adaptation procedures and leave no room for programming experiments during economic activity, there remains a strong dichotomy between those who deliberately pro- duce knowledge and those who use and exploit it. When an activity moves to higher forms of learning, and where the individual can programme experiments and obtain results, the production of knowledge becomes much more collectively distributed. . . . With the emer- gence of experimental learning, the feedback and reciprocal links that tie 'on-line' learning processes and in-house R&D together—and whereby a potential creative activity effect- ively contributes to the production of knowledge—become crucial.   (OECD 2000: 25)

While for Lundvall, the issue is a matter of convergence between knowledge practices that start out as different, our argument is that the ontological distinction is less obvious, because both epistemic communities and communities of practices are deeply implicated in processes of non-deliberate learning that are rooted in doing, despite the varying degree of the intentionality of knowledge within each. As Nooteboom (2000*b*) observes, all forms of thought develop out of active inter- action with the physical and social environment, thus 'experimentation' too grows out of 'exploitation'. There is a circular and reinforcing relationship between big and small leaps in novelty.

Learning in Doing

The modes of unintended learning are revealed in Wenger's longitudinal study (1998) of insurance claim processors in a corporation. The study is a detailed anthropology of learning rooted in the everyday practices of horizontal and ver- tical interaction, supported by an elaborate techno-structure of technologies, artefacts, and routines. For Wenger, this and other communities of practice are marked above all by different dimensions of repeated interaction. One is *mutual engagement*, involving doing things together, establishing mutual relationships, and maintaining community. This dimension chimes with the emphasis on social capital raging through the US-inspired literature on corporate perform- ance, but significantly, in Wenger's hands, it is seen as the product of the act of social interaction, not any (pre-given) culture or psychology of trust and reci- procity. In addition, for Wenger, there is more to interaction than mutuality of engagement. A second dimension of interaction is *joint enterprise*, involving the negotiation of diversity within a community, the formation of a local code of practice, and a regime of mutual accountability. A third dimension is *shared repertoire*, supported by a variety of media such as stories, narratives, concepts, and historical accounts, all of which mark a history of engagement against which existing and new practices can be evaluated.

For Wenger, the infrastructure of each form of interaction is also an infrastructure for learning. Learning based on *engagement* draws on mutuality, supported by such things as joint tasks and interactive spaces, on competence, provided through training and encouragement of initiative and judgement, and on continuity, with the aid of stored data, documents, storytelling, and meetings with past employees. *Alignment* is a second basis for learning, through convergence facilitated by common focus, shared values, and leadership, through coordination helped by procedures such as standards, information feedback, division of labour, and deadlines, and through arbitration facilitated by rules, policies, and conflict-resolution techniques. Finally, for Wenger, *imagination* in a community of practice is another infrastructure for learning, in that it facilitates orientation, with the help of aids such as visual representations, analogies, symbolic expressions, and organizational charts, reflection (helped by retreats, time-off, conversations, and pattern analysis) and exploration (facilitated by scenario building, prototypes, play, simulation, and experimentation).

Wenger's work is important in three senses. Firstly, it reveals how unintentional forms of learning are grounded in habituated but structured interactions. Consequently, secondly, it shows how the varied organizational orientations and tools that structure daily interactions also constitute a socio-technical sphere that supports learning. Learning, in this sense, is organizationally instituted and supported by infrastructures that are not normally associated with knowledge generation, innovation, and creativity. Thirdly, in that the infrastructures enrol and align a very wide range of facilities, tools, routines, and conventions, some of which are expressions of tacit knowledge and some of which embody codified knowledge, it is practically impossible to attribute a learning outcome to tacit or codified knowledge (in the way that Nonaka attempts, for example).

These are also the mechanisms that support radical learning within communities of practice, even when circumstances require snap decisions. A revealing example is Hutchins's study (1996) of how a navigation team arrived at a new procedure when, upon entering a harbour, a large ship suffered an engineering breakdown that disabled a vital piece of computer-based navigational equipment. Following a chaotic and unsuccessful search for a solution through thought experiments and computational and textual alternatives, the team developed an answer through doing, with the aid of analogue devices. As local tasks were found for individuals distributed across the ship, the ensuing sequence of actions and conversations, drawing on experience and experimentation, led to the construction of a solution based on trial and testing. On this occasion, a solution was found on time. Although Hutchins describes what happened as 'cognition in the wild', the central point is that radical innovation also occurs through engagement and enactment and through the alignment of elements—human and technical—in a new script of organizing and acting.

The same sociology of learning based on interaction and alignment is evident on the so-called higher rungs of explicit knowledge work, even when the interactions of the community of practice are spatially distributed. An illuminating example is provided by Orr's anthropology (1996) of Xerox's highly skilled technical reps who work at customer sites to service or repair the corporation's copiers. Orr found that the information and training provided to the reps, who tend to work alone, seemed inadequate for all but routine tasks. Instead, he found that a forcing ground for new learning was the avidly attended breakfast or lunch, when reps would come together and intermingle eating and idle chat with endless talk about work—discussions of problems, solutions, experiences, customers, technical standards, and so on. These occasions allowed the reps to learn through discussion of common problems, narration of experiences, joint problem solving, and reflexivity through interaction. Similarly, he found that often seemingly intractable problems were resolved when two reps with different expertise came together to work on a machine, hitting on a solution after hours of talk involving recollections of past problems and their solutions, gradual alignment of respective repertoires, and the emergence of a logic of diagnosis and step-by-step problem solving based on the talk and alignment of narratives.

Importantly, and echoing Wenger, Brown and Duguid (2001) have argued that such learning, 'off the road and without maps', is underpinned by sociality in quite crucial ways. They highlight three forms. The first is collaboration, which they see as allowing information sharing and the construction of a common pool of knowledge. The second is narration, which they see as facilitating understanding, as disparate pieces of information come to be ordered sequentially as stories, the transmission of rule of thumb principles, as stories are retold, and the formation of a common interpretative framework. The third form of sociality they highlight is improvisation 'inherent in practice' (p. 108), which permits the separate knowledges of actors to be confronted and combined in emergent ways. For these reasons, 'the talk and the work, the communication and the practice are inseparable' (p. 125).

What of the sociology of epistemic communities, of work deliberately organized to produce new knowledge? Are sociality and interaction significant in communities of practice because learning is an unintended consequence, and therefore a by-product of the social engagement involved in routine joint work? Are sites of formal scientific discovery somehow different, and more reliant on the 'cognitive conscious' and related structures (for example, codified knowledge and formal training programmes), and, for this, less reliant upon sociality? We find this sort of distinction in evolutionary economics, based on the assumption that sources of tacit knowledge, such as craft experience or face-to-face interaction, are appropriate for product and process refinements, while path-breaking innovations are driven by science and technology, dedicated educational and research organizations, theorists, and thinkers. Each is said to involve a different learning repertoire.

We would argue that the social processes of learning in doing outlined by Wenger and Orr also apply to strategists, scientists, and 'big' discoveries. Indeed, a remarkable early insight of studies in the sociology of science was that the practices of R&D laboratories were not that different from those leading to innovation in the Breton fishing industry or the learning in doing described by Wenger and Orr. In the laboratory, too, the production of novelty draws upon routines, conversations, meetings, scripts, memory, stories, and other soft technologies, grafted onto the technologies of formal knowledge acquisition and application (Latour 1986*b*). So entangled is the knowledge chain that it is virtually impossible to assign the moment of discovery to a sudden brainwave, a retraining programme, a conversation at a coffee break, or a technology-driven prompt. This is also the daily sociology of learning in universities, as students and researchers combine intuition, conversations, reading, laboratory experiments, tuition and experience, paper, pen, and computers, quiet moments, play and relaxation, in order to produce new knowledge. Here, too, learning occurs through doing and through social engagement of some form. Linking the two— laboratory scientists and academics—surely Rabinow is right in implying, as we saw earlier, that occasions such as conferences and their murmurings, chatter, and social display, are as deeply implicated in knowledge exploration as work in the laboratory. This is when ideas are tested, tracked, and incorporated, when allies and converts are acquired, when new alignments and adjustments are made, when display is used to convince, and when power and influence are mobilized to naturalize new knowledge. All this is part of the chain of making new discoveries.

There are many studies of the sociology of knowledge in epistemic communities, all of which reveal the centrality of the everyday, of recursive interactions, of sociality, of the inseparable entanglement of body, mind, and thing, in producing experimental knowledge and radical discovery. Knorr Cetina's book (1999) *Epistemic Cultures*, which compares the laboratory worlds of molecular biology and high-energy particle physics, details this ontology of knowledge through a catalogue of revealing examples. She shows how experimental knowledge is based on the painstaking and meticulous organization of detail, routine, mundane facts, and small-step incremental experiments, on endless talk, jottings, and rearrangements of material, on bold and simple displays in front of conferences and potential funders, on mixtures of everyday conversation and obsessive discussion of technical material, on interactions carried across virtual networks, social occasions, and private spaces, and on a strong commitment to both teams and projects that carries long and often tedious experiments forward. No part of Knorr Cetina's account is intended to play down the exceptional intelligence, expertise, and experience of the scientists involved in the experiments, the large resources they need to mobilize, and the sophisticated power and capabilities of the elaborate range of equipment they use. Instead, it shows that these qualities and the everyday mundane are woven together in an unbroken and recursive act of knowledge generation through social action.

Where, then, should we locate the difference between epistemic communities and communities of practice, or between the exploration of new knowledge and the exploitation of existing knowledge? The difference might well lie in the remit and organizational structure of the communities, in the terms on which engagement occurs. We have already seen that epistemic communities are heterogeneous, deliberately experimental, goal-oriented, and procedurally organized, while communities of practice are spontaneous, largely homogeneous, socially based, and self-organizing. These definitional differences and the organizational means by which community is reproduced might be the significant variable, rather than differences in the balance between the cognitive unconscious and the cognitive conscious in each type of community.

Callon (1999*a*), for example, explains how the architecture of organization can affect learning outcomes in stable or routinized networks and emergent or experimental networks. In the former, innovation objectives and goals are known *ex ante* and expectations are rationally ordered, with an emphasis placed on combining known and complementary competences with codified or tacit knowledge, in pursuit of programmable action. Network stability, in terms of composition, duration, replication, and length, is a key property. Emergent networks, in contrast, yield identities, interests, and competences as the outcome of 'temporary and experimental translations [*traductions*, in the original French]' (p. 29). In emergent networks, actors with different knowledges come together into an uncertain venture, with ill-specified objectives (only experimentalism is the goal). In order to work, equivalence (linguistic and cultural) needs to be established between interests that are distant, incommensurate, unstable, and uncertain. 'A sustained effort to interest, enrol, and form alliances is needed before the usefulness is accepted by agents other than A, agents who in the process of translation often change their identity' (p. 32). In emergent networks, 'actors are condemned to interaction' (p. 32) and the organization of difference through translation and enrolment plays a crucial role in supporting the production of experimental knowledge.

How the interplay between the organizational set-up and collective goals can affect the status of a community and the type of learning within it is well illustrated by the story of the Linux computer operating system (Cohendet et al. 2002).[5] In the early days, as the student project of Linus Torvalds, the programme developed as the work of a community of practice. People who joined the endeavour to write a new software programme did so to improve their skills and

---

[5] The example of Linux also highlights the relevance of virtual communities, originally thought of as largely non-interactive and procedural. There is growing research that shows that some, especially programmatic communities, display (albeit at a distance) a number of the characteristics of 'normal' epistemic communities or communities of practice. Through repeated and frequent virtual contact, the use of intermediaries in order to orient participants as well as maintain momentum, and some face-to-face meetings, these communities are capable of surprisingly high levels of relational intensity and proximity, and, through this, knowing through interaction.

to gain reputation. The Linux community that emerged spontaneously, with little overall coordination and organization, was not seeking to enhance the body of knowledge in computing science. Slowly, however, as the project began to look like a potential competitor to Windows NT, and as the flow of contributors grew, a committee to manage the interactions emerged above and apart from the mêlée of developers. The rise of a procedural authority and the reorientation of the work towards a deliberate knowledge product gradually shifted the virtual network towards an epistemic community (but without any loss of the original hacker enthusiasm that characterized the community of practice). The search for radical novelty became more deliberate as well as more organized. The central point, however, is that the shift, which entailed a significant leap in the quality of the knowledge product, did not entail any significant alteration of the knowledge practices—the mind–body–thing acts of cognition—of the subjects involved. These remained the same. What changed was the balance between the tacit/ informal and deliberate/formal purpose of the knowledge exercise (see Box 4.1 for a fuller account of Linux).

Box 4.1. *Linux: from a community of practice to an epistemic community*

The *open-source operating system Linux* has been developed on the Internet, outside any formal organization, by the community of 'hackers'. Linux successfully competes with proprietary softwares that follow a traditional business model, where licensing fees yield a return on development and marketing investments, and where development is processed following a 'cathedral' organization (Raymond 1999), through well-designed projects groups. By breaking most of the rules that prevail in the proprietary model, open-source software heralds a 'new economy' (Dang Nguyen and Pénard 1999; Zimmermann 1999), and illustrates the possibility of a process of knowledge creation based entirely on communities.

The initial Linux community of hackers as a community of practice

Hackers constitute a community of passionate programmers. Anybody with the required technical skills and the desire can participate. The Linux community too, thus, emerged spontaneously. What holds hackers together and what makes them cooperate in a collective endeavour is passion and reputation building. Their objective is to solve problems, refine competences, and exercise intelligence. An essential rule is that no problem should have to be solved twice: hackers must therefore share and make their work publicly available. This, plus the desire of a hacker to develop personal competences, is a reason to belong to a community within which resources (for example, pieces of codes) are publicly shared.

According to Raymond (1999), 'if you are part of this culture [i.e. of expert programmers and network wizards], if you have contributed to it and other people in it know you and call you a hacker, then you're a hacker' (p. 2). Members are chosen according to their commitment to and participation in the identity of the community: 'Most central and traditional [for one's status] is to write programs that other

(continued)

Box 4.1. *(continued)*

hackers think are fun or useful, and give the program sources to the whole hacker culture to use' (p. 5). In this sense, this community is self-organized, since no external factor shapes its structure. By the same token, it is the commitment to this culture that binds members together, subject to the acquisition of certain programming skills. To know HTML, to master Unix, and so on are minimum requirements of membership of the community. We find here the two properties of shared values and required individual skills that define a community of practice.

The evolution of the Linux community towards an epistemic community

The Linux story also reveals another feature of community: that through time the nature of the community can change and that the dynamic of community can lead to new forms and new rules of cooperation between members. In the case of Linux, the change has been towards the formation of an epistemic community. In order to cope with the flux of inputs, a committee in charge of evaluating the incoming contributions was created. This committee stood apart and above the community of developers, representing a procedural authority to judge progress towards the desired objective (which changed from the enhancement of a student project to the building of a competitor for Windows NT).

The introduction of a collective project, on the one hand, and of a procedural authority, on the other, sparked the emergence of a different type of knowledge and new learning modes. Indeed, the knowledge created is no longer individual oriented. Instead, the knowledge is now voluntarily put outside the individual and made both explicit and available to all members of the community. Unlike procedures within communities of practice, the impetus here is towards creating and accumulating a stock of knowledge about the operating system. In addition, the procedural authority guides the process of knowledge creation and accumulation at the community level, rewarding the 'good' contributions and discarding the 'bad' ones.

Source: Adapted from Cohendet et al. (2002)

CONCLUSION

What we have questioned in this chapter is the dominant assumption that there exists a discernible hierarchy of cognitive processes that can be matched to knowledge acts of varying quality and impact. We have placed our emphasis, both in general terms and in the context of organizational learning, on the cognitive unconscious, on the everyday interactive, on social embedding, and on learning in doing as equally important to all types of knowledge. Our aim has not been to deny the existence of different types of knowledge or knowledge communities, but to argue that experimental or radical learning and routine or incremental learning draw on much the same sociology of knowledge practices, which, in addition, cannot be easily separated into bundles of tacit or codified knowledge or bundles of rational versus experiential knowledge.

The implication of our approach is that the hierarchy of social and corporate knowledge outputs and achievements might need to be explained through weakly cognitive variables. At the level of the knowledge work done in communities of different sorts, this would include consideration of the degree of knowledge intentionality and organization for it, the degree of variety and spontaneity in the community, the incentives in place to favour experimental or procedural learning, accumulated experiences, achievements, and socio-technological trajectories, and the organizational routines and specific actor-network configurations that have come empirically to prevail in any given setting at any given moment in time. These, together with chance, serendipity, and the unforeseeable contingencies of everyday interaction, are more likely explanations of why the knowledge achievements of different communities vary. These variables—and there may well be others—need to be critically investigated and evaluated in a grounded and practice-based theory of organizational learning that is still at the stage of youthful promise.

What we can be certain about is that linear or rationality based models of learning—speculating on the delivery of knowledge from an Olympian height or from a more lowly zone of mental activity—place far too much emphasis on the fictive cognitive conscious. Equally, the recent turn towards purely humanist and over-socialized accounts of learning—captured in metaphors of trust, face-to-face engagement, and social capital—is also an exaggeration of the anthropomorphic properties of communities over the imperatives of capital in shaping corporate learning parameters. How to make things count and how to make the complexity of everyday practices count in a theory of organizational learning remain a challenge that we have only begun to meet in this chapter. One of the challenges raised by the idea of knowing through relational practices relates to whether relational proximity necessarily implies geographical proximity, or, conversely, whether transactions conducted at a distance do not lend themselves to the ontology of learning that we have mapped out in this chapter. We take up the question of the spatiality of practices of knowing in the next chapter.

5

Spaces of Knowing

All our arguments in the previous chapter on innovation and learning as a situated practice embedded in distinctive communities and actor networks suggest that the powers of context—spatial and temporal—should be placed at the centre of any theorization of knowledge formation. The vector of time has long been recognized by heterodox economists from Marx and Kondratiev to Schumpeter and Veblen, through notions such as historical shifts in modes of production or technological paradigms, knowing through evolving technological paths and knowledge trajectories, and the significance of time-instituted determinants in both the selection environment and what counts as knowledge, and the significance of knowledge accumulated over time. This vector has lain at the heart of the evolutionary strand of the knowledge-based approaches in economics discussed earlier in the book. The vector of space, in contrast, has remained comparatively undertheorized.

This imbalance has improved in recent years, following recognition by institutional and evolutionary economists, economic geographers, and scholars of business organization of the geographical embeddedness and specificity of business innovation systems, and of the increasing returns and competitive advantage associated with such localization. The interest in the spatiality of innovation and learning has risen rapidly since the 1980s, partly owing to increased dialogue on matters geographical between scholars from a range of disciplinary backgrounds (see, for example, Issue 4 of the journal *Industrial and Corporate Change* in 2001, focusing, in its entirety, on the Geography of Innovation). In these still early beginnings, the dominant inclination has been to define spaces of learning rather too narrowly, with discussion and emphasis placed primarily on the powers of spatial proximity and territorial mooring. This is slowly changing, as evidence comes to be offered of innovation and learning based in distant networks and communities linked through cultural ties, travel, and sophisticated communications, in the travel of ideas and knowledge, and in the links of localized clusters with sites many thousands of miles away.

This chapter seeks to work with an expanded definition of space, one that recognizes territorial placements but also other arrangements, in order to explore the spaces of learning in firms. It does not assume that knowledge falls into bundles organized along neat geographical scales and contours (for example, that tacit knowledge requires spatial proximity while codified knowledge is ubiquitous or that knowledge externalities are spatially agglomerated). Instead, it defines spaces of knowledge and learning in terms of the traces of corporate organization and communication—that is, as organized spaces of varying length, shape, and duration, in which knowing is dependent upon the ways in which actants—human and transhuman—are mobilized and aligned in pursuit of particular corporate goals. The spaces are defined by the contours and forcings of actant effort and by organizational architecture. Depending on circumstances and the resources at hand, they can involve all manner and combination of spatial mobilizations, including placements of task teams in neutral spaces, face-to-face encounters, global networks held together by travel and elaborate communications networks, virtual communities, and corporate thought experiments, symbolic rituals, and cultures of belonging. All of these count as potential spaces of learning, along with traditional geographies affecting learning such as local technological spillovers, national knowledge infrastructures, and global communications networks.

The first part of the chapter traces the geographical sensibility in studies of business innovation and learning that has emerged in recent years. We engage, in particular, with a central claim that spatial proximity and territorial agglomeration generate distinctive and superior learning advantages. In the second part we offer an alternative spatial sensibility, one that incorporates the possibility of achieving relational proximity—a key requirement for learning—at a distance, one that is consistent with the plural geographies and indivisible knowledges—tacit and codified, social and embodied—that firms mobilize in practice to gain learning advantage, and one that maps geographies of knowledge formation—ever changing geographies—through organizational traces rather than the other way round.

ISLANDS OF INNOVATION?

Two forms of territoriality or spatial proximity have come to be seen as influencing the innovation and learning potential of firms. The first, based on the rising influence since the early 1980s of Schumpeterian, institutional, and evolutionary approaches in economics, is the embeddedness of firms in *national* systems of innovation (Lundvall and Johnson 1994; Amable 2000; Gertler, Wolfe, and Garkut 2000; Hollingsworth 2000). It is now widely accepted by national policy-makers as well as international organizations such as the OECD and the European Commission, that firms are profoundly influenced by the quality of 'home-base' institutions that act as a collective resource for both technological and non-technological innovation and learning.

A varied set of institutions is recognized to constitute the national system of innovation. This includes the science and technology base, the quality of education and training and links with the business system, the information and communications infrastructure, the policies of financial institutions towards innovative or risky business ventures, public policies on trade, industry, and technology, the norms, values, and practices ingrained within the national business and industrial-relations cultures, and the nature of knowledge linkages and flows in inter-firm networks and supply chains.

This institutional set-up, which varies from country to country and from region to region, is said to constitute the location-specific supply base of technological and knowledge externalities that firms draw upon for their competitiveness. There is no suggestion that these externalities substitute for firm-specific learning capabilities, for firms too are path-dependent and context-specific learning agents. As Coriat and Dosi (1998: 109) note, 'given any set of technological competences and techniques of production which a firm can master, particular organizational structures and strategies affect both the actual efficiency that a firm displays and the rates and direction of accumulation of innovative knowledge'. However, the claim is that the slow-to-evolve, hard-to-transfer, 'home base' of institutional entanglements also shapes the ability of firms to learn and the type of learning that takes place. So, for example, where these entanglements are research intensive and supportive of long-term, experimental or strategic behaviour, firms are likely to be engaged in innovation-driven or path-moulding competition, while, in locations with more constrained access to advanced technologies, skills, and infrastructure, and non-experimental business cultures, firms are more likely to seek markets reliant on incremental and path-dependent innovative behaviour.

The home institutional base, thus, seems to matter, and this not only for businesses with linkages primarily in the national economy. Importantly, several studies of innovation within multilocational firms such as transnational corporations (TNCs) have argued that the home base remains important not only as the prime site of major or strategic R&D activity and certain core competences, but also as the cultural template for international business behaviour, including the knowledge and learning dynamics of overseas operations (Nelson 1994b; Gertler, Wolfe, and Garkut 2000). In this first interpretation, therefore, proximity refers to the links of firms to the institutions of a national system of innovation. It is a proximity to territorially defined institutions.

The second form of spatial proximity that has come to be emphasized, largely through parallel research in economic geography on local innovation systems, relates more directly to the perceived benefits of *industrial agglomeration and spatial proximity* between firms. This research builds on a long tradition of work on agglomeration economies, now applied to the implications of industrial clustering for innovation and learning, and expanded to cover in particular the social and cultural dimensions of co-location and collaboration that support competition. Its focus falls on micro-scale interactions in industrial districts or within cities and regions.

There are two main lines of argument associated with this second interpretation of spatial proximity, each linked to distinctive learning or knowledge effects. The first, which is closest to mainstream economic thought and which draws on studies of product specialization and clustering primarily in urban centres, weaves technological and know-how effects into older and more familiar theorizations of agglomeration. Clustering is said to help raise productivity by reducing transport and transaction costs (Glaeser 1998); to stimulate economies and knowledge flows through the formation of upstream and downstream linkages between firms (Porter 1995); and to increase demand and further spin-off through cumulative causation (Krugman 1991, 1995). It is also said to raise local know-how through labour pooling and product specialization; to allow the circulation of ideas and know-how through local labour mobility and inter-firm contact (Glaeser 1998; Breschi and Malerba 2001); and to generate knowledge spillovers in the local industrial atmosphere (Marshall 1920) associated with product specialization.

An extension of this kind of thinking can be found in contemporary work on the geography of the knowledge economy, which finds in cities—city centres to be more precise—the contact networks and cultural amenities that are said to sustain the creativity and lifestyle of the fast-paced knowledge worker (Leadbeater 1999; Grabher 2001), as well as the density of codified knowledge that sustains excellence and variety through the fruits of science, technology, and education lodged in corporate HQs, research establishments, higher education, arts, and cultural organizations, and the media industries.

The second line of argument concerns the role of codified and tacit knowledge in competitive advantage and how the two affect the geography of corporate organization. One influential idea that has been circulating is that codified knowledge can be dislocated from its originating setting and made ubiquitous through its formal scripting, standardization, and global transmission by the feats of advanced communications technologies and media. This, plus the growing pressure constantly to innovate and to learn in the new economy of knowledge-based competition and constantly changing markets, is said to be putting a premium on learning and innovation based on tacit knowledge (Maskell et al. 1998; Nooteboom 2000*b*). Tacit knowledge is said to facilitate learning in doing, knowing through application, information sharing, and collective understanding and agility. These are the vital assets for competitive advantage.

Adherents to this view—inspired by the experience of craft-based Italian industrial districts, or centres of engineering excellence such as Baden Württemburg, and high-tech regions such as Silicon Valley—stress that tacit knowledge is formed relationally, and for that is 'context-dependent, spatially sticky and socially accessible only through direct physical interaction' (Morgan 2001: 15). The important conceptual step here is that tacit learning is a form of social learning, which, in turn, is dependent upon particular relational conditions, such as networking and interaction, face-to-face contact, ties of trust and reciprocity, and cultural proximity in localized business networks. Lorenzen and Foss (2002: 10) explain, for example, that 'social learning processes work smoothly between entrepreneurs in a cluster compared to the outside world, because of an abundance of strong and weak ties . . . facilitated by the geographical proximity of local entrepreneurs. Proximity promotes face-to-face interactions along with monitoring and gossip, and hence shared experiences and points of reference.' Thus, 'co-located firms . . . tend to experiment with a variety of approaches and solutions to similar problems, spurred in this activity by the incentives and the opportunities provided by the possibility of constantly monitoring, comparing, selecting, and imitating the solutions chosen "next door"' (Breschi and Malerba 2001: 827).

Others, instead, argue that the learning is nourished by the social capital that is generated by localization, as Ettlinger (2000: 27) explains:

the intensity of instability associated with hypercompetition suggests that place-based 'anchors' of open networks may more readily facilitate social capital because of pre-existing localized social relations. Localized clusters of firms have the potential advantage of frequent face-to-face interaction and social cohesion . . . thereby providing opportunity to transfer tacit knowledge . . . It is the combination of social cohesion and openness to new knowledge . . . followed by ability to integrate that knowledge and reconfigure existing knowledge that defines competitiveness notably, under hypercompetition.

It has also been argued that, in certain sites, notably those that are host to industries characterized by strong 'untraded interdependencies' (Storper 1997) between firms in a locally interlinked business system, such interdependencies may spill over into the wider fabric of these places as collective social conventions. Through specialization, the industrial atmosphere converges with the social atmosphere, through such processes as everyday social talk about the dominant industry, the overlap between work cultures and domestic and public cultures, the rise of industry-specific organizations and associations, the inflection of values and programmes in local educational and training institutions, and media and other symbolic constructions of local society as trust-based, interactive, and cohesive (Amin and Thrift 1992; Amin 1999). In such cases, the locality itself—not just its business system—is said to be involved in mobilizing tacit knowledge and social learning, through strong communalist or shared traditions, high levels of trust and social exchange, institutional convergence, social familiarity and a shared sense of place, and other social virtues associated with common purpose. Here, learning and innovation are cast as regional properties, with spatial proximity and local belonging read as the vital economic asset for learning-based competitiveness (especially in high-tech regions, according to Lawson and Lorenz 1999). As Florida (1995: 19) boldly claims, 'regions are becoming focal points for knowledge creation and learning in the new, global, knowledge-intensive, capitalism. In effect, they are becoming learning regions. These learning regions act as collectors and repositories of knowledge and ideas, and provide the underlying environment or infrastructure which facilitates the flow of knowledge, ideas and learning.'

The fundamental insight provided by both the national systems of innovation perspective and the local agglomeration/proximity perspective is that territorial context matters for business innovation and learning, in the shape respectively of national or regional institutions of knowledge formation and transmission, and of the learning-enhancing properties of clustering and local attachment. This is an important insight. It compensates for the blindness in mainstream economics towards spatial context in explaining economic behaviour and competitive potential and it recognizes very real differences in competitiveness between

nations and regions that can be linked to local influences on knowledge formation and acquisition by firms. This emphasis on local influences extends well
beyond a simple recognition of the powers of proximity in easing transaction
costs (for example, processes of learning facilitated by face-to-face contact, dense
local interaction patterns, and interpersonal ties). The new geographical thinking, with its emphasis on local untraded interdependencies, shows that learning
takes place not only under conditions of frequent interactions and transactions,
but also in the absence of transactions, facilitated by a regime of local conventions of business behaviour, awareness, and monitoring.

This new spatial awareness has been boosted considerably by the general turn
in the literature on learning towards the sociology of tacit knowledge practices.
Even the literature on communities of practice has begun to address the question
in terms of the powers of spatial proximity. After years of research on communities of employees within organizations, Brown and Duguid (2000) in *The
Social Life of Information*, acknowledge that local clustering of firms possessing
complementary and rival knowledges, as in Silicon Valley, can be vital for
innovation and learning. They describe such clusters as 'ecologies of knowledge',
'fertile for the growth of knowledge because . . . knowledge that sticks within
firms quickly finds ways to flow between them' (p. 165). In the 'dense, cross-hatched
relationships' (p. 165) that characterize clusters, 'firms keep a constant benchmarking eye on each other [and] the ecology develops as a whole. Both invention
and innovation develop rapidly and together, turbocharged by feedback loops
that run both within and between firms' (p. 165). Thus, 'for the ecology to flour-
ish', conclude Brown and Duguid, it 'needs not just a range of capabilities, but a
close range' (p. 168): spatial closeness keeps firms on their toes or reassures
them of potential dangers through the circulation of ideas in business and associational networks, movement of employees, observation of rivals, and high
standards resulting from local product specialization.[1]

A similar spatial awareness is growing in social studies of science, which, along
with other approaches discussed in Chapter 4, have emphasized for well over two
decades the social and anthropological foundations of scientific discovery. In a
paper on why Russian measures of the quality factor of sapphire made twenty years
ago have only recently been replicated in the West, Collins (2001*b*) argues that
much of the inability has been due to differences in tacit knowledge between the
Russian and US or Scottish laboratories, rather than differences in formal knowledge, expertise, or measurement technologies and techniques. Collins shows
that successful replication has depended on Russian experts spending some time
in Western laboratories, which has allowed rather small but significant differences

---

[1] Similar arguments are emerging in other studies of high-tech industries. For example, Powell,
Kogut, and Smith-Doerr (1996) have shown that learning and innovation in the emergent field of
biotechnology did not start with any explicit geographical focus, but have become increasingly clustered due to the 'stickiness' of venture capital, networks of reputation built around local knowledge,
and other localizing pulls.

in procedure to emerge and be noted, and for tacit knowledge to be communicated through working together and, most importantly, establishing trust. What is interesting is that the older language in this approach to science, emphasizing the role of informality, trust, and relationship building, is now accompanied, as Morgan (2001) notes, by explicit recognition of the powers of co-location, of being there, of the social space of face-to-face contact.

In summary, the 'spatial turn' in studies in innovation and learning has come to offer a powerful set of arguments—and considerable case evidence—in support of the argument that businesses are locked into territorially defined institutional arrangements and social relations that nourish/hamper their creativity and adaptability. Earlier observations on the integration of firms in national systems of innovation have been accompanied by a new interest in the powers of local clustering and networking, but what seems to underlie both perspectives is a reading of innovation as an 'island' activity. The geography of innovation is seen in terms of islands of innovation, in which internal links or 'home-base' characteristics, distinguishable from external and distant or omnipresent forces, drive business creativity and performance. And, precisely on the basis of such a spatial awareness, Morgan (but see also Gertler 2001) has rebuked scholars who 'devalue the significance of geography' (2001: 14), including those geographers who have asked if relational proximity can be reduced to spatial proximity (Amin and Cohendet 1999, 2001; Oinas 2000).

In the rest of this chapter, our aim is not to take issue with matters geographical, because we too believe that space lies at the heart of knowledge formation. Nor is it our intention to question the valuable insight that has been gained on how spatial proximity can support business innovation and learning.[2] Instead, our aim is to appeal to an expanded geographical imagination, one that is not constrained to conceptualize 'being there' or 'near' in terms of island properties. What we take issue with, thus, is the *kind* of geography that is mobilized to grasp the spaces of knowing (incorporating innovation and learning) within businesses.

We ask if thinking of spaces of knowing has to be a geography of points, lines, and boundaries, of islands linked by distances, based on the intuitive distinction between *place* defined as the realm of near, intimate, and bounded relations, and *space* defined as the realm of far, impersonal, and fluid relations. It is just this kind of opposition that has allowed commentators to associate the tacit/contextual nature of knowledge with spatial proximity, or far away places and global connections with knowledge dissonance and discontinuity. But such associations are highly selective and partial.[3] We suggest the possibility of imagining spaces of

[2] For example, Saxenian's pioneering work (1996) has shown how the success of Silicon Valley cannot be explained without an understanding of the regional institutional frame of representation, collaboration, and socialization that has evolved, serving as a unique catalyst and support for innovation and knowledge diffusion.

[3] For example, Lissoni (2001) argues that, in Brescia's highly successful engineering industrial district, the key learning factor has been the local circulation of highly codified forms of knowledge, a finding that is at odds with the assumption that local clusters draw on the premium of tacit knowledge.

knowing topologically, where the folds and undulations of lines drawn as contours bring into close proximity sites that might appear distant and uncon-nected on a linear plane, and that also allow the possibility of no relational links between co-located sites. We propose, against a geography of scalar nesting, a map of knowledge practices as tracings in criss-crossing and overlapping net-works of varying length and reach, thus allowing an understanding of individual sites as a node of multiple knowledge connections of varying intensity and spatial distance, as a place of trans-scalar and non-linear connections, and as a relay point of circulating knowledges that cannot be territorially attributed with any measure of certainty or fixity. This is an important dimension of spatiality that we wish to add to the rich vein of work that has grown in economic geography on the territorial moorings of knowledge.

A DISTANCIATED SOCIOLOGY OF LEARNING

We attempt to develop this alternative spatial ontology in the rest of this chapter. Given the emphasis on communities in this book, our prime aim is to argue that relational or social proximity involves much more than 'being there' in terms of physical proximity: face-to-face contact, local ties, the home base, and the like. Crucially, if the sociology of learning is not reducible to territorial ties, there is no compelling reason to assume that 'community' implies spatially contiguous com-munity, or that local ties are stronger than interaction at a distance. Of course, many communal bonds *may be* localized, as in a community of practice made up of employees in a given workplace, but many other communal bonds—of no less commitment and intensity—rely on a spatially 'stretched' connectivity (Amin and Thrift 2002). This includes communities of enthusiasts with like interests (for example, vegetarians, DIY groups, road protestors, clinical psychologists) held together by cheap travel, the Internet, and specialist literature. It includes diaspora communities based on migratory ties and transnational cultural connections, which may contribute to different local systems of innovation.

These distanciated ties and the organizational architectures and infrastructures that support them are highly significant knowledge spaces, involving forms of learning and a unity of tacit and codified knowledge that cannot be described as inferior or radically different from the putative powers of face-to-face presence and spatial proximity. For, as Allen (2000) comments:

What matters in such situations is not the fact of local embeddedness but the existence of relationships in which people are able to internalize shared understandings or are able to translate particular performances on the basis of their own tacit and codified under-standings. Some such understandings and their symbolic system of meaning are likely to be bound up with particular artefacts and ways of doing that are firm or place specific. But many other relationships may involve learning-by-detection [or learning by search], where unformed ideas are picked up through distanciated contacts and translated in new and novel ways. Such 'thick' relationships may span organizational and spatial bound aries, as can the puzzles and performances which constitute them.   (p. 28)

Spaces of Knowing

These 'distanciated' relationships describe another spatiality of knowing, one that cannot be reduced to a spatiality of bounded places:

The translation of ideas and practices, as opposed to their transmission, are [*sic*] likely to involve people moving to and through 'local' contexts, to which they bring their own blend of tacit and codified knowledges, ways of doing and ways of judging things. There is no one spatial template through which associational understanding or active comprehension takes place. Rather, knowledge translation involves mobile, distanciated forms of information as much as it does proximate relationships. (p. 28)

This provides the possibility, as we argue below, of recognizing spaces of relational proximity that draw on far more than spatial proximity to influence the formation of territorial clusters. It also provides the possibility of identifying long chains and circulations of embodied knowledge that 'activate' knowledge practices in individual sites.

Knowledge in Relational Spaces

Nonaka and Konno (1998) have suggested that the Japanese philosophical concept *ba* (roughly, 'place' in English) helps to highlight that the 'shared space for emerging relationships' is the 'foundation in knowledge creation' (p. 40). Implicit in the typology of different forms of *ba* they identify is an acknowledgement of the varied spatiality of these forms of engagement. According to Nonaka and Konno, *ba* 'can be physical (e.g. office, dispersed business space), virtual (e.g. e-mail, teleconference), mental (e.g. shared experiences, ideas, ideals), or any combination of them' (p. 40). Thus, while they acknowledge that physical proximity, say in the form of face-to-face contact, does undoubtedly support relational proximity, they are clear that virtual spaces as well as cultural or ideational spaces also count as spaces of *relational* knowledge. They are not somehow less social, less tacit, less sticky, less negotiated.

They do, however, suggest that each type of space is conducive for a particular phase in the cycle of tacit to explicit knowledge conversion and back. Each space performs a specific knowledge act. So, '*originating ba* is the world where individuals share feelings, emotions, experiences, and mental models', and here, according to Nonaka and Konno, 'physical, face-to-face experiences are the key to conversion and transfer of tacit knowledge' (p. 46; emphasis in original). Then, '*interacting ba* is more consciously constructed . . . Selecting people with the right mix of specific knowledge and capabilities for a project team, taskforce, or cross-functional team is critical. Interacting *ba* is the place where tacit knowledge is made explicit. . . . Dialogue is key for such conversions' (p. 47, emphasis in original). Thirdly, there is '*cyber ba* . . . a place of interaction in a virtual world . . . Here, the combining of new explicit knowledge with existing information and knowledge generates and systematizes explicit knowledge throughout the organization' (p. 47). Finally, '*exercising ba*' . . . facilitates the conversion of explicit knowledge to tacit knowledge' and is 'enhanced by the user of formal knowledge (explicit) in real life or simulated applications' (p. 47).

We are not convinced that each of these relational spaces can be described so clinically as doing a particular form of knowledge work (for example, that virtual networks do not transmit tacit knowledge or that physical contact is somehow less involved in generating codified knowledge). This is for two reasons. First, as we argued in the preceding chapter, embodied knowledge and knowledge practices operate in such a way that it is virtually impossible and also meaningless to separate codified (or explicit) knowledge from tacit knowledge—each one is needed to instantiate the other, tacit knowledge is inscribed into the artefacts of codified knowledge (in codes, jottings, software, notes on the margin), and, in turn, these artefacts are always present in the act of thinking in action or learning in doing. Secondly, therefore, particular spaces cannot be separated as spaces of tacit or explicit knowledge other than, possibly, for heuristic purposes, nor can the spaces be said to exist in sequential steps in the knowledge conversion process, as conceptualized by Nonaka and Konno, since each space is doing more than that permitted by the two scholars (for example, the office, as we illustrate in the next section, is the meeting point of a variety of knowledge forms, local and distributed, and, for this, is neither a sequencing site nor a privileged location of 'originating' or 'interacting' *ba*).

Corporate Spaces

Nonaka and Konno's notion of place, liberated from territorial/physical connotations, is compelling, in that it allows the possibility of seeing relational learning at a distance. It certainly clears the ground for grasping knowledge practices within multilocational firms, by allowing such firms to be seen as both sites of decentred learning in local communities of practice (as currently emphasized in the literature on corporate learning) as well as organizational structures that allow distanciated learning to take place (of both an explorative and an exploitative nature).

In the 'islands-of-innovation' perspective, now gaining considerable ground in theorizations of innovation and knowledge creation within multilocational firms such as TNCs (Dunning 2000), the diagram of knowledge drawn is decidedly decentred, composed of local R&D, local competences and capabilities, and local knowledge networks exploiting the powers of proximity (Zander 1999; Howells 2000). While the 'home base' is still considered a significant site of strategic innovations and patenting activity (Cantwell and Iammarino 2001), it is argued that the old corporate model of centralized and hierarchically transmitted knowledge has been undermined by the rise of differentiated markets, shortened product life cycles and product-to-market times, and increased demand for knowledge inputs. These changes are seen to be encouraging the rise of the heterarchical firm—decentralized and immersed in a web of global and local alliances, partnerships, and supply relationships with other firms—reliant upon a system of dispersed (and locally rooted) knowledge resources. In this account, corporate knowledge is mapped as a loosely held string of islands: each island generating its own specific, but especially tacit, knowledge (Cantwell and Santangelo 1999), with everything in between—from management devices and organizational arrangements to logistics and communications networks—concerned with aligning, converting, or transmitting the diverse local knowledges.

However, it could be argued that part of the purpose of modern organization has been to make 'everything in between' do more than align dispersed competences, to make it count as a formative space: to enable proximity at a distance, in the service of the various forms of relational *ba* outlined by Nonaka and Konno through the organization and mastery of space. Without doubt, one of the achievements of corporate form, the rules and practices of technological ordering and spatial distribution, and the conventions of communication, command, and control, is to hold varied knowledge architectures in place and establish knowledge coherence across different spatial sites. But, through complex network formation and network management devices, another important achievement has been to find ways of 'being there' through regular and frequent contact between distributed communities, the formation of task forces and project teams dislocated from their sites of regular work, the travels of tacit know-ledge carried by executives, scientists, and technicians, the movements and transmissions of knowledge embodied in varied technologies, the insights generated during occasional meetings, teleconferences, and telephone conversations, or in e-mail messages sent in transit.

Aided by the architecture and tools of corporate organization, a disconnected spatial ecology of knowledge has become aligned as relational knowledge. 'Being there' is no longer a constraint of geographical proximity. This is not to suggest that the nature and quality of near and distanciated relational links are the same. Malmberg (2003: 00–00) notes, for example, that, in the 'local circuit', 'the likelihood of regularly meeting, and gradually developing a relation, with another person is infinitely greater' (p. 157), and that 'interactions are characterized not just by being unstructured, unplanned, but also relatively broad and diffuse and sometimes unwanted and often seemingly of little immediate use'. In contrast, for Malmberg, interactions in the 'global circuit' do not come by chance: 'they are often the result of devoted and targeted identification of specialist people' (p. 158), and they require 'a lot (time, money, energy) in order to establish their relations'. Whatever the accuracy of this comparison between 'local buzz' and 'pipeline hum', its significance lies in illustrating that both spaces are interactive spaces, conceived of as circuits of supporting relationally based knowledge.

Indeed, within given corporate parameters, and with the aid of varied mechanisms for distributed organization, these two circuits fold into each other into one space of more or less long, more or less frequent, interactions. The result is a blurring of the distinction between relations in the local circuit and those in the global circuit and a growing interdependence between them. Thus, for example, the serendipity of casual contact during transit, on a visit to an affiliate unit, or through free surfing or discussion groups on the intra-net, might match the serendipity that Malmberg reserves to the local circuit.[4] Most importantly, as part of a distinctive set of corporate connections and obligations, these travels— physical and virtual—blend into the rhythm of work, such that the practices of knowing in any single site can no longer be described in terms of a 'local' versus 'global' distinction (see Box 5.1).

Box 5.1. *The geography of Swedish pop creativity*

The Swedish pop industry, agglomerated in Stockholm, is a major contributor to national economic competitiveness, earning around $411 million in exports in 1997 (Power and Hallencreutz 2002). There are at least 3,000 professional musicians, composers, and producers in this small nation, most of whom are clustered in Stockholm. Along with a far higher number of amateur musicians, these professionals constitute the core of musical creativity.

There is no question that the creativity draws on strong agglomeration economies. The Stockholm region houses around 200 record companies, seventy musical publishing companies (half of the national total), an extensive network of specialist service firms such as music video production companies and multimedia firms, a whole series of post-production firms, a multiplicity of retail outlets and publicity companies, a dynamic music and club scene, a sophisticated media technology and telecommunications infrastructure, protective associations, and a well-developed property-rights infrastructure. The urban milieu nourishes and supports the creativity of the artists and ensures that the commercial rewards and reputational effects follow.

It would be easy to conclude that the creativity of the Swedish pop industry is the product of strong local linkages and dense local inter-community relationships. But this would be only a partial reading, since the music cluster is sited in a series of global relationships and networks that cannot be subtracted from the creativity of the industry, let alone its competitiveness. First, as Power and Hallencreutz (2002: 12) note, 'the strength of the Swedish music scene seems to lie in producing Anglo-American music that is better than the "real thing". By singing in English and fitting well into established rock, pop and dance genres many Swedish artistes have produced products easily palatable to international markets and enjoyed considerable commercial success.' Thus, international cultural and linguistic engagement, through travel, the media, consumption norms, what is taught at school, and so on, remains a central factor. Secondly, all the majors active in the global recorded industry have subsidiaries headquartered in Stockholm. The space, money, technology, expertise, contacts, and global cultural connections that they provide feed into the creativity of the artists (as do the various other corporations that are present in the

(continued)

---

[4] This is not to deny, as Gernot Grabher has pointed out to us, that the intentionality and effects of light talk do not vary between local and global circuits of communication. For example, in email conversation, saying 'hi' keeps open communication channels for more substantive purposes, while, in the context of face-to-face communication, saying 'hi' might not imply a similar substantive intent (Sarbrough-Thompson and Feldman 1998). These differences are important social dynamics in the formation of interpretative communities. Our emphasis on the blending of global and local circuits, therefore, is not intended to neglect different knowledge *practices* in the two media.

consumption spaces of Stockholm, and that nourish the artists in one way or another). Thirdly, the successful independent production companies may be Swedish in ownership, but they are global in orientation. In fact, they have been responsible for launching and promoting many international artists, and it is this global expertise and experience that feeds back into the 'home base' through advice to Swedish artists on latest genres, tastes, technologies, and performance standards.

A 'local' versus 'global' perspective does not help in understanding the geography of creativity in this industry. The local connections are intricately woven into the global connections, and to such a degree that it becomes meaningless to describe one set as particularly 'indigenous' and the other as especially 'exogenous'.
Source: Adapted from Power and Hallencreutz (2002)

In emphasizing spatial blending here and in the examples that follow, our intention is not to flatten the power dynamics of distributed corporate networks. Our focus is on the quality of relational possibilities at a distance and in close proximity. The power dynamics are never matters of blending or a continuum between major players and others battling for independence and dependent on ecologies of creativity and experimentation that are organizationally, culturally, and symbolically *de*coupled from the corporate ties. Rarely are the networks—and therefore also their learning dynamics and distribution of rewards—composed of smooth and neat complementarities and mutual benefits between actors that are linked in the overlapping global and local circuits.

Spatial Strategies

The enrolment of actors at a distance into a relational field is a prime feature of the history of 'long-distance corporations'. In an innovative paper on scientific discovery in sixteenth-century Europe, Harris (1998) shows that long-distance corporations such as the Spanish colonial House of Trade, the Dutch East India Corporation, and the Society of Jesus—all possessing considerable global reach—played a critical role in instituting medical, cartographic, biological, and botanical discoveries through a 'kinematics of scientific practice' based on the to and fro of knowledgeable people and a vast variety of knowledge objects such as maps, quadrants, dials, chronometers, compasses, logs, descriptions, and correspondence. Harris explains:

the long-distance corporations—that is legally constituted corporations that had more or less mastered the operation of long-distance networks—had immediate institutional need of certain forms of natural knowledge and therefore incorporated knowledge-gathering and knowledge-producing mechanisms into their social fabric. These practices, though directly related to academic and bookish disciplines we think of as scientific, were situated in the *vita activa* of a corporation's membership and were necessary tools in the prosecution of corporate agendas. Moreover, the dedicated channels of communication required in the operation of long-distance corporations facilitated the movement of personnel, texts, and objects in both the pre- and postproduction phases of knowledge-making. . . . the long-distance corporation is an especially promising research site for the integration of local or embedded knowledge on the one hand and geographically distributed practices on the other.   (p. 271)

The modern corporation is a masterly achievement along these lines, now doing most of the above within its own corporate boundaries and through other networks under its control and influence. And, as such an entity, it may well face distinctive challenges, such as how to shape path dependencies and inertia based on accumulated knowledges, how to manage a system of distributed knowledge, and how to balance exploration of new knowledge with exploitation of existing knowledge. But, like the long-distance corporation of old, it draws upon a fine network architecture and a whole array of governance technologies to make sense of varied, often conflicting, knowledge domains, each with its own spatiality. Like the old long-distance corporation, it seeks to achieve relational proximity through translation, travel, shared routines, talk, common passions, base standards, brokers, epistemic and community bonding, and the ordering and orientation provided by files, documents, codes, common software, and so on. Thus, there is no compelling reason, as Harris notes, that when 'one speaks of "local", "situated" or "embedded" knowledge, the implication' must be 'that the narrative is somehow confined to a small "space"—if not in the literal sense of a geographic metric, then at least in the sense of a restricted social, cultural, and temporal metric' (p. 296). Corporate organization, with all its devices, is the banal means by which knowledge spaces made up of bits and pieces from all over are mobilized.

Through the tools of organization, corporations have been able to develop complex spatial strategies in service of innovation and learning, strategies that involve more than reliance on the powers of proximity and avoidance of the perils of distance (Yeung 2001). Gupta and Govindarajan (2000) go so far as to claim that 'the primary reason why MNCs [multinational corporations] exist is because of their ability to transfer and exploit knowledge more effectively and efficiently in the intra-corporate context' (p. 473). They readily acknowledge that this 'does not in any way imply that such knowledge transfers actually take place effectively and efficiently on a routine basis' (p. 474), but are dependent upon local knowledge capabilities, subsidiary–parent and subsidiary–subsidiary relations, richness of transmission channels, local motivational or absorptive capacities, and so on. These skeletal elements are 'worked' in different ways by different types of corporation; so, for example, Gupta and Govindrajan find that knowledge inflows from peer subsidiaries are higher among subsidiaries that are integrated more tightly with the rest of the corporation through formal mechanisms and subsidiaries 'whose presidents have been involved in lateral socialization mechanisms with peer subsidiaries to a greater extent' (p. 488). The point we wish to draw for our purposes is that 'nodal' knowledge—that is, the know-how of individual units—is not a 'local affair' but is shaped by flows from

elsewhere in the corporation, parent policies and cultures, inter-nodal socialization patterns, and other spatial strategies of corporate mobilization for innovation and learning. These spatial strategies are also a means through which
dispersed knowledge communities can be linked together.

The spatial strategies come in many forms that are hardly recognized in
theorizations of the spatiality of corporate knowledge. One of these is the strategy of displacement. There are sites set up for new epistemic communities or
projects that cannot be boxed into existing spatial arrangements, but that are
crucial for generating path-breaking innovations. For example, Schoenberger
(1999), who supports the new localism thesis that the multilocational firm can
no longer ignore local corporate cultures as sites of learning, is quick to note that,
when the firm 'realizes it needs to change', it may 'consciously set out to create a
new kind of place within the firm', including 'organizational and geographical
separation from the centre' (p. 216). Project teams and task forces are a typical
example, dislocated from usual places of work or established R&D centres, and
bringing together project-centred specialists from different locations within the
firm. Lee (2002), for instance, shows that some of the Korean conglomerates that
have had to restructure and adapt radically after the East Asian crisis, are increasingly relying on such sites, where teams constructed from different locations in
Korea live together for weeks or months to develop new ideas.

Of course, the sociology of learning in these temporary and displaced
communities draws centrally on co-presence (as argued by proponents of the
localization thesis), but mobility is also built into the act of displacement, knowledge transfer, and application of new knowledge. Old and new knowledge translates back and forth from these sites with the specialists and the artefacts they
carry with them, and through the communications networks they use. This
process of translation is very much part of the circuit of knowledge creation, not
least because new insights and discoveries need to be understood and aligned at
destination sites. Placement is tied up with mobility, and which aspect is privileged (by scholars and firms) is a matter of emphasis. For example, in the
McKinsey corporation, project development teams, reveals Hargadon (1998: 218),
'are not traditionally co-located or isolated from the rest of the firm', but 'consist
of consultants working out of offices across the country' as this 'gives the team
access to the most resources within the organization because each individual
team-member knows and regularly talks to their colleagues back at the office'.

The corporeal space of displacement as a stimulus for creativity can be light
and performative, which adds another interesting twist to the relational versus
physical interpretation of knowledge spaces. Hatch (1999), for example, writes of
'empty spaces' in organizations, to distinguish spaces for creative action that
are not regulated by rules and norms and act as working and thinking spaces that
are not easily located spatially or structurally. Hatch argues that organizational
creativity can be viewed in terms of the achievements made possible by ambiguity
and emotion (and also tempo) exploited during the empty spaces of improvisation in jazz. Innovation in jazz occurs when the openness in a structure of a tune

'permits any of the musicians to take the tune in a variety of directions' (p. 85) and use of the ambiguity opened up by empty spaces in the tune. For Hatch, the strategic use of ambiguity in organizations can have a similar effect, if structure and script are moulded in a way that allows the most to be made of the open space between common orientation and overarching purpose, on the one hand, and different beliefs and incommensurable actions, on the other hand.

Similarly, Hatch argues that, just as 'groove and feel' are built into the rhythm and tempo of jazz (that is, a structural aspect), organizations can mobilize 'structure as emotion' (p. 89) by attending to 'liking and interpersonal attraction', 'intimacy based in shared action', and emotional 'performativity' (p. 89) as a way of allowing emotions to be communicated, and, through this, of unlocking creative impulses. She explains:

If work processes have rhythm, harmony, groove and feel, then the jazz metaphor suggests developing emotional and bodily sensitivity to work. One place to look for evidence of the effectiveness of such a strategy might be the outdoor development programmes in which many organizations have invested considerable time and money. . . . The contributions of such programmes can be perhaps better understood using concepts such as rhythm, harmony, groove and feel that are connected by the jazz metaphor to concerns for entrainment and flow. That is, team members who are in touch with their bodies and emotions may be better able to develop rhythm, harmony, groove and feel in their work processes which will enhance communication and the collaborative potential of their teamwork. (p. 90)

The use of emotions has become big business in the field of organizational mobilization of creativity, occupying centre stage in magazine accounts of fast companies, class time in MBA programmes, the attention of corporate training and performance units, and the imagination of a whole new industry of allegedly creativity-unlocking consultants and event providers. Things have moved far beyond crude attempts to inculcate loyalty through company songs and company jollies, into the realm of sophisticated uses of spaces of emotional performativity to generate novelty and 'groove and feel'. These include enactments of plays, simulations of problems, musical performances, role playing, deliberate and aggressive group confrontations, exhortations of guilt and exaltation, and application of softer 'new-age' therapies such as meditation and spiritual chanting (Spinosa, Flores, and Dreyfus 1997; Thrift 2000).

In all of the above examples of knowledge generation, it is relational proximity, achieved through a variety of spatial mobilizations, that stands out. We are beginning to see a similar shift in register in the literature that has grown emphasizing the learning effects of joint ventures and strategic alliances. Hitherto, it is the transfer of formal knowledge (for example, R&D, product specifications, new jointly developed codified knowledge) that has been stressed, possibly influenced by the assumption that non-sticky knowledge is best suited to travel over the long distances that normally characterize such forms of inter-firm collaboration. Now, however, the networks of collaboration are seen as possessing inimitable resources that are derived from the structure of the networks themselves, resources with learning advantages associated normally with relationally generated social capital. For example, Gulati, Nohria, and Zaheer (2000: 212) argue that:

Firms are highly alert when they create and utilize wide-ranging information networks with plentiful weak ties, high centrality, and wide geographical scope, and together with responsiveness, this capability translates into superior performance. The private and invisible nature of the ties renders the network inimitable, and thus too the information that it provides.

Inkpen (1996) has developed this thinking further by providing an illustration of how the 'soft' infrastructure of alliance knowledge works. In answering why 'some firms actively seek to leverage alliance knowledge while others make only a minimal effort' and why 'some firms are more effective at leveraging alliance knowledge' (p. 131), he identifies six factors (on the basis of evidence drawn from international joint ventures in the auto industry). The first is flexible learning objectives and expectations—that is, an open attitude to the venture. The second is leadership commitment to the joint venture, which can drive the experiment forward when exit tendencies prevail. The third is a climate of trust between partners, often enhanced by a history of ties between them. The fourth is tolerance for redundancy, or a 'conscious overlapping of company information, activities, and management responsibilities' (p. 134) that serves to lubricate dialogue and understanding, and, through this, stimulate collective learning. The fifth is 'creative chaos'—that is, the ability of managers to channel conflict, difference, and misunderstanding between partners for creative ends. The sixth factor he identifies is the avoidance of 'performance myopia' and acceptance of the joint venture as a firm-bending experiment with a longer-term pay-off.

What is striking about Inkpen's list of factors (whether we agree with it or not) is that it replicates—now over very long distances—many of the relational qualities claimed by the exponents of the islands-of-innovation perspective as properties of local clusters. Conceptually, the overlap of knowledge work in physically proximate and distant networks (aided in the case of the latter by corporate organization, virtual communications, travel, displacement, and new inter-firm networks) forces reconsideration of the territorial moorings of knowledge.

Circulating Knowledge

One clear implication of the argument we have been developing is that knowledge is not fixed to particular sites (geographical locations or network sites). The 'stickyness' of knowledge in these sites, be they clusters or R&D units or brainstorming events, stems from the unique interactions and combinations of bodies, minds, speech, technologies, and objects that can be found there, crystallized in a set of local practices of doing, interpreting, and translating or perhaps even in a momentary flash of inspiration. It has little to do with 'native' practices or locally confined assets. If there is a boundedness to the knowledge generated in each site, it is a feature of its entrapment and nodal position within specific actor networks of varying spatial composition and reach, not a feature of local confinement.

This is how we interpret the awareness of situated knowledge that has grown in recent years thanks to the literature on the sociology of science (as we saw in Chapter 4). This literature has been concerned 'to show in concrete detail the ways in which the making, maintaining, and modification of scientific knowledge is a local and mundane affair' (Shapin 1995: 304): a reading with profoundly different policy implications than current emphases on top-down science (see Chapter 7). Interestingly, though, what is meant by 'local' is not reducible to geographical location. Shapin, for example, has noted four dimensions of this 'localist' turn in science studies: first, science making as a 'mundane matter', accounted for by human cognitive capacities and ordinary forms of social interaction; secondly, the work of persuasion and enrolment through various means in translating and generalizing findings from any one site; thirdly, the 'embodied character of scientific knowledge', 'reposed in skilled people, in scientific instruments, or in the transactions between people and knowledge-making devices'; and, fourthly, the 'physical situatedness of scientific knowledge-making' in sites that can vary from 'the personal cognitive space of creativity, the relatively private space of the research laboratory, the physical constraints posed by the natural or built geography . . . the local social spaces of municipality, region, or nation, or the "topical contextures" of practice, equipment, and phenomenal fields' (p. 306).

The local, or bounded, nature of knowledge here is taken as the entanglement of human and non-human practices that make up the everyday—knowledge in action—drawing upon a varied spatial ecology of impulses and inputs. The local is not the spatially confined. The sites are recipients, combiners, and transmitters of what can be considered to be travelling or circulating knowledge, coming in bits from a number of distances and directions and in varied forms. Viewed in this way, the knowledge work and challenges of individual sites might be seen as focused less on mobilizing and taking advantage of local tacit knowledge or other indigenous capabilities than on working with and making sense of knowledge—in all its forms—as an immanent and circulating force. But their task should not be seen as that of pinning this circulatory force down or through other metaphors of fixing, slowing down, or containing, but as a task of making, aligning, and ordering relational networks made up of a multitude of potential knowledge actants. It is about acting at a distance and managing circulating knowledge by bringing into play (or onto site) dispersed inputs through relational connections, holding them in place, and making them count in distant places as new (and attributable) knowledge. Box 5.2 exemplifies this point through an actor-network-based account of the spatial connections of a laboratory office.

The discussion so far has explored the idea of knowledge circulation in terms of the distributed and distanciated workings of actor networks. But the idea also has a literal meaning, involving the deliberate use of mobility as a means of maintaining the 'potential for creating unexpected connections' (Hargadon

Box 5.2. *The office as a network node*

In their account of a UK commercial laboratory, Law and Hetherington (2000) conceptualize the Managing Director's office as a significant site in a circulatory knowledge network made up of heterogeneous elements. For them, Andrew, the Managing Director, can be thought of

not just as a man but more specifically as a *knowing location*. Or a point of surveillance. But he's only a point of surveillance—he only knows—because *he is at the right place in a network of materially heterogeneous elements*. This is the argument, then, about material heterogeneity. We might number: his computer; its software; the figures typed into the spreadsheet; the process of collating those figures carried out by people in the finance department . . . And then we can extend the network: into the power company (no electricity, no surveillance). The work of the programmers both locally and at Microsoft, the decisions by previous directors to implement a time-booking sheet . . . and then the car that Andrew drove to work; the fact that he and the other employees are paid; the telephone and the e-mail that allow him to summon the other senior managers to an emergency meeting. For yes, the point of this . . . analysis is that the relations that produce knowing locations, information, are endless. That they are materially heterogeneous. And, one way or another, they all have to be in more or less working condition if there is to be such a thing as a 'knowing location'. We're saying, then, that *knowing is a relational effect.* (pp. 37–8; emphasis in original)

Knowledge work in Andrew's office is all about making and managing globality, so that the knowledge network can be made to work:

[The office] is linked to other locations on the globe, to be sure. It is located in a world-geographical space. But—and—this is because of the work involved in making and maintaining all the e-mail, telephone and transport links which join it to other offices and laboratories around the globe. The work of keeping up the materially heterogeneous links, which maintain the mobilities between places, and define their distances. The materially heterogeneous enactments and performances, which create a global geographical space on the one hand and locations in that space such as Daresbury Laboratory [Andrew's company] on the other. Again, then, we want to say that the possibility of globality—and location in globality—is sustained in that work.

The success of the site lies in its ability to mobilize nodal privilege in a mobile and dispersed system of knowing. This can be achieved through delegation or 'sending something [like a spreadsheet] out which will hold its shape—so that the centre does not have to do the dirty work itself' (p. 41). It can also be achieved by becoming 'an obligatory point of passage' (p. 41) within the knowledge network. In Andrew's office, this is helped by knowledge held in unique software, or the offer of laboratory facilities that others are obliged to use. The spatiality of knowledge is not one of nested scales (cores and peripheries) or bounded containers of knowledge, but a spatiality of manipulation involving the passage of distant objects and flows through nodal centres that may or may not be a geographical centre:

This means that that which is large in the geographical sense, spread out over time and over space, gets reduced to a report, to a map . . . or, in the case of Andrew, to a set of figures in a spreadsheet. Everything—or representatives of everything—is being brought to one place, all at one time. That which was big is thereby being rendered small. And, as it is being rendered small, it generates a capacity to see far for the privileged centre. (p. 42)

> As a consequence, finally, Andrew's success is '*the effect of the performance of a particular version of spatiality and temporality*, in which proximity or distance take a network form that has to do with the rapid transmission of immutable mobiles' and also '*the result of the intersection of that network form of proximity with other and different spatial and temporal form*—and in particular geographical distance and elapsed time' (p. 46; emphasis in original). Knowledge is a product of spatial enactment involving, on the one hand, geographical manipulation and geographical mobility, and, on the other hand, the empowerment of things to travel and act at a distance.
>
> *Source*: Adapted from Law and Hetherington (2002)

1998: 219). Increasingly, as Thrift (2000) notes, 'new means of producing creativity and innovation are bound up with new geographies of circulation which are intended to produce situations in which creativity and innovation, can, quite literally, take place' (p. 685). These are geographies supported by a rich and diversified infrastructure of global travel and communications, including rapid and frequent trains and flights for mass transit, meeting places and residential sites for those on the move, sophisticated logistics networks to keep freight and people on the move on a just-in-time basis, easy access to a variety of real-time and interactive communications media, and new possibilities for voice-and-visual contact at a distance.

Thrift provides three examples of such circulation. The first is the familiar 'constant quartering of the globe by executive travellers' (p. 685) to attend in person meetings where face-to-face contact permits brainstorming, sealing deals, checking credentials, renewing trust, inspiring passion. Such travel has become routine in business and knowledge transactions—an out-of-office activity no longer confined to meetings with local suppliers and customers or confidences in local clubs and associations. It covers aspects of 'being there' that are not easily achieved through remote interaction, but, at the same time, it does not demand enduring face-to-face interaction and local embedding (in fact very many meetings are in neutral places). The meetings are one element in a continuum of relational interaction at a distance, over the wire, through past contact, based on reputation and recommendation, and so on. Their temporary duration and intensity—their increasing routinization as a transactional mode—have allowed the spatial span of creative interaction to be stretched without loss of the intimacies normally associated with face-to-face interaction.

The second example cited by Thrift of circulation as a means of creativity is the 'construction of office spaces which promote creativity through carefully designed patterns of circulation' (p. 686). The task of designing offices to encourage informality, casual contact, and surprise encounters has become an important tool in the management toolkit to help engineer creativity. Layout has become a visual symbol of how serious companies are about encouraging creativity, and is increasingly used in business chat and in the media to rank high performance and innovative companies. One trend, for example, is the replacement of offices by 'hot desks' that busy employees constantly on the move may book for a finite period. While this move has been driven in part by a desire to cut out wastage in the use of office space, it also aims to normalize circulation, exploit the possibilities of new desk partners and conversations, and inculcate a sense of attachment to projects and broader corporate goals rather than to a particular office and its trappings of security and ownership. Another trend has been the creation of common spaces such as atria, gyms, café offices, green spaces, streets, and squares—all within a building—in order to encourage serendipitous contact and conversations away from the heat of the moment, as a means of circulating information, sparking new ideas, and developing new socialities. This trend plays on the classical expectations of free social interaction, relaxation, and civility in widely shared public spaces (see Box 5.3 for some examples).

The third example cited by thrift of circulation as a means of creativity relates to new possibilities opened up by advances in virtual communication. He notes the rise of Internet 'thinking studios' or 'innovation exchanges', which 'promote knowledge exchange and sharing by bringing different actors together via

Box 5.3. *Experiments in office layout*

New designs

- Orticon, the hearing aid firm, has rebuilt the office space to create broad stairwell landings with coffee machines and places to sit to encourage people to extend out-of-office conversations.
- Alcoa has designed its offices around escalators or central open stairways where people can see one another. 'The Lowe and Partners Advertising firm in New York describes its three-storey central staircase as the "communal heart" of the agency' (Cohen and Prusak 2001: 87).
- Viant and BT has moved towards open offices for everyone, including senior managers, and on single levels.
- At Unipart, the resource centre of the corporate university is located next to the reception area of the group headquarters building, to publicize the central status of this thinking space.

New takes on traditional space

- Viant's open offices cluster around the focal point of a kitchen and a play area with a pool table and video games, Alcoa has introduced kitchens, and Boeing's St Louis leadership centre has living-room-style sitting areas.
- Waterside, the British Airways headquarters in London, consists of six buildings arranged along a central covered street with trees and fountains, a library, café, bank, supermarket, and restaurant. Bridges, glass-walled elevators, and open stairwells give people a view of this public area.

- The f/x Networks office in the Fox Tower in Los Angeles has introduced a central post office, where employees go to collect mail and refreshments, and, if they choose, hold informal meetings and carry on conversations.
- Chiat/Day, followed by London-based advertising agencies, has pioneered hot-desking facilities in order to stimulate circulation of project-driven personnel freed from permanently allocated desks and offices.

Source: Adapted from Cohen and Prusak (2001: 86–91)

information technology' (p. 687). These are highly interactive 'virtual clusters' that involve a considerable transfer of information over considerable distances. They are geared up for visual contact, memorization, and coding of past conversations, digitization of data, drawings, jottings, 'mood', and 'atmosphere', sequencing of conversations, trust, commitment, and enthusiasm for given projects, and so on. They act as virtual knowledge communities, enrolling knowledge workers at individual sites and workstations into a wider everyday net of highly creative relational interactions. There has been an explosion of virtual communities, communities that can no longer be seen as somehow less able than physically proximate communities. These communities have built up all sorts of routines and conventions, as well as organizing structures (for example, gatekeepers, web managers, orientation maps), that allow meaningful interaction and communication, sequence and memory, trust and compliance, and a whole series of other aspects of the 'soft' architecture of learning normally reserved for face-to-face communities. The upshot is that knowledge work has to be seen also as an immanent force with a virtual spatial structure.

A fourth literal example of circulating knowledge that can be added to the list relates to the increasingly transnational span and mobility of epistemic communities. We saw in Chapter 4 how these communities are crucial sources of emergent and radically new knowledge based on focused projects, and how, like communities of practice, they draw on a rich anthropology of human and non-human entanglements and relational practices to generate understanding, insight, and creativity. Many are distributed communities, with knowledge production dependent upon a considerable degree of international collaboration and exchange, manifest in a variety of spatial expressions of 'being there', local and global.

In molecular biology, for example, laboratory presence—hence localization and located practices—is without doubt of central importance, owing to the nature of the work, which requires close, ongoing experimental work with physical objects and complex instruments. As Knorr Cetina (1999: 86) summarizes, the 'many forms of intervention in material objects, and the laboratory protocols summarizing them, illustrate the object-oriented processing taking place', which conveys the importance of the continuous daily interactions with material things, of the need to establish close relationships with the materials, and of the experience bench scientists can gain from them'. But, importantly, laboratories talk to each other and there is a considerable international flow of information and people between them. This is especially so with the rise of large and expensive ventures such as the Human Genome Project, which draws on experts, and laboratories scattered around the world. Thus, as Rabinow (1996: 24) notes, molecular biology 'has taken up the current conjuncture through an increased use of electronic means of communication, of data storage, of internationally coordinated projects like the human (and other organisms) genome projects. The circulation and coordination of knowledge has never been more rapid or more international.'

Bodily or physical presence is interwoven with circulation in epistemic communities. High-energy particle physics is another scientific field that is based on large-scale and complex mega-experiments. Much of the work centres around significant sites such as CERN in Switzerland, which house massive detectors and other spaces for high energy experiments—sites that gather scientists from around the world and that depend on strong local communitarian procedures. But there is more to this epistemic community. It is also global, but held together; as Knorr Cetina (1999: 160) marvels in the context of one mega-experiment: 'how is it possible to conduct an experiment with 100 (UA2), let alone 2,000 (ATLAS), participants over the course of twenty years? What organizational policies are needed to keep 200 physics institutes—located all over the world and representing virtually all major languages, national scientific systems, and cultures—focused on a common goal?' We will return to what these organizational policies are in the next chapter when we discuss the management of distributed communities. Here all we wish to note is that 'distributed cognition' has involved building commonalities and a sense of the whole beyond the individual laboratory, through the constant exchange of information and people, frequent meetings, bonding at conferences, skeletal presentations that members from other teams can contribute to, and so on—in short, the circulation of knowledge.

CONCLUSION: DISTANCIATION AND GEOGRAPHICAL CLUSTERS

The thrust of our argument in this chapter has been, to paraphrase Oinas and Malecki (2002: 103), that 'innovation systems are worked out differently in space; they exhibit different spatial configurations. They may originate in one place, but often they are spread beyond local, regional, and even national borders.' The everyday possibility of striking and maintaining distanciated links, the everyday possibility of action at a distance, the everyday possibility of relational ties over space, the everyday possibility of mobility and circulation, the everyday organization of distributed systems, make mockery of the idea that spatial proximity and 'being there' are one and the same. There are many spaces of relational proximity, which is why we should be wary of claims privileging the special powers of place in the production of that rare asset called tacit knowledge.

The emphasis on relational proximity also forces a reconsideration of what is at work in those sites such as Silicon Valley or other Marshallian industrial districts where relational proximity is secured locally. These can be seen as spaces where the innovative thrust comes from the intertwining of communities (of engineers, entrepreneurs, financiers, computing experts, advertisers, and so on). Thus the dense relations or ecology of interlinked communities act as the field of innovation and creative thrust, so that, when a firm or venture fails, the ecology remains unthreatened, and able to push new projects, adjustments, and opportunities. The 'secret', thus, of local clusters may reside much more in the relational aspects of community (that is, as one spatial form of knowing through communities) than on the balance between tacit and codified knowledge.

But there is more at work in these clusters. We end this chapter by illustrating, with the help of two well-known examples, that their knowledge work is dependent upon translocal connections and mobilities. The first example concerns the famous high-tech cluster Silicon Valley, commonly cited as a paradigmatic example of the powers of local economies of agglomeration and association. In a challenging paper, Saxenian and Hsu (2001) show that a transnational technical community of US-educated Taiwanese engineers is increasingly responsible for the technical excellence of Taiwan's premier technopole—Hsinchu Industrial Park—and increasingly that of Silicon Valley, where, by 1999, 17 per cent of the companies started in the region since 1980 were run by CEOs from Chinese backgrounds, with the majority from Taiwan. On the back of a history of Taiwanese students travelling to Silicon Valley for graduate courses, setting up firms in the Valley, returning to start up new businesses, owning businesses across the Pacific, travelling regularly to both regions and treating them both as the 'home base', and developing a strong and well-supported diaspora network, a 'community of Taiwanese returnees, "astronauts" and US-based engineers has become the bridge between Silicon Valley and Hsinchu' (p. 911). Here are some telling facts:

Silicon Valley's Taiwanese engineers and scientists continue [to] travel to Taiwan regularly (7.3% travel to Taiwan more than five times a year for business purposes, 22% travel between two and four times a year). The great majority (85.3%) have friends and colleagues who have returned to Taiwan to work or start a company, with 15.8% reporting more than 10. They regularly exchange information with friends and colleagues in Taiwan about technology and about job opportunities in both locations. More than one third (38.9%) have helped to arrange business contacts in Taiwan, one quarter of them (24%) have served as advisors and consultants for Taiwanese companies, and one fifth (19.2%) have invested their own money in start-ups or venture funds in Taiwan. (p. 916)

An elaborate transnational structure of business links, family and friendship ties, shared technical and tacit know-how, venture capital, ethnic social networks, and business and cultural associations bridges the two regions. Consequently, Saxenian and Hsu note that, 'just as the social structures and institutions *within* these regions encourage entrepreneurship and learning at the regional level, so the creation of a transnational technical community facilitates collaborations between individuals and producers in the two regions' (p. 916). The consequence is that 'what was once a one-way flow of technology and skill from the United States to Taiwan has become a two-way thoroughfare allowing producers [in] both regions [to] collaborate to enhance distinctive but complementary strengths of these comparably decentralized industrial systems' (p. 911). The distanciated network is responsible for knowledge generation and excellence in both technopoles.

The second example comes from Soho, London. A widely held view is that the media and advertising cluster in Soho—increasingly an international power-house in the industry—is a typical Marshallian industrial district, providing firms with their critical knowledge inputs through the local industrial atmos-phere and clusters of specialist and related firms (Nachum and Keeble 1999). Concept-based companies are said to put together teams of talented young people around specific projects, working late into the night, and spilling over into Soho's many twenty-four-hour bars and dives of one sort or another to feed their creativity and ideas. In turn, the branding of Soho as the place for designer media products, fast creativity, and hyper-sociability is said to attract customers, more talented people, and consumers of the Soho lifestyle. Soho's strong sense of place and its networks of creativity are said to reinforce each other, thus making the district a significant island of innovation.

But this tale is only partial. It leaves out another organizational space—not reducible to place—that is crucial for knowledge formation and creativity in Soho. Grabher (2001), has argued that Soho's leading firms are international 'heterarchies', dependent on project teams around the world linked up virtually and through international placements. These project teams are firm specific but also composed of people from different organizations brought together for specific projects, and regularly recruited from across the globe as well as quickly assembled and dis-mantled. Grabher shows that there is no systemic or systematic linkage between firms in Soho and that the local industrial atmosphere is not a free externality in the service of local firms but is tightly woven into a wider architecture of organ-ization. The intense meetings in Soho and the exuberant local sociality feed into wider 'ecologies of creativity' (p. 351) that include international project teams, the reputation and might of internationally organized firms, and considerable con-nectivity between Soho and other international sites. Soho is a key nodal point through which a lot of things travel: people, aesthetic styles, genres, and so on.

Consequently, the geography of 'heterarchic novelty' includes, yes, face-to-face meetings, sociality, and casual contact in the knowledge-rich 'village' of Soho, but it also draws on distant objects such as drawings faxed between offices around the world, global travel to form temporary project teams, and daily Internet/tele-phone/video conversations with distant clients and collaborators. Soho without its role in this wider economic space makes no sense. Stripped of its place in a complex spatial ecology of creativity, stripped of its incorporation into highly decentred international media and advertising firms, Soho's Marshallian atmosphere would deliver very little in this extraordinarily volatile and competitive industry.

The corporate policy implications of an ontology of knowledge that recognizes the near and the far, the possessed and the practised, the role of competences and communities, are discussed in the next chapter.

6

Communities and Governance of Knowledge in the Firm

A central hypothesis in this book has been that an important element of knowledge generation, accumulation, and distribution relates to the work of communities of people acting under conditions of voluntary exchange of and respect for the social norms that are defined within each group. Accordingly, communities—with all their human and non-human entanglements—can be considered as key building blocks in the organization and management of corporate innovation and creativity. This statement raises a critical question concerning the conceptualization of knowledge governance in the firm. The perspectives considered in Chapters 2–4 clearly suggest two main competing modes of knowledge management.

The first mode is *management by design*, suggested by the strategic knowledge-based approach to the firm (Prahalad and Hamel, for instance), which tends to focus on appropriate coordination mechanisms and issues of organizational design. This type of management is a renewed version, in the context of a knowledge-based economy (KBE), of classical management principles based on managerial intervention, hierarchy, orders, and blueprints. The appropriate managerial tools in a KBE context may be different from those used in the classical case of transaction-cost economies (where the firm is conceived of as a processor of information), but the intention is the same (as we have seen in Chapter 3). The governance of the firm is conceptualized from a top-down vision of the firm, suggesting a 'hard' infrastructure of learning where managers use *extrinsic* incentives mechanisms (such as stock options) to align the knowledge activities of employees to the vision they seek to promote. For example, Grant (2002) emphasizes mechanisms that enable the integration of distributed, specialized, and individual knowledge in the firm, including rules and directives, time-patterned sequencing, routines as 'grammars of action', and group problem solving and decision making. He also suggests that complex product development can be facilitated by the modular organization of subsystems and standardized interfaces to allow the modules to work together, and that codifiable knowledge can be centralized, while tacit knowledge requires localized management because it is sticky (Grant 2002). In such a vision of the firm, communities are considered similar to any other groups within the firm (functional groups and project teams, for instance) that *hold* specific forms of knowledge (according to the 'epistemology of possession' underlined by Cook and Brown 1999).

The second mode is *management by communities*, suggested by the perspective that emphasizes *learning in doing*, of both an experimental and a path-dependent nature. This mode takes us in a different management direction, into the realm of how the practices of engagement/enrolment/translation can be supported. This shift of focus springs from the interest in the process itself of how knowledge is formed and made explicit, something that the knowledge-based perspective tends to take for granted. The governance of the firm relies on a bottom-up vision of the firm, where managers, promoting a 'soft' infrastructure of learning, permanently 'enact' new forms of organizational devices suggested by the social dynamics of communities. The nature of incentive mechanisms used in such a context is essentially *intrinsic*, embodied in current practices. In such a context, communities should not be considered as basic *loci* that hold specific pieces of knowledge, but as active entities of *knowing* that make specific forms of knowledge through their daily practices ('epistemology of practices', according to Cook and Brown 1999).

In this chapter, we suggest that the second mode of management captures the very essence of the governance of firms in a knowledge perspective. We propose that communities, considered as a mode of coordination, can correct major 'learning failures' characteristic of hierarchical organizations, and can provide specific advantages in terms of coordination that cannot be fulfilled by a hierarchical approach ('management by design'). However, we also critically examine the conditions under which a new type of governance that encourages and supports communities in a decentred mode of learning can be implemented. Like any coordination problem, coordination through communities also faces certain risks of failure. We suggest that in practice circumventing these risks implies exploration of hybrid forms of management able to find complementarity between 'management by design' and 'management by communities'.

MANAGEMENT BY COMMUNITIES

The first and obvious 'management' step implicit in a model of learning by doing is clear recognition of the limits of management by design, of the top-down inculcation of creativity. This is not an argument against organizing for innovation, simply an appreciation that the social dynamics of learning in communities cannot be engineered with the tools of hierarchical or transactional governance in the firm. As Cohen and Prusak (2001: 23) note:

Recent work on communities and various aspects of knowledge management promote a kind of managerial intervention that encourages natural developments, that orients rather than orders, that provides nourishment rather than blueprints. Some describe the difference in terms of a distinction between management and leadership. Some use the analogy of gardening or husbandry, the stewardship of an ecology as opposed to the construction or maintenance of a machine.

Questions of style and tone of management are crucial. The social dynamics of communities, based, as they often are, on serendipity (Nonaka 1994), trial and error, social interaction, experience, and enactment, cannot be tackled by a mindset of rationalist or calculative order. They cannot be neatly disassembled into a set of factors that can be slotted into a management of innovation tool box, as we find so frequently in the strategic- or knowledge-management literature. A typical example is Tushman and Nadler's list (1996) of devices at different levels of the firm to manage innovation. These include: at the level of individual attributes, the encouragement of specialization, bolstered by skills in problem solving, communication, conflict resolution, and team building; at the level of formal organizational arrangements, the use of internal linking mechanisms (for example, teams, task forces, project managers), designs for venturing and entrepreneurship, incentives linked to innovation, schemes for job rotation and career development, and active education programmes; and, at the level of informal organization, such factors as a clear set of core values, norms that stress informality, rewards for risk-taking behaviour, informal communications networks, and promotion of idea generators and champions.

Individually, these factors are crucial for innovation, but it can be questioned whether they can be gathered into an innovation management toolbox, which, once in place, can unlock innovation. These factors might be capable of steering the learning that goes on in communities, but they are not likely to generate the practices of community themselves—the everyday, recurring, and evolving social practices that fold together the conscious and the unconscious, the tacit and the codified, into a complex assemblage of learning through action.

Enactment

An appreciation of the social anthropology of learning takes us in a different management direction, towards understanding how the practices of engagement/enrolment/translation can be supported, and in ways that respond to the details and dynamics of context. The challenge here lies in intervening with a light touch in the process itself of knowledge formation, and being clear about what knowledge management is about. A first step is the acceptance that organization and management are about recognizing and publicizing the powers of *enactment.*

Vicari and Troilo (1998) go so far as to suggest that firms make sense of the environment—as the basis of learning—only through enactments of the environment with the help of varied 'cognitive schemata' (for example, scripts, maps, data, stories). Through simulation exercises based on interpretations of raw data, expectations of customer and competitor behaviour, time and motion studies, scenario building, and so on, firms build a picture of themselves in the world. The performance of these enactments—rather than the rational anticipation of external signals—is the basis upon which firms know and act, and there are identifiable management implications that follow from this perspective. Vicari and Troilo (1998: 211) argue that one possibility is explicit organization for the 'production of errors'. Distinguishing between chance errors (for example, generated by alterations in market circumstances or behavioural mistakes) and intentional errors based on deliberate dissonance (for example, critical customer surveys, firing old management) or experimentation (for example, acquisitions, the launch of new product lines), Vicari and Troilo suggest that firms should encourage the managed production or error as a basis for learning.[1] This suggestion, of course, is as debatable as those proposed above by Tushman and Nadler in terms of its learning outcomes, but our central point is that the meaning and expectations of knowledge management are altered in the context of learning envisaged as a grounded social praxis. We propose the need to recognize and support the soft architecture of learning within communities.

Managing the Soft Architecture of Learning in Communities

The soft architecture of community practices is not reducible to the technological, cognitive, or rational characteristics of communities. Instead, its key aspects are maintaining the social engagement and aligning the bits and pieces—animate and inanimate—that hold a community together, and, as a result, stimulate learning. We can revisit some of the elements discussed in Chapter 4 that are open to management.

First, close to the cognitive end of the spectrum, efforts to retain *slack* as well as stimulate *memory* and *forgetting* are clearly of crucial importance in moves to push communities towards non-routine learning. Slack, involving the retention of skills and capabilities in excess of those needed for immediate use, helps 'innovative projects to be pursued because it buffers organizations from the uncertain success of these projects, fostering a culture of experimentation' (Nohria and Ghoshal 1997: 52). Memory, facilitated by remembering exercises or intergeneration mixture, mobilizes the fruit of experience, including consciousness of past trials and errors, and past routines. Forgetting, through employee rotation, new training and the establishment of new work routines, helps to weed out practices that may no longer be suitable for changing market or operational circumstances (although the danger of removing redundancy has to be avoided).

Secondly, as is so clearly evident from the work of Wenger, Snyder, Orr, and Brown and Duguid, management has to be about encouraging the practice itself of community. But, what is it about community that needs to be recognized and supported? This is by no means self-evident. For example, in the burgeoning

---

[1] The management implication of stressing the role of error could be twofold: either that there is only so much that can be done in order to overcome the ever-present gap between autopoetic knowledge and market preferences; or, as argued by Vicari and Toniolo, that firms should foster learning through error production, for example, by developing procedures to detect and amplify market signals (e.g. benchmarking to detect the size of error, or acknowledgement of error throughout the firm). Perhaps both implications are valid, especially if we take seriously the claim that learning occurs in communities of practice that combine procedural and recursive knowledge, exploration, and exploitation.

US literature on social capital in organizations (e.g. Cohen and Prusak 2001), the emphasis tends to fall on community cohesion, reciprocity, and trust as the sources of innovation and transactional efficiency. It is argued that a culture of consensus, trust, loyalty, and group belonging permits the free flow of knowledge and information as well as collective or shared learning. Accordingly, corporate leaders are invited to focus on such virtues of community, perhaps through group bonding exercises of one sort or another, or interventions designed to increase trust (for example, through novel training programmes or joint working).

However, in our reading of the management implications of community, the emphasis falls on *engagement itself* rather than on the values or ethics of a collaborating group. The practice itself of the community does not necessarily mean consensus or trust and loyalty (if the latter two are meant to imply lack of conflicts and dissonance). What counts are the daily practices of a group held together by shared purpose and expertise, which yield learning as the product of shared expertise, talk, sociability, argument, and disagreement. As Wenger, McDermott, and Snyder (2002) claim in their recent book *Cultivating Communities of Practice*, 'a well-designed community of practice allows for participating in group discussion, having one-on-one conversations, reading about new ideas, or watching experts duel over cutting-edge issues' (p. 50). It is the architecture for certain types of interaction that needs attention. If a culture of trust and reciprocity exists, this is the *product* of sociality, and so it is engagement that needs 'engineering', rather than particular cultural dispositions like trust.

For Wenger, McDermott, and Snyder, community design should seek to evoke 'aliveness', based on actions that 'bring out the community's own internal direction, character, and energy', to find ways of helping an institution that is by definition natural, spontaneous, and self-directed, to 'realize itself' (p. 51). They recommend, thus, that communities should be helped to evolve in a natural and self-reflexive way, perhaps through the offer of open systems such as web sites, community coordinators, or problem-solving meetings; they advocate open boundaries, so that knowledge from the outside can help community members to see new possibilities; they suggest that communities should allow for differentials of participation among members, so that novelty and change are generated through varied inputs from core, active, and peripheral members of the community; they recommend that ways are found to help members realize the value of community-based knowing and action (for example, through efforts to make explicit or evaluate the value added from teleconferences or informal gatherings); they suggest that familiar collective events and gatherings are interwoven with exciting events, so that the community can generate novelty through both exploitation and exploration; and they invite managers to help communities to find a rhythm of engagement (based on a cycle of events, from informal lunches to web-site meetings) that is neither too fast nor too sluggish. All these designs are aimed at recognition and publicity, rather than the engineering of community.

There is no shortage of specific interventions that can help support 'aliveness' (as summarized in Box 5.3). Cohen and Prusak (2001), for example, stress the value of carefully engineering common spaces as sites of 'chance meetings and casual conversation' (p. 86). They dismiss the current fashion for 'hotelling' and 'hot desking' as being inimical to the formation of social ties and obligations. Instead, they praise new uses of traditional meeting spaces—including kitchens, open offices clustered around central kitchens and play areas, in-door streets, town squares, and neighbourhoods—as serious attempts to deploy conviviality and serendipitous contact as a rich source of ideas.

There are clearly limits to how far the sociality that underpins communities can be encouraged through such an engineering of semi-public spaces. Locational fixes do not generate social interchange, but gestures of the sort Cohen and Prusak describe can provide powerful corporate endorsement of the value of informality and slack/idleness for knowledge generation, through the time and opportunity provided for casual conversation, exchanging notes, tracking novelty. Cohen and Prusak suggest that 'telling and listening to stories, chatting, sharing a little gossip, are the main ways that people in organizations come to trust and understand one another' (p. 104). But the talk achieves more than trust and mutuality. Stories of corporate successes and failures, for example, serve to order the cognitive unconscious into an explicit frame of sense making, to align disparate interests and competences, and to cement collective memory. 'Investments' in storytelling can take many different forms, from encouraging everyday exchanges regarding jobs done among employees, to enactments of corporate histories at big occasions, and deliberate attempts by corporate leaders to weave together dispersed workforces through particular tales of the company.

An emphasis on sociality, rather than trust, as the key asset of communities broadens the scope far enough to recognize also the role of dissonance and friction in the process of learning. Creative communities are those that are able to confront and channel difference and disagreement. Learning within them is clearly partly a matter of exploiting existing competences, but it is also both about retaining variety so that new opportunities are not lost and renegotiating the creative play of dissonance, ambiguity, struggling with otherness, and rivalries.[2]

The key management challenge, thus, is to strike a delicate balance between existing routines and the exploration of novelty. Many management tools now exist in order to encourage and steer dissonance. These include the use of competitions between groups for new ideas, supported by prizes and other rewards; the employment of internal or external intermediaries or personnel transfers to help groups to adopt new routines or adapt existing ones; encouraging groups to play experimental games, build scenarios, develop new metaphors and framing concepts, enact new scripts at such events as away days; and the creation of project-specific teams or peer groups from disparate groups of experts, supported by various group-bonding measures to secure commonality and commitment (Pfeffer and Sutton 2000).

---

[2] We are grateful to Gernot Grabher for reminding us of the significance of dissonance and rivalry.

But there is much more. According to Thrift (2000), a whole new management culture valuing dissonance and enactment in its own right as a source of creativity has arisen, with firms increasingly drawing on cultural projects of one sort or another, and on performativity in general, as a means of encouraging innovative thinking and practice. This ranges from the re-engineering (by new business magazines and management consultants) of executives and professionals as fast, youthful, and urbane figures of business creativity and inventiveness, to the growth of management training courses that get participants to perform in plays, stories, historical enactments, and musicals to unlock the imagination (Pine and Gilmore 1999), and the deployment of drama, speech techniques, and rage by flamboyant business consultants to broker intent and novelty among clients (Spinoza, Flores, and Dreyfus 1997).

The Advantages of Management by Communities over Management by Design

There are two major advantages of management by communities along the lines described above, when compared to management by design.[3] The first is that communities absorb some critical costs of the process of generation of knowledge that hierarchical entities cannot afford to bear (for example, skills, experience, routines). In particular, one of the main characteristics of communities is that they 'freely' absorb the *sunk costs associated with building the infrastructure needed to produce or accumulate knowledge,* either in a completely non-deliberate manner embedded in their daily practices, or in a more deliberate manner related to their willingness consciously to contribute to building knowledge. Viewed from the perspective of a hierarchical organization, the building (or reproduction) of an infrastructure to accumulate knowledge (definition of a common language, definition of dominant learning processes, and so on) entails significant costs.

As we have seen in Chapter 2, the process of codifying knowledge entails three distinct but related steps: creating models, creating languages, and creating messages (Cowan and Foray 1997).[4] Each of these aspects has its own costs, and at each level, as the process unfolds, typically, new knowledge is created. The first two steps in the process of knowledge codification generally involve high fixed costs. Indeed, they require time and effort to implement standards of reference (numerical, symbolic, geometrical languages, and taxonomies of many kinds), standards of performance, a vocabulary of precisely defined and commonly

---

[3] This section relies on intense and rich discussions that Patrick Cohendet had with Frédéric Creplet, Morad Diani, Olivier Dupouët, and Eric Schenk. We are grateful to all of them for their comments.

[4] For example, when referring to the barcode system, Cowan and Foray (1997) reveal that it took more than twenty years for the community of the developers of the system to define the 'model' and the 'grammar' of the model, before messages (barcode information) could be widely exchanged at very low cost.

understood terms, and a grammar to stabilize the language. Once these steps have been achieved, a 'code-book' becomes available, and agents are able to carry out knowledge operations at low marginal costs, since messages are reproducible.[5]

Members of communities can absorb, through passion and commitment to a common goal or practice, the irreversible (sunk) costs of the process of genera- tion or accumulation of specialized knowledges. Communities are developers and repositories of useful knowledge embedded in their daily practices and habits. A related characteristic of communities is that, once knowledge is accum- ulated in the practices of a given community, the degree of inertia of routines and the power of replication of the routines kept by the community are much stronger than the power to replicate routines encapsulated in a given hierarchical unit. Routines 'stick' to a given community, while a hierarchial unit must deploy considerable effort to replicate deliberately the knowledge contained in an organizational routine (Cohen et al. 1996).

The second advantage is that, as the incentive schemes of communities are internal to the practices of communities, they do not require (costly) external schemes to be implemented. From an economic perspective, unlike other insti- tutions, communities do not need 'alternative bundles of contracts understood as mechanisms for creating and realigning incentives' (Langlois and Foss 1996: 1). There is often no visible or explicit central authority that controls the quality of work or enforces compliance with any standard procedure. The notion of contract is meaningless for members of the community, and in particular, there is no a priori motive for any financial or contractual incentive to align the behav- iour of the members of the community. The behaviour of participants is guided by respect for the social norm of the group. Thus, an effective community monitors the behaviour of its members, rendering them accountable for their actions (Bowles and Gintis 2000).

The Limits of Communities

Governance by community, however, does not come without limits. One of the major causes of failure in communities is the risk of parochialism, discrimina- tion, or vengeance on other communities, or incompatibility with the hierarch- ical imperatives of organizations. A second limit is the risk of lack of variety, as noted by Bowles and Gintis (2000: 14):

The personal and durable contacts that characterize communities require them to be of relatively small scale, and a preference for dealing with fellow members often limits their capacity to exploit gains from trade on a wider basis. Moreover, the tendency for com- munities to be relatively homogeneous may make it impossible to reap the benefits of

---

[5] As noted by Steinmueller (2000), this simplified vision of the process of codifying knowledge as a three-step process does not encompass all the cognitive issues associated with the codification process. In particular, there may be problems in aligning cognitive understanding with the language by which models and messages are constructed.

economic diversity associated with strong complementarities among differing skills and other inputs.

Here perhaps lies the main potential disadvantage of communities when compared to deliberate governance. Most of the time the attention of the members of a given community is focused on a specialized topic, but the emergence of diversity requires in general the creative interaction of different communities. Working by community can stifle knowledge fit across the organization (for example, integration of several heterogeneous professional bodies, cross-fertilization, and so on).

Thirdly, the hypothesis that incentives and hierarchy are weak within communities should not be taken at face value. Recent work, in particular on virtual communities, has shown how communities develop specific structures of organization (such as the community 'kernel', community 'developers', 'browsers'), which implicitly signal the existence of an 'invisible' hierarchy or power structure in the division of work and command. Some communities progressively build a 'procedural authority', such as professional codes of conduct, that helps to resolve potential disputes and also provides a reference point for recognizing the completion of various stages in the process of generation of knowledge. Similarly, recent literature (Lerner and Tirole 2001) has emphasized that some of the motives that guide the behaviour of members of the community can be seen to be of an economic nature, the main one being the search for reputation. Thus, if some characteristics of communities strongly deviate from classical ways of understanding organizations in terms of principles of hierarchical order and incentive devices, others can be reinterpreted through an economic lens.

To summarize, when compared to management by design, management by communities offers strong advantages, but also certain limits. This necessitates enquiring into the ways in which different modes of govenance can be integrated A first imperative is to find ways of linking different communities.

LINKING COMMUNITIES

By viewing, along with Brown and Duguid (1991), a firm as a 'community of communities', or, more accurately, as an organizational matrix that cuts through or bundles together different (professional, local, etc.) communities, we can begin to analyse how a given organization can cope with the communities that form its base. As we shall see, this poses the tension between hierarchical rules and the governance dynamics of communities as a key management issue.[6]

Managing a Collective of Communities: A New Way of Looking at Variety in Organizations

In the knowledge-based economy, the firm can be viewed as a community of communities that at most times are complementary in terms of their contribution

---

[6] This section relies on a series of research and works in progress that Patrick Cohendet is carrying out with Morad Diani. He is particularly grateful to Morad Diani for suggestions and comments.

to knowledge generation and accumulation. Management can be seen as the management of different 'shared spaces of emerging relations' in which organizations are implicated (Nonaka and Konno 1998), for example, through 'facilitating the voluntary construction of highly homogeneous social networks of scientific (or other, say, political) communication therefore allows individuals to filter the potentially overwhelming flow of information' (Cowan and Jonard 2001: 19).

According to Brown and Duguid (1991), an obvious, but central, management aim in a 'community of communities' perspective should be to encourage, value, and support a varied ecology of communities within and beyond the boundaries of the firm:

Within an organization perceived as a collective of communities, not simply of individuals, in which enacting experiments are legitimate, separate community perspectives can be amplified by interchanges among communities. Out of this friction of competing ideas can come the sort of improvisational sparks necessary for igniting organizational innovation. Thus large organizations, reflectively structured, are perhaps well positioned to be highly innovative and to deal with discontinuities. If their internal communities have a reasonable degree of autonomy and independence from the dominant worldview, large organizations might actually accelerate innovation.   (p. 54)

At one level Brown and Duguid's suggestion is an argument for maintaining a varied selection environment for innovation (most evolutionists would agree)— one that allows learning along different paths suitable for specific needs and specific community contexts, as well as the possibility of new learning through friction between communities (more on linking up communities below). At another level, it is an argument for the autonomy of small and decentred groups left to their own devices and their own routes into learning. Management by design of learning (for example, via training courses, R&D, new technologies, project development teams, task forces) is not a most likely route for generating novelty. Nor is the deliberate establishment of communities for innovation, as evident in the growth of project-based teams that bring together specialists across and beyond the firm into limited life ventures.[7]

As we have seen in the previous chapters, the myriad of communities at the base of the firm that Brown and Duguid are referring to covers a large spectrum of heterogeneous and overlapping groups, from the traditional hierarchical groups such as functional units and team projects, to autonomous groups, such as communities of practice or epistemic communities, which are founded on the principle of voluntary adherence to a number of common features. Within a given community, members find a setting that provides them with grids of general rules that help coordinate actions.

---

[7] Grabher (2002) shows that beyond the manifest pattern of productive ties (which consitute a project) lie latent networks of reputation, professional communities of practice, local interpretive communities, and so on. These wider ecologies are the constituent elements of project-based organizing, and are not deliberately established or managed.

Such a perspective opens up a new way of looking at the governance of the firm. As we outlined in the first section of the chapter, some of the elements of the 'soft' infrastructure of learning in communities are increasingly recognized and worked upon by companies as legitimate tools in the management of innovation. But, in what sense can we say that this myriad of heterogeneous groups interacting with one another constitute *a* community, underpinned by certain global norms and a unique organizational culture? Communities are disparate and dispersed. The constituent communities of an organization are neither homogeneous nor convergent towards a common objective. The risks of inter-communal conflicts or parochial partitioning are always latent. Therefore, a key management challenge is the need to align and establish coherence between the different types of community within and beyond the firm. This might include thinking in terms of combining soft and hard structures of learning within a given organization.

Tentatively, we wish to suggest that, in such a context, the governance of the firm becomes *an act of integrating aspects of management by design with aspects of management by communities*. This immediately raises the problem of how autonomous communities can be made to 'stick' to the hierarchical domain of a given organization. However, before examining the nature of these hybrid forms, we outline the ways in which different communities (whether hierarchical or autonomous) can interact.

The Interaction of Heterogeneous Communities

In dealing with the problem of aligning heterogeneous communities, two factors are of crucial significance: the degree of repeated interaction between communities, and the nature of communication between communities.[8] Some communities may meet frequently (for example, workers and managers using the same canteen), and this can generate some benefits for the firm (for example, formation of a certain common knowledge, circulation of news that 'something isn't going well'), even though the nature of communication can remain poor (for example, minimal common language or grammar to improve the circulation of knowledge between the communities). Conversely, some communities can be joined together through a rich texture of communication, even if the 'degree of repetition' of interaction is weak. Minzberg (1979), for example, quotes the well-known example of operations in hospitals, where the members of the different communities involved (surgeons, anaesthetists, nurses) meet infrequently, but, when they do so, they know exactly what to do and how to work together (thanks to the possibility of communication provided during their respective training).

The *degree of repetition of interactions* between communities stimulates processes of learning and common knowledge. It helps resolve conflicts and encourage

---

[8] Before exploring these two phenomena in more detail, it must be emphasized that we consider the firm as constituted of *existing* communities that overlap, and we do not take into account the process of emergence of new communities or demise of communities in place.

'interested interiorization' (Patry 2002: 18; translated from the French). One important insight of game theory is that cooperation is a rational option when an individual contemplates the losses that might follow from sanctions resulting from non-cooperation. In this case, coordination is achieved through a procedure of reciprocal adjustment. The degree of repetition of interactions between communities within the organization could favour the development of routines between agents located in heterogeneous communities of routines. In fact, the constitution of routines and their evolution is expressed in the development of a collective base of knowledge, and in the definition of a set of rules, codes, and common languages. Therefore, devices—for example, group projects or frequent meetings encouraging sharing of experiences—are regularly introduced by the management to compensate for the lack of spontaneous interaction between heterogeneous communities (to compensate for the insufficiencies of the communal coordination mechanism). This enables us better to understand the importance given to the construction of privileged learning platforms by firms (*ba* in the sense meant by Nonaka and Konno 1998).

The *quality of communication between different communities* of the organization cannot be reduced to 'systems of information' that prevail in the firm. Such communication is not a simple matter of information flow within and beyond a firm, as stipulated in the classical contract-based model as a means of minimizing transaction costs and other frictions impeding information processing. As Nohria and Ghoshal (1997) stress, the attention to communication in a system of decentred learning is principally a matter of ensuring that there is effective communication between self-governing, and, as we saw in Chapter 5, increasingly distributed, communities. It is crucially a matter of relational or cognitive proximity (Nooteboom 2000*a*) between distributed units, requiring attention to linguistic and semantic communication, shared tacit knowledge, flow and interpretation of information, and trust or other conventions of collaboration.

In such an 'architecture for interaction', the use of state-of-the art communication technologies to facilitate real-time and two-way interchange across the boundaries of the firm is one aspect, but not the only aspect. What matters above all, as we have explored in earlier chapters, are the cognitive efforts made by each community to contribute to the circulation of knowledge, particularly of that type of knowledge embodied in the routines it practises. In this respect, organizations are confronted with big obstacles—for example, the alignment of the knowledge and routines acquired by members of a team project when they come back to their original functional community. Another example is the impulse of formation of routines between agents not belonging to the same communities. The circulation of knowledge in an innovating enterprise rests essentially with the sharing of codes and languages allowing the various communities to interact.

What does it take to align different communities within the firm? In orthodox management terms, the answers are unusual. Our earlier emphasis on knowing through talk also suggests the need to secure effective communication between various knowledge/language communities. Nohria and Ghoshal (1997: 87) argue, for example, that in a decentred organization 'the real leverage lies in

creating a shared context and common purpose and in enhancing the communication densities within and across the organization's internal and external
boundaries'. Interestingly, though, here too it is the soft infrastructure that
Nohria and Ghoshal highlight, choosing to emphasize the role of socialization
(for example, via corporate encounters, conferences, recreational clubs), normative integration (for example, via incentives such as access to health care or travel
concessions, company rituals, inculcation of corporate or brand standards), and
effective communication between self-governing units (for example, via both
Internet and relational or cognitive proximity).

Similarly, Ichigo, Krogh, and Nonaka (1998) argue that tacit knowledge does
not readily translate beyond its generative context, but can be nudged through
the use of 'knowledge enablers' (for example, ongoing dialogue with customers,
personnel exchanges with suppliers, intra-organizational conversations through
block conferences, newsletters, and inter-divisional exchanges of plans). Probst,
Büchel, and Raub (1998) highlight the role of 'languaging' devices that enable
knowledge integration across boundaries. They note that 'boundary-spanning'
informal networks (for example, associations and clubs that cross divisional
boundaries) and individuals (for example, brokers and intermediaries, employee
exchanges between firms) help to intermediate linguistic transfer and the introduction of new practices. Similarly, Nooteboom (1999) has emphasized the role
of third-party 'go-betweens', who help to sediment trust, resolve conflicts, reveal
mutual advantage, and introduce novelty without destabilizing established competences within each firm. Brown and Duguid (1998) draw on the work of socio-
logists Star and Griesemer (1989) to note the role of 'translators' such as external
mediators and consultants, who 'can frame the interests of one community
in terms of another community's perspective' (Brown and Duguid 1998: 103);
'in-firm knowledge brokers', who work with overlapping communities in order
to loosen strong internal ties that restrict exploration; and 'boundary objects'
such as contracts, plans, blueprints, and other technologies and techniques that
'not only help to clarify the attitudes of other communities, they can also make
a community's own presuppositions apparent to itself, encouraging reflection
and "second-loop" learning' (p. 104).

Much of all of this is about the management of space, in all its organizational configurations. Relational proximity may be struck through the alignment of routines
and conventions between geographically proximate units, within and between
firms, through the use of the devices mentioned above. But, in this case, face-to-face
presence and maximization of the benefits of co-presence are the key management
objective, underpinned by agglomeration-specific efforts, such as cross-community
social events, local linkage programmes and exchanges, appeals to a local commons, and so on. But relational proximity is also a matter of alignment over
distance, with its own particular forcing tools such as virtual communities underpinned by multiplex advanced communications technologies, frequent
business travel, regular conferences and workshops, project teams that draw
from dispersed communities or that are displaced from the main sites, and careful

attention to protocols, standards, and conventions that help alignment at a distance. Distanciated organization, as we saw in Chapter 4, has its own management tools— tools that are less hierarchical than interactive in their nature and intent.

In summary, the degree of repetition of interactions combined with the likeness of representations due to rich communication modes between communities will be essential elements in fixing states of knowing in the future, the convergence of actor anticipations, and adaptation to common norms.

Corporate Culture and Knowledge Management

The simultaneous functioning of the two main mechanisms of sense construction and collective beliefs within the organization (degree of repetition of interactions and the nature of communication between communities) detailed above can, to a large extent, be related to the key notion of 'corporate culture'. This is a complex and elusive concept, but corporate culture can be summarized as a common grammar, allowing agents to give sense in the world, to code history and past experiences, and to develop their actions there. It corresponds to a process of co-construction of sense between communities, a co-construction of a 'common vision' (Weick 1995).

The culture of an organization is the global vision of the organization, its objectives, and its everyday and typical mode of behaviour. It refers to the role of representations, collective beliefs, and common enactments in the sharing of strategies and objectives (mechanism of convergence). Coordination here is devised or negotiated, taking substance within routines, conventions, focal points, and corporate culture. This mode of coordination can be distinguished from the two others in that it is spontaneous and includes the element of trust. It may in addition remedy the cognitive insufficiencies of agents and act as a mode of attention saving. The passage from an explicit relation to a spontaneous one allows cognitive economy, because the conventional agreement requires limited information synthesized into convention. From this perspective, the organization can be defined as the place where rules and conventions are established and where a corporate culture emerges, required for decision making and for functional efficacy (Orléan 1994; Gomez 1998).

The two levels of coordination—structuring beliefs and representations—can be linked. On the one side, the existence of a common knowledge base is essential to sediment informal interaction structures: 'Common knowledge not only helps a group coordinate, but also to some extent can create groups, collective identities' (Chwe 2001: 11). On the other side, the emergence of small groups or communities is a prerequisite for sharing representations and mental models: 'Sharing common mental models requires that individuals form communicating groups' (Cohendet et al. 1999: 11). The system of transverse coordination through communities is, therefore, evolutionary, since the agents, while referring to a given system of beliefs, envisage its evolution. Thus, the system corresponds to a continuous learning process.

In a framework of coordination oriented towards organizational learning based on the explicit mobilization of corporate culture, we must consider corporate culture or the referential system as cognitive devices (corporate culture in its own right, of course, is never purely cognitive). This is a condition of 'situated rationality', designating the dependence of agent behaviours on past experiences and past networks of interaction, such that the individual is helped 'in seeing a certain rule implemented in a social community within which he operates' (Vanberg 1994: 21). The situated rationality draws on the tacit knowledge specific to particular agents and particular contexts. Thus, the construction of sense and collective beliefs is a procedural process: through the process of translation, individuals and communities construct sense. This sense remains intimately bound to the action and is not fixed in time (Marmuse 1999).

Through such an understanding, corporate culture can be regarded as a weakly formalized and codified entity, one in which the experiences and the history of the organization resulting from various modes of coordination (from market and hierarchy to community) come pouring. The mode of coordination *ex ante* by leadership is necessarily conscious and purposeful, whereas the mode of coordination *ex post* by communities is essentially spontaneous. Thus, by its procedural construction (as the non-intentional and tacit result of repeated interactions), corporate culture takes its origin essentially in the communal and inter-communal dimensions of the organization.

A consideration of the three modes of coordination (market, hierarchy, and communities) poses the question of their consistency and their complementarity. As Foss (1998: 28) stresses, 'there are both cognitive and incentive aspects to these coordination problems. For example, the problem of adapting to an unexpected event has the cognitive dimension of categorizing and interpreting the event, and it may also have the incentive dimension of avoiding that one of the parties to a contractual relation utilizes the unexpected contingency to effect a hold-up.'

It is thus vital for an organization to establish governance mechanisms that strive for complementarity between the three modes of coordination. On the basis of our definition of corporate culture, a spectrum of different corporate cultures can be distinguished, depending upon the degrees of interaction and repetition, and the quality of communication between communities (see Fig. 6.1). Each implies different coordinating imperatives, and, in particular, each implies a different way of looking at the coupling between management by design and management by communities.

In *Case 1*, communities in the organization do not frequently interact and cannot rely on a rich cognitive architecture (common jargons, codes, and so on) to communicate. In this case of a weak communicative culture, an opening arises for the rules of hierarchy to find coherence, through prescriptions of procedures and methods and through a common unified language imposed by the hierarchy. Classic incentive and coordination mechanisms such as Taylorist time-and-motion management principles drive decision making. Management by design

	Weak repetitiveness of interactions between communities	Strong repetitiveness of interactions between communities
Poor quality of communication between communities (lack of common codes, jargon, languages)	*Case 1* Weak communicative culture	*Case 2* Strong tacit culture
Strong quality of communication between communities (existence of common codes, jargon, and languages)	*Case 3* Strong codified culture	*Case 4* Strong communicative culture.

Figure 6.1. *Different forms of corporate culture*

Source: Adapted from Cohendet and Diani (2003)

clearly dominates management by communities, although local mechanisms of learning in communities (for example, at shop-floor level) can transmit learning-by-doing effects at the global level of the organization.[9] Also, in such a context, as Foss (1998: 28) suggests, a 'weak' corporate culture may emerge to fulfil a classical role:

The firm may have an implicit contract (or corporate culture) that solves incentives coordination problems by signalling to employees that management will not opportunistically take advantage of them in case of unforeseen events, although nothing specific is said (or can be said) about the event. Likewise, we can have shared interpretative schemes that solve other types of coordination problems by allowing employees to categorize unexpected events as being the same overall type and therefore reacting in a coordinated manner. Here, there is the creation of a 'convergence of expectations' that Malmgren (1961, quoted by Foss 1998) saw as a primary benefit of firm organization, but only convergence of expectations with respect to typical features.

In *Case 2*, the weak quality of communication between communities, especially noticeable in emergent relations built around many communities, can lead to an expensive search for cognitive alignment between communities. Coordination by leadership (necessarily conscious and intentional) appears to be the ideal solution in instances when the costs of communication or compatibility are onerous or when the resolution of coordination problems is urgent. Therefore, a script of

[9] All these phenomena have been widely recognized and identified by the management theory of 'human relations', in particular in the perspective of the researches done by Mayo (1945), who advocated that managers should develop 'social human skills' to facilitate interpersonal communication within formal groups of the work organization.

leadership emerges, charged with coordinating intricate actions or beliefs while producing sense. Foss (1999) has shown that, in some circumstances, leadership can offer less expensive solutions than complex mental processes or formation of conventions. It can, particularly, facilitate coordination of beliefs:

Leadership is designed to coordinate the interlocking actions of many people through the creation of common knowledge. . . . It is the ability to resolve social dilemmas, by influencing beliefs. . . . Leaders may create a common knowledge when none exists previously. They also may solve co-ordination problems that persist even in the presence of common knowledge.   (Foss 1999: 8)

This type of situation also requires a specific coupling between management by design and management by communities. Part of the solution might reside in the hands of middle management, who play, for authors such as Nonaka and Takeuchi, a decisive role in the innovative quality of the business. The middle managers can be seen as mediators who know the norms and habits of the communities sufficiently well to translate messages of the hierarchy into a jargon intelligible to different communities, and, in turn, to translate for the hierarchy the messages coming from communities. As noted by Schelling (1960: 144), 'a mediator can do more than simply constrain communications—putting limits on the order of offers, counter-offers, and so forth—since he can invent contextual material of his own and make potent suggestions. That is he can influence . . . expectations of his own initiative. When there is no apparent point for agreement, he can create one by his power to make a dramatic suggestion.'

Case 3, marked by a strong codified culture, involves the existence of a common cognitive architecture that links communities together (for example, different communities of work in a hospital—nurses, surgeons, anaesthetists). The existence of such an infrastructure of knowledge (common grammar, common codes, common languages) may be due to very different historical factors (a type of education that has anticipated the cognitive forms of relationships between heterogeneous communities, shared experience that has lasted long enough to permit a common grammar to be built, a decision taken by the hierarchy to build a modular platform of knowledge, and so on). But, whatever the reason, the common infrastructure of knowledge has taken time and sunk costs to be built. It not only defines what the communities have in common, but it also implicitly defines what they do not have in common.[10] Standardized interfaces between each community and the common platform of knowledge allow each community to work independently from others. This implies specific advantages, in particular the fact that, provided that the platform holds, the need for coordination by hierarchy is significantly reduced. In this case, management by communities temporarily dominates management by design.

---

[10] This can be related to well-known developments suggested by Bourdieu on the fact that more important than the notion of common knowledge is the notion of acceptance by one community of what we 'do not want to know' (about what the other community is doing). For economists, this suggests a radical reconsideration of the way to perceive the notion of asymmetries of information.

However, if the constraint of the interfaces cannot be respected, then the efficacy of the common platform becomes severely questioned. This could happen, for example, when emergent innovations in one community imply the reformulation of the whole cognitive platform. In such a context, 'sense-making' interventions by the hierarchy may arise, to decide if the novelty produced needs reformulation of the common platform. If deemed so, then a new cognitive process of definition of common codes, jargon, and languages has to be initiated.[11] In summary, the role of the hierarchy is to intervene at critical moments when the need to reformulate a common platform of knowledge between communities is perceived as essential. *Case 3* is thus a case when management by design and management by communities sequentially alternate as dominant modes of coordination.

In *Case 4*, characterized by a strong communicative culture based on interaction between communities, memory, and the quick coordination of divergent interests, the organization can largely operate in a self-organized manner (including the determination of its core interests, which can occur without excessive market or hierarchical intervention) in either a consolidated or an emergent context. It is probable that, in such a situation, the unceasing bubbling of communities allows the organization to innovate constantly, since it does not disrupt corporate integrity (this dimension can be related to the creative spiral as conceived by Nonaka and Takeuchi 1995). In such a context, where management by communities clearly dominates management by design, the main role of the hierarchy is to enact the innovative outcomes produced by the constant interactions of communities, along the lines that have been described in the first sections of this chapter.

The implications, in the area of product management, of this fourfold typology are illustrated in Box 6.1.

Box 6.1. *Managing product creation processes: a typology based on the nature of interactions between communities*

In a seminal paper in the *Strategic Management Journal*, Sanchez and Mahoney (1996: 63) propose a typology of the different ways of managing product creation processes:

- The *traditional sequential process*, characterized by sequential staging of design and development tasks after defining the product concept, and by the fact that the information structure of component interface specification (the new product architecture), is the output of the design and development processes.
- *Overlapping problem solving* calls for greater sharing of information through joint problem solving, which allows interrelated component development to proceed

(continued)

---

[11] This corresponds to a process of codification in the sense that has been described in Chapter 2.

Box 6.1. *(continued)*

more quickly and reduces information losses between stages. It requires influential project managers who have the authority to make design and specification decisions and adjudicate disputes between development groups.

- *Modular organization*, which seeks continuously to 'change and solve problems through interconnected coordinated self-organizing processes' (Daft and Lewin 1993). Modularity allows component-level learning processes to be carried out concurrently and autonomously by geographically dispersed and loosely coupled development groups.

Sanchez and Mahoney show that each type of management approach for product creation is adapted to a specific environment or context (for example, the traditional sequential approach is well adapted for a very stable environment). They emphasize that, in a turbulent and competitive environment where flexibility is required, modularity is superior to more classic forms of management of knowledge in product creation processes: 'A firm using a modular product architecture to coordinate development processes has a means to quickly link together the resources and capabilities of many organizations to form product development resource chains that can respond flexibly (i.e. broadly, quickly and at low cost) to environmental changes' (p. 63). In particular, they stress that the learning processes at stake in a modular product architecture create a complete information structure (fully specified components). This information structure provides the 'glue' of embedded coordination that allows the development of a loosely coupled organization. 'Embedded organization is the coordination of organizational processes achieved by any means other that of continuous exercise of managerial authorities' (p. 63). Sanchez and Mahoney acknowledge that the concept of 'embedded organization' may include forms of coordination other than modularity, such as, for instance, 'clan coordination through tradition' (p. 66).

What Sanchez and Mahoney suggest in the idea of 'embedded organization' can be extended to the development of product creation processes by viewing the organization as a myriad of communities interacting together. It can be argued that the active units of analysis in a product creation process are those small groups of people that interact directly, frequently, and in multifaceted ways in the process of generating, exchanging, and distributing knowledge within a given organization. From our perspective of the firm as an architecture of interacting communities, we can distinguish distinctive modes of managing product creation processes (see Fig. 6.2).

The first category corresponds to the traditional sequential process mode of management (as in a typically Taylorist organization). The strong division of work relies on specialized units that do not interact on a frequent basis, and do not develop rich modes of communication. Coordination is dependent upon intensive management, involving *ex ante* top-down rules and procedures to be followed by the entire organization, and centralized global vision of the product creation process.

The second category corresponds to the overlapping problem-solving mode (as in a matrix type of organization). The division of work includes repeated informational exchanges between specialized groups in the organization. The absence of a rich architecture of communication between the groups leads to an expensive search for a cognitive

	Weak repetitiveness of interactions between communities	Strong repetitiveness of interactions between communities
Poor quality of communication between communities (lack of common codes, jargon, languages)	*Category 1* Traditional sequential process Intense managerial decisions (full design and specification decisions, and control decisions)	*Category 2* Overlapping problem solving Strong managerial decisions (partial design and specification decisions and adjudication of disputes)
Strong quality of communication between communities (existence of common codes, jargon, and languages)	*Category 3* Modular organization Managerial decisions ex-post to redefine the platform if radical innovations needed	*Category 4* Evolutionary organization Managerial decisions to enact the organizational forms that emerge from auto-organized process

Figure 6.2. *Modes of managing product creation processes based on the nature of interactions between communities*

Source: Cohendet, Diani, and Lerch (2002)

consensus between communities, and necessitates active managerial involvement, mostly *ex post*, to resolve disputes and conflicts between communities, but also to implement common knowledge and to coordinate beliefs while producing sense.

The third category corresponds to modular organization (organizational structures with existing cognitive platforms that allow loose-coupling systems to function efficiently). In such contexts, learning at the component level is insulated against disruptions by unexpected changes in product architecture caused by development projects. The role of hierarchy is to define *ex ante* the nature of the platform, and *ex post* to redefine the platform if radical innovations are unavoidable (see Langlois 2002).

Our typology leads logically to a fourth category (strong repetitiveness of interactions and strong possibilities of communication between communities), which is not envisaged by Sanchez and Mahoney. In this mode of management, we can envisage governance by community alone, with hierarchy needed only to 'authorize' or 'enact' the organizational forms produced by the interacting autonomous communities. The organization can operate largely in a self-organized manner. It is probable that, in such a situation, the unceasing efflorescence of communities allows the organization to innovate constantly. This mode can be called management by enactment, after Ciborra (1996), who describes the 'knowledge platform' at Olivetti in such terms.

Source: Adapted from Sanchez and Mahoney (1996)

An interpretation in terms of spatial arrangements

Significantly, the four categories of interaction between communities outlined in Fig. 6.1 can be related to the spatial concerns discussed in Chapter 5, allowing us to link different management styles with the nature of inter-community interaction in particular spatial arrangements. For example, in co-located communities:

- *Case 1* (weak interactions, poor communications), exemplified by localized groups of firms that depend on a large group (for example, Michelin City, Leverkusen BASF), is likely to yield a management culture that is more or less completely shaped by the large group, which defines the procedures to be followed, the language, the corporate ethos, and so on.

- *Case 2* (strong interactions, poor communications) is exemplified by industrial parks, where companies are placed together in the expectation[12] that from repeated interactions innovative sparks will emerge. If a strong tacit culture does emerge from repeated interactions, this still leaves the problem of weak communications, thus there is a particular role for central efforts to improve the park's informational and communications circuitry, through local IT networks, newsletters, local cultural events, common services, and so on.

- *Case 3* (weak interactions, rich communications) is exemplified by industrial clusters where there is a common platform of knowledge and semantic understanding, but a weaker structure of interaction between firms. Certain craft industrial districts that lack a detailed division of labour between firms share a strong communicative culture based on local community (social and kinship ties and a shared public culture and shared public spaces and institutions—for example, educational, engineering centres that irrigate the different firms), but they lack transactional interdependence. Here, the challenge lies in attempts to encourage the latter through task specialization, joint ventures, linkage programmes, subcontracting, and so on.

- *Case 4* (strong interactions, rich communications) is exemplified by Silicon Valley as well as industrial districts with strong interdependencies between firms. Here, interacting communities (of engineers, software designers, specialist firms, and so on) are genuinely self-organizing, and in such a way that organization emerges from the interactions rather than the reverse. The management of these clusters is largely autopoetic, and dependent upon the structure of interaction and communication; thus, for example, if a firm goes bankrupt, the collective interaction of communities takes charge, to ensure that new organizations are formed and that the competences and experience of individuals are redistributed. Redundancy is maintained and sunk costs are not lost as a result of a systemic vibrancy that emanates from strong local ties.

---

[12] An expectation held by local authorities and planners, often against the findings of research in economic geography, that shows that levels of interaction within industrial parks tend to be relatively low.

We can conclude, therefore, that it is the culture of communication that influences spatial management strategies. Spatial proximity (or for that matter distance) on its own, to return to the concerns of Chapter 5, is a poor indicator of the relevance or not of particular governance mechanisms, contra recent writing on clusters that assumes that spatial proximity tends to privilege communicative or interactive strategies. A geography of organization based on a weak communicative culture is likely to rely on traditional coordination mechanisms, regardless of the spatial proximity between communities and other units of a network. Similarly, the heterarchical relations that characterize a strongly communicative culture can be as much a feature of firms in an industrial district as of a business network straddling across several countries (for example, the entrepreneurial networks between Silicon Valley and Taiwan or the global science networks discussed in Chapter 5).

Neither type of organization is dependent upon traditional hierarchical incentives to manage distributed knowledge.

Combining the hard and the soft architecture of learning

To summarize, the governance of the firm as a community of communities seeks to benefit from the diversity of interactions between communities (the innovative 'sparks from interacting communities', as described by Brown and Duguid). It seeks to bridge the hard architecture of learning, which exists in many visible forms, and the soft architecture of learning. The four types of organizational culture described in Fig. 6.1 suggest that the nature of the governance of the firm—more precisely, the balance between management by design and management by communities—strongly depends on the relational context of the organization. In a context of weak frequency of interactions and weak communications between communities (*Case 1*), the coherence of the firm is drawn entirely from the tools of hierarchy. The hard architecture of learning dominates. In *Cases 2* and *3*, the nature of interaction between communities shapes the balance between management by design and management by communities. For example, *Case 3* implies a 'loose coupling' corresponding to modular governance approaches, where the role of hierarchy might be to intervene (*ex post*) in the case of too innovative a project. This is a hybrid form with a strong learning platform associated with a soft learning architecture (the communities working independently, provided they respect the standard interfaces linking them to the platform). It is only in *Case 4* (strong interactions and strong possibilities of communication between communities) that we can envisage governance by community alone, with hierarchy needed only to 'authorize' the organizational forms produced by the interactive autonomous communities. The soft learning architecture is prevalent.

Whatever the organizational culture, in the context of a KBE, governance of the architecture for dissipated learning remains the central management challenge in the domain of resource mobilization, alongside, of course, managing the domain of resource allocation. Reconciling this difference will be no light matter, for, at the level of communities of practice, ongoing activity tends to generate a hybrid culture that is capable of both experimentation and routine response, while, at the level of designated corporate management, groups tend to be specialized in either the preservation of routine or the search for novelty.

MANAGING NETWORKS OF COMMUNITIES

A partial answer to the paradox of simultaneously decentring and recentring knowledge management might be found in the workings of innovative networks of communities that interact directly between themselves beyond the boundaries of organizations (for example, Linux, as described in Box 4.1). Their terms of governance are different from those characterizing communities in a given organization, since hierarchy is no longer explicit.

In such a system of distributed learning, a key management challenge is to hold the network in place, to align autonomous centres of innovation towards common goals and core priorities. The rules of hierarchy are largely inappropriate, because the distributed communities are not open to top-down management, and neither are some of the procedures of intra-firm alignment of communities that we have discussed above, owing to the absence of overarching corporate obligations and repertoires. Networks of independent communities, such as epistemic communities, are driven by common projects, common passions, and varied expertise, with a considerable degree of overlap or misalignment of tasks between the communities. The people who work on a project may belong to a number of communities. How are such networks held in place, and with what means of governance?

Connectivity, implying the integration and alignment of (humans and non-humans) in a network, rather than network coordination or ease of communication between the dispersed groups, appears to be a key concept. In their book on the genius of 'great groups' of innovation over the last half century, Bennis and Biederman (1997: 66) observe:

In an interview in *Wired* magazine, Steve Jobs [founder of Apple] made a shrewd observation about creativity. 'Creativity is just connecting things,' he said. 'When you ask creative people how they did something, they feel a little guilty because they didn't really *do* it, they just *saw* something. It seemed obvious to them after a while. That's because they were able to connect experiences they've had and synthesize new things. And the reason they were able to do that was that they've had more experiences or they have thought more about their experiences than other people.'   (emphasis in original)

Jobs emphasizes the experience and reflexivity of individuals in the process of making connections. But we can go much further, into the character of network connectivity itself in aligning interests and persuading actors to play particular roles within a network. In the terms of actor-network theory, successful project management is a matter of aligning, heterogeneous associations into a seamless web, based on all entities adopting roles that help to hold the actor network together (Garrety, Robertson, and Badham 2001). There is no formula for network management and alignment, but an illustration of the processes involved is provided by Garrety, Robertson, and Badham, who describe the formation of an Intelligent Manufacturing System (IMS) project network involving 'different communities of practice, with different routines, expectations, vocabularies and sets of skills' that were also 'more than 1,000 km apart' (p. 12). For example, this particular IMS project entailed 'enrolling' the factory manager by convincing him that the developers at the test site were working in his interests, it drew in academics as brokers between the conflicting/disparate communities of practice, it involved considerable mobility of workers in order to embed the new system and align it to existing practices, and it required paying careful attention not only to the human–technology interface, but also to the interface between objects along the string from project design to implementation phases. As the authors note, it is adjustments of this nature, in service of a 'viable artefact that works in the context for which it was designed and built' (p. 15) that '*constitute* the learning components of a technology development project' (p. 15; emphasis in original).

More complex epistemic networks, or 'machineries' as Knorr Cetina (1999) calls them, pose an even greater challenge of network enrolment and alignment. Knorr Cetina asks, in relation to communities of scientists and laboratories working on joint high-energy particle (HEP) experiments, 'what organizational policies are needed to keep 200 physics institutes—located all over the world and representing virtually all major languages, national scientific systems, and cultures—focused on a common goal?' (p. 160). For her, 'the hallmark of the HEP experiments . . . is not that they organize a workforce of employees in industry-like ways but that they bring about truly collective forms of working: they entice participants into some form of successful cooperation' (p. 163). What enables cooperation?

Knorr Cetina finds the answer in two related steps of organization. The first she describes as 'post-traditional communitarian structures—as structural forms attempting to implement collective ways of working that downgrade the individual as an epistemic subject and that emphasize instead such communitarian mechanisms as collective ownership and "free" circulation of ideas' (p. 165). This involves decoupling the work from the individual scientist, shifting authorship to the experiment, featuring individual scientists as representatives of the whole, and building an emotional attachment that arises from the individuals' awareness of their collective responsibility. The individual becomes part of a collective project and part of a distributed network of research institutes and laboratories. This step establishes a 'communal life-form . . . based neither on altruism nor on commonality' (p. 165), but on structuring the experiment, rather than the individual, as epistemic subject. The management challenge, thus, lies in maintaining this structure of organization (for example, by reinforcing commitment to the experiment, by reinforcing the convention of multiple authorship, and so on).

The second step—facilitated by the structuring of the experiment as an epistemic subject—is management by content. For Knorr Cetina, 'the idea of management by content can be captured by two principles: it is management that maintains participants' proximity to objects or to the substance of scientific work; and management that substitutes, where possible, object-oriented structures for social authority structures' (p. 171). Thus, 'organizational governance crucially works through the manipulation of problem content rather than solely through people and structures' (p. 172). For example, traditional vertical lines of command between people in hierarchical organizations are replaced by horizontal links between scientists and objects, so that information or knowledge 'resides, and remains, in the immediate environment of technical objects, where it is transported by the scientists engaged with these objects' (p. 173). But, as a consequence, a second level of management by content is required in order to ensure that 'local' technical objects can be grasped elsewhere in the network and configured as complex wholes. This is management by discourse:

Discourse runs through HEP experiments; it provides the experiment with a massive spectacle of object features, of their story lines and technical dramas, which are held by and spill over from computer displays and printouts, transparencies, internal notes, 'documents' and together with all these, talk. Through discourse, the proximity with physical objects is extended beyond the individual subject's object relationship to working groups and larger sets of experimental participants, and eventually to 'all' participants. Discourse channels individual knowledge into the experiment, providing it with a sort of *distributed cognition* or a stream of (collective) *self-knowledge*, which flows from the astonishingly intricate webs of communication pathways . . . The HEP experiments . . . are marked by a constant humming of the experiment with itself, about itself. If these experiments do not need cumbersome organizational structures, it is not only because of the object circuits with which they replace lines of command. It is also because in addition to these circuits they create a discourse within which features, reactions, and requirements of technical objects are continually exhibited and expressed . . .   (pp. 173–4; emphasis in original)

The hum of experiments is sustained by numerous and diverse discourse spaces, ranging from the incessant local technical talk over lunch, during jogging and bus rides into town, to virtual face-to-face occasions created on computer terminals, a plethora of formally arranged meetings between distant partners and collaborators, and very frequent status reports at larger meetings and conferences.

The management implications of work done in this way are novel indeed. The distributed communities are held together by a collective consciousness that acts as a strong 'moral' force. Leaders are not managers or heads of experiments, but spokespersons, representatives of the experiments or their parts, and information gateways. Groups are self-organizing, but held together through a rich ecology of discourse, acceptance of the experiment as epistemic subject, a principle of community that is not reducible to altruism or trust, and considerable travel between sites and projects.

CONCLUSION

In this chapter we have examined the mechanisms of, contexts for, and balance between, management by design and management by community of distributed learning networks. Despite the thrust of our argument in this book towards privileging the work of communities in the KBE, we have argued that management by community alone—except in the context of a richly interactive corporate culture—does not secure the transcorporate or transnetwork coordination and alignment that are required in order to avoid diversity degenerating into conflict of purpose or confused business orientation. Here, the rules of hierarchy, in familiar and novel guises, also help. However, we have also argued, on the basis of our observations of networks of communities, that other centering and alignment devices do exist, which have little in common with the tools of hierarchical management (for example, management by content or new divisions of labour).

In discussing the various alternatives, we have tried to retain the emphasis on search and incertitude. The management proposals are ideal types, not fixed and guaranteed solutions. There is too much of the noise of context, grey balances between centred and distributed activities, unique histories and diverse corporate cultures, to allow the suggestions to be used as a template for action. We say this to warn against the promises of so much current writing in business studies concerning what it takes to promote organizational learning and corporate creativity. Equally our return to questions of hierarchy serves to warn against excesses in the same literature on the promises concerning the soft architecture of learning.

7

Public Policy Implications

The central focus of this book has been on knowledge practices in firms and related organizational networks. We have emphasized *community* as the basic unit of knowledge formation and organization and we have explored the challenges thrown up by competing corporate governance imperatives. At the end of our journey, we cannot resist the temptation to look beyond the frontiers of firms, to glance at the public policy implications of learning in communities. Many questions are raised by the interpretative framework developed in this book. For example, what implications does the conceptualization of learning as a distributed, weakly cognitive, and practice-based phenomenon have for public policy efforts intended to encourage the 'knowledge economy'? Or, what can public policy do directly to support communities and actor networks, when so much of the governance of learning in doing lies in the hands of firms, organizations, and networks?

Our analysis in this book suggests that policy attempts to steer the internal dynamics of firms and networks will not work, as they are too remote from the precise, grounded, and evolutionary processes behind knowledge formation in individual contexts. But, this is not to say that certain general principles of public policy action cannot be identified. For example, a product-specific, cluster-specific, technology-specific, or know-how specific approach to science and technology policy risks missing more than it captures, and may be less preferable than a programme of sustained generic support—through generous and long-term investment in universities, technical colleges, public research institutes, basic science and technology programmes, arts, media and cultural industries, and centres of experimental and future knowledge. Such a programme would help to secure not only a varied ecology of knowledge but also a foundation for emergent, new, and unanticipated discovery.

Similarly, technology transfer policies between research centres and firms should explore beyond their current focus on technology and business management, to address insights on community-based organization, industrial democracy, and network alignment as the core elements of learning. Similarly, they should recognize the powers of lay knowledge (as we saw with the example of patient organizations in French muscular dystrophy cited in Chapter 4) as well as other lateral sources of knowledge (for example, the work of neural psychologists or the experience of redundant and retired workers). A key task of public actors in a distributed model of knowledge management, then, would be to broker links between different stakeholders together, rather than providing policy support only to the collaborative ventures that seem to be the most innovative.

These examples suggest that an understanding of innovation and creativity based on community has profound implications for public policy thinking. This is why, in full awareness that we risk overstretching the brief of this book, in this final chapter we focus on some of the radical implications of placing the notion of learning by community at the very centre of public policy.

KNOWLEDGE-INTENSIVE COMMUNITIES

A start is to delineate precisely the type of community we are considering. The clarity of the term at the level of the firm is not matched by a similar clarity at a more general level, where the idea of community has become fashionable in many disciplines. This interest can be related to a significant degree to the concept of social capital, which has taken a firm hold across the social sciences and within the public policy realm, as Bowles and Gintis (2000) explain:

the social capital boom reflected a heightened awareness in policy and academic circles of real people's values, which are not the empirically implausible utility functions of *Homo economicus*, of how people interact in their daily lives, in families, neighborhoods, and work groups, not just as buyers, sellers, and citizens, and of the bankruptcy of the ideologically charged planning-versus-markets debate . . . Perhaps social capital, like Voltaire's God, [needed] to be invented if it did not exist. It may even be a good idea. A good *term* it is not. Capital refers to a thing that can be owned, even a social isolate like Robinson Crusoe had an axe and a fishing net. By contrast, the attributes said to make up social capital describe relationships among people. 'Social capital' has attracted so many disparate uses that we think it better to drop the term in favour of something more accurate. 'Community' better captures the aspects of governance that explain the popularity of 'social capital', as it focuses attention on what groups *do* rather than what people *own*. By community we mean a group of people who interact directly, frequently and in multifaceted ways. People who work together are usually communities in this sense, as are some neighborhoods, groups of friends, professional and business networks, gangs, and sports leagues. The list suggests that connection, not affection, is the defining characteristic of a community. (p. 3)

Seen in these terms, community can be acknowledged as a concept that pre-dates the modern values of market and planning, but condemned to history as 'the anachronistic remnant[s] of a less enlightened epoch that lacked the property rights, markets and states adequate to the task of governance' (p. 15). In particular, the parochialism of community has been considered antithetical to modern institutions, an old-fashioned idea in the context of market and state institutions. However, communities have survived the emergence of modern social institutions, not least because of their important contribution to governance, when market contracts (in the provision of local public goods, for example) and government fiats have failed. Associations, neighbourhood groups, and other forms of grouping offer efficient arrangements that are not plagued by the usual problems of moral hazard and adverse selection, or by the illusion that governments have both the information and the inclination always to offset market failures.

In this book, the strong hint of the modern that we find in Bowles and Gintis is reflected in the claim that an important part of the process of generation, accumulation, and distribution of economic knowledge is achieved through communities acting as 'a nucleus of competence through the daily practices of the community' (Cowan and Jonard 2001: 19). The types of knowledge problems that communities solve, and that escape governmental and market solutions, are those that arise when individuals interact in forms of knowledge exchange that cannot be regulated by complete contracts or by external *fiat*. However, their generic value lies in their ability to absorb a significant proportion of the unavoidable sunk costs associated with building and exchanging knowledge.

Such a role of communities to knowledge formation forces the public policy discussion to go well beyond the traditional 'market-versus-public-intervention' dualism. In what follows, we outline the general principles of a new policy approach through a reconsideration of the domain of science and technology policy in community terms. Then we consider the growing significance of lay knowledge communities and their interaction with communities of expert knowledge, a phenomenon that raises some of the most critical issues for public policy towards economic knowledge today.

RECONSIDERING PUBLIC POLICY IN THE DOMAIN OF SCIENCE AND TECHNOLOGY-BASED INNOVATION

In fairness, it has to be acknowledged that public policy has moved on from the model of top-down, science- and technology-based innovation and learning that dominated policy discourse during the 1980s.[1] Much of this shift has been supported by the OECD, which has come to accept insights from evolutionary and institutional economics regarding innovation as an embedded, path-dependent, bottom-up, and tacit process. There is now explicit recognition of innovation and adaptability based on craft, apprenticeship, learning in doing, work routines, informal networks, employee competences, basic and applied learning, experiential knowledge, and other dimensions of learning as an ongoing and grounded process. Thus, for example, the recognition of informal local conventions and tacit knowledge in both craft industrial districts and high-technology regions such as Silicon Valley has forced a re-evaluation of models of innovation and learning based only on science.

In practical terms, this has led to policy suggestions aimed at strengthening technical and craft colleges, continual learning, employee participation, vicinity between research institutes/academic organizations and the world of entrepreneurship and work, and policy learning based on reflexivity and ongoing monitoring of goals and routines. No longer is policy practice confined to

---

[1] This section relies on intense discussions Patrick Cohendet had with Frieder Meyer-Krahmer during the TIPIK project on codification of knowledge carried out for the European Commission.

support for the production of new codified knowledge, the transfer of technology, or reforms to the formal education and training system.

The traditional vision of public policy in this area dates back to the seminal contribution of Arrow (1962*a*) on knowledge creation in the firm. For Arrow, the process of invention can be interpreted as the production of new knowledge, which in turn is comparable to information. Arrow stressed that, in such a context, the production of new knowledge faces the key problem of appropriability. He argued that it is difficult or even impossible to create a market for knowledge once it is produced, so it is difficult for producers of knowledge to appropriate the benefits that flow from it. Arrow argued that, if the producers of knowledge cannot appropriate the benefits of new knowledge, then they have no incentive to produce it. Thus, without external intervention, the level of research in a society will be below optimal.

The consequences of this vision have been considerable, a key one being the justification for government subsidization of science, technological and engineering research, and innovative activity more generally. This vision shaped the conception of public intervention in R&D for decades. It justified the role and creation of public laboratories and research centres, public R&D programmes, public institutions (for example, patent offices), and public infrastructure for technology transfer. It explained why public efforts in R&D were generally disconnected from applications and why arguments concerning the existence of spillovers from public research programmes were so important in justifying public money spent on R&D. It suggested in fact that scientific production was exogenous to the economic sphere, and governed by rules and behavioural norms (reputation effects, peer reviews, and so on) that were drastically different from the norms and behaviours of industry (seeking profit and technical efficiency). In particular, in this perspective, the choice of research themes by academics was to remain independent of the objectives of industry.

The idea that research produces only codified information has been increasingly questioned in recent decades. Pavitt (1984) and Dosi (1988), amongst others, have shown that research does not produce information, but knowledge, some of which is codified and some of which remains tacit. Cohen and Levinthal (1990) have argued that the degree of spillovers and imitation depends on both the nature of knowledge and the absorptive capacity of firms. Research activity has two complementary facets: it contributes to the creation of information and knowledge, but it is also a learning process that helps to increase absorptive capacity. Not only are externalities unevenly distributed, but they increase when the knowledge bases of firms are similar. In such contexts, external research cannot be substituted for internal research. The two are complementary. All things being equal, the more knowledge is codified, the easier its absorption will be. But, even in the case of codified knowledge, the user or imitator needs certain know-how and technical ability to benefit from the knowledge. To appropriate the results of academic research, even when it is codified, one has to know the code.

For these reasons, a new approach to science and technology support has been developing, one based on the following premisses, which summarize many of the arguments advanced earlier in this book:

- Knowledge is not a pure public good, but comes in varying forms, from the completely appropriable to the completely public.
- Appropriation is not the only incentive for knowledge production. Firms have alternatives to the direct exploitation of monopoly rent, the sale of licences, or the advantages in negotiations offered by patents. The willingness to maintain the firm on the technological frontier, the search for reputation, the need to build absorptive capacity or enter into networks, and more generally the endeavours of agents in building competences, are amongst the main other incentives for firms to invest in R&D.[2]
- The production of knowledge is not a solitary venture, as amply argued in this book. Knowledge is generally produced within a community. Thus the validation of knowledge takes place, in the first instance, within a given community. In the same way, the interpretation of knowledge provided externally (in particular by the hierarchy) is examined, criticized, and reprocessed (leading sometimes to creative adaptations) within communities.
- The producer of knowledge does not face the market, but a specific structure of interaction among economic agents. As Nonaka and Takeuchi (1995: 59) note, 'knowledge creation should be understood as a process that organizationally amplifies the knowledge created by individuals and crystallizes it as a part of . . . an "expanding community of interaction", which crosses intra- and inter-organizational levels and boundaries'.
- The producer of knowledge has emitting capacities. An agent (or a group of agents) producing new knowledge will generally select between communities: on the one hand, the communities to which the new knowledge is addressed, and, on the other side, the communities to be excluded. This highlights the centrality of *disclosure and secrecy*.[3]

---

[2] In particular, the growing number of publications by industrialists working in firms can be interpreted (Hicks 1995; Meyer-Krahmer 1997) as an attempt to find access to new external knowledge and to signal the existence of tacit knowledge and other non-codifiable resources. By becoming a member of the 'club' of academic activities, by paying an implicit fee to access the epistemic communities of researchers, the firm clearly expects a right of access to the academic tacit knowledge in a given field.

[3] 'The extent of disclosure is a continuous variable bounded by full disclosure at one limit and total secrecy at the other. The degree of disclosure required is not uniform across intellectual property rights regimes, and even with a given regime, different kinds of text may be protected by varying completeness of disclosure. Computer software, for example, may be copyrighted without revealing the source code, and in some instance even the full body of object code does not have to be disclosed. Standards of disclosure may be defined not only by the statute laws and intellectual-property agencies such as patent offices, but also by the policies of the journals in which scientific papers are published. For example, professional journals may or may not insist upon the exact co-ordinates of complex proteins whose molecular structure is being reported, or required disclosure of the computational algorithm used in analysing experimental observations' (David and Foray 1995).

- Other agents do not have the full capabilities to absorb innovative ideas emitted by the producer of knowledge. In order to absorb new external knowledge, firms need to develop what Cohen and Levinthal (1990) called absorptive capacity. Firms need to build a knowledge background, based on knowledge previously acquired, to be able to absorb the external knowledge. Thus, spillovers do not necessarily have a negative impact on R&D.[4]
- The epistemic content of knowledge matters. As noted by Callon (1999*a*), we should distinguish knowledge with a high degree of generality (knowledge that can potentially be used in various contexts by a large variety of agents) from knowledge that can be absorbed and used by few other agents.

New Policy Directions

The above hypotheses about conditions for the production of innovative ideas imply that traditional policy understandings of how best to encourage and protect commercial knowledge need to be reconceptualized. As we have seen, the traditional instruments are based on sole consideration of the individual agent. The question now is how to place communities at the centre of a new policy model. We address this question below by focusing on the role of patents in stimulating and protecting knowledge.

Revisiting the Role of Patents

In the traditional theoretical context that has been described above, the agent at the centre of the scene of knowledge production is the individual. Thus, the institutional setting, as expressed by the norms, rules, and standards, is entirely focused on enhancing individual motives in the production of knowledge.[5] The main (even sole) problem that is considered to be hampering the individual

---

[4] As Saviotti (1998: 848) observes, 'even a completely codified piece of knowledge could not be used at a zero cost by anyone. Only agents who know the "code" can use the piece of knowledge at zero (imitation) cost. Agents who do not know the "code", if they realise the economic value of a given piece of knowledge, have to know the code before being able to retrieve and to imitate. The cost of learning has to be included among the costs of imitation. The concept of absorption capacity tells us that in order to be able to access a piece of knowledge, we must have done R&D on something similar.'

[5] For instance, as Stephen and Levin (1997: 55) note, 'why have researchers in the US focused so extensively on individuals *as* opposed to groups and why has this focus persisted despite widespread evidence that science is becoming increasingly a collaborative effort? It is virtually impossible for a scientist to survive and have a career at a university without becoming a "principle investigator" (PI) and directing a lab. The research the PI directs is collaborative, but the majority of the collaborators are graduate students and post-docs statuses which by their very definition are temporary. This individualistic vision of incentives is in accordance with the Mertonian model of scientific activity, where the individual trajectory of the researcher and his/her capacity to accumulate a stock of credibility is the main driver of the academic domain. This leads for instance to the well-known "Matthews effect": as public funding of scientific research is related to previous accomplishments, the system may give disproportionate recognition to scientists who attained early discoveries.'

agent is the risk of not being able to appropriate the new knowledge produced. The policy emphasis falls emphatically on patents, which are seen to resolve this problem of appropriability as well as favour global knowledge production.

In contrast, a conceptualization of knowledge production based on the notion of community suggests an entirely different set of policy principles. Acknowledging the key role of communities[6] in the production of knowledge indicates the need for institutional norms that can support communities. Public policy instruments are still very far from this aim. In many research settings (including the academy), the style of public incentives is still to focus on individual publications and publicity, which, in our view, is a strong barrier to the diffusion of the community-based knowledge economy. But some change is discernible. For example, a very different approach to incentives has been adopted recently in the UK, where the 'lab' is increasingly seen in science and technology policy as the unit of reference for reputation-based and other non-financial incentives. A focus on communities suggests the desirability of extending incentives beyond the boundaries of the lab, to reward the *network* of research centres and laboratories that produce new knowledge. A revealing example cited by Joly (1997) is an article in *Nature* on the sequence of chromosome III in yeast, that was signed by 147 researchers from forty different research institutions—one among many signs of the need for research and science policies to acknowledge and reward knowledge chains.[7] How far incentives can move in this direction will play a crucial role in determining whether the trend of indisputable achievements in complex and large-scale experiments can become a dominant mode of production in research.

The focus of public policy on the sole question of appropriability of knowledge is far too limited. The significance of other factors in the knowledge production

---

[6] It should be made clear that such a position does not deny the role of individuals in knowledge production. It accepts that there are individual entrepreneurs and that there are individuals within communities who are located at the kernel of innovation. But it is clear that the active unit of knowledge production is the community, where the elementary activities related to the production of knowledge (acquisition and accumulation of knowledge, elaboration of new knowledge, validation of emerging ideas, replication, etc.) are essentially made.

[7] A redefinition of incentives should carefully investigate the nature of individual incentives within a given community before being in a position to derive a set of global incentives to stimulate the functioning of communities. An example of individual incentive within a community is delayed reward. Following a career-development argument, Lerner and Tirole (2002) suggest that contributing to open-source projects can be used by programmers as a signalling device for their competences. A programmer who has made major contributions to the Linux kernel, for instance, is more likely to find a rewarding job in the future. Hacker communities (as in most communities) are not anonymous. Conversely, contributors are well known and they are often ranked in status (for instance, according to the amount of code released or to the popularity of their code). But career concern is probably not the most important incentive device in communities. Other incentives for participating in a community include ego gratification, peer recognition, and reputation building. Though less concrete than the former, these benefits too can be seen as delayed rewards from contributions to community activities.

process (signalling, voluntary disclosure, building of absorptive capabilities) that have been discussed above needs recognition. Let us take one example. An important factor in the production of knowledge is the degree of *trust* between different agents. Following Zuscovitch (1998), as we have seen in Chapter 3, trust in networks can be considered as a tacit agreement in which partners take a longer perspective on transactions, instead of seeking out the best opportunity at every instant. Agents agree to increase their specialization in a given form of knowledge, because they are confident that the other agents will increase their specialization in complementary forms. This arrangement relies intensively on the building of mutual trust in the production of knowledge, which is why one of the key issues that shapes the efficacy of innovative networks is constant mutual negotiation of *rights of access* to complementary forms of knowledge. Much of the work of decentralized economic units within a given network is concerned with building a carefully negotiated system of rights of access to knowledge.

Public policy has to find a way of building trust between economic units, or at least acknowledging that this is what some initiatives are about. For example, stimulating the participation of public labs, private firms, or public research units in complex networks of innovation (such as the industrial networks financed by the EU programmes) can be considered as a way of increasing the level of trust in the daily functioning of the network. Individual units, in such a network of collective knowledge formation, can actively build trust by taking the risk of high specialization, while remaining open to the wide dissemination of results throughout the network (following the rules of 'open science communities'). They can also absorb the sunk costs of building a common architecture of knowledge within these networks, thus facilitating the building of a common trust. These aspects require in-depth investigation to formulate the appropriate direction of public policy.

In the new knowledge context, patents naturally keep their essential feature of protecting the innovator, but the above discussions reveal new roles linked to the practices of the active communities that develop the new knowledge. Patents come to possess, for instance, a more and more important strategic role in negotiation. Very often patents are the first side of cooperation or knowledge exchange. In this capacity, they determine the balance of power between the members of the network. Patents may also be used by a community as signalling devices about the existence of a given competence, in order to enter complex negotiations related to building networks.[8] These multiple potential uses of

---

[8] As Foray (2002: 3) notes, the intensity of signalling depends on the institutional context: 'the institutional articulation of [patents] that can vary a great deal across countries. For example, the information disclosure rules matter: the Japanese system is effective for sending signals and placing a large amount of information in the public domain, thus contributing to the essential objective of "collective invention". While the European system tends also to have an effective signalling function (though less powerful), the US system, until recently, was not effective in terms of signalling. Minor

patents can be linked to the overlapping interactions that lead to innovation. The property rights nature of the patent can be tied to the 'innovator', traditionally viewed as the embodiment of 'possessed knowledge'. The strategic role in negotiation can be recognized through the organization that owns the patent (for example, a patent can be an important asset for a start-up company when dealing with financial institutions or seed capital companies). The signalling nature of patents can be acknowledged through recognition for the specific community involved in the innovation, which needs protection of its competence in order to enter into collaborative ventures with other communities.

The need for appropriation might even be marginal when incentives to build knowledge within a given community are already strong (for example, the desire to belong to specific communities of practice). In this case, at least temporarily, members of the community might voluntarily focus on building a common architecture of knowledge, without any explicit regard to appropriation. An extreme example, as we saw in Box 4.1, is the case of the 'free software' development by Linux. The participants of this network strongly believed that property rights were a threat to user freedom and the dynamics of innovation in industry. In order to allow free use of each software, Linux adopted the 'copyleft' system in opposition to the principle of copyright.

Communities, thus, can be seen as semi-public entities, holding something in common but not available to all. This is a key aspect in the production of knowledge that public policy needs to grasp. The growth of 'copyleft' systems, and also the rise in many industries of 'knowledge platforms', show that, in the emergent stages of innovation, when the boundaries and definitions of products and objects are still fuzzy, there is a strong need for a common platform of knowledge, from which interfaces, standards, and designs will progressively emerge. Thus, at first glance, certain aspects of the behaviour of communities, in particular their willingness to give freely of knowledge as a *semi-public good*, contradict or reinterpret standard micro-economic rules.[9]

---

institutional differences are important to explain the disparities of the value of patents as a source of information and, thus, as a mechanism for efficient coordination. When information is properly disseminated (as in the Japanese system) and when the nature of the protection granted is specified in ways that encourage patentees to make their innovations available for use by others at reasonably modest costs (narrow patent as well as weak degree of novelty are crucial in this way), the patent system becomes a vehicle for coordination in expanding informational spillovers, rather than for the capture of monopoly rents.'

[9] A plausible explanation for knowledge offered as a free public good is that the cost of contributing is actually low (in contrast to the altruism argument, which fails to answer why such offerings are found in only certain economic domains). For example, it appears that programmers who offer free tutorials to Internet user groups spend little time actually answering questions (see Lakhani and Hippel 2000). This 'cost' saving (in terms of the time needed to find the answer to a question) might raise programmer inclination to diffuse (almost) common information. A slightly less straightforward explanation for free public goods relates to expectations of potential feedback or return from the community of users, as, for instance, users of open source software, who can see the code itself, and may be able to fix it or to see what the problem is.

All these arguments force fundamental reconsideration of the traditional view of patents, which historically have been criticized for hampering the diffusion of innovation owing to their emphasis on individual appropriation. What the above discussion suggests is that strong patents could also hamper the *production* of knowledge. As Foray (2002: 3) remarks,

an excess of privatization relates to excessive fragmentation of the knowledge base, linked to intellectual property rights on parcels and fragments of knowledge that do not correspond to an industrial application. This situation is described by the concept of an anti-commons regime and illustrated with the case of biotechnology: when private rights are granted to fragments of a gene, before the corresponding product is identified, nobody is in a position to group the rights (i.e. to have all the licences) and the product is not developed.

Box 7.1 summarizes Foray's suggestions on property-rights policies in the new knowledge context. In the same vein, what the example of Linux suggests is that in certain contexts, when some emerging technological developments need common cognitive platforms of knowledge, the 'price-free' development by communities could be an efficient solution to the production of new knowledge.[10]

Box 7.1. *Intellectual property-rights policies in the knowledge-based economy*

In the knowledge economy: 'good fences do not make good neighbours'

As Paul David (2001) claims, good fences probably make good neighbours where the resource is land or any other kind of exhaustible resources. But simple considerations of the 'public-goods' nature of knowledge suggest that this is not so when the resource considered is knowledge. Knowledge is not like forage, depleted by use for consumption; data-sets are not subject to being 'over-grazed', but, instead, are likely to be enriched and rendered more accurate, and more fully documented, the more that researchers are allowed to comb through them.

Thus, the shift towards a new policy mix is raising many problems and may lead ultimately to major social losses. In most research fields, 'creative discovery comes from unlikely journey through the information space'. If too many property rights are assigned to the micro-components of the information space, travelling through it proves to be extremely costly, even impossible, because at every point the traveller must negotiate and buy access rights. We are facing here a great paradox that intellectual property rights (IPRs), which are traditionally used to support the exploitation of knowledge, are becoming ultimately a way to shrink the knowledge base.

Of course, the new system of knowledge production generates its own regulation, which can bring about a certain equilibrium in some instances. We can list four classes of solutions, dealing with the various problems developed below.

(continued)

---

[10] Referring to Linux, one should remember that initially the development of software was considered as a public good. The researches on software were financed by public universities or the defence public sector. The emergence of collective endeavours such as Linux could be interpreted as a collective reaction (through the functioning of communities) against the attempt to 'privatise' research in that domain.

Box 7.1. (*continued*)

1. Mechanisms are devised to support, in certain circumstances or for certain classes of economic agents, the fast dissemination and free exploitation of private knowledge. There are three main mechanisms:

   (*a*) Compulsory licensing (compulsory diffusion of private knowledge for the general interest).

   (*b*) The state or international foundations buy patents to put them back in the public domain. To illustrate this mechanism Kremer (1997) uses the historical case of Daguerre, the inventor of photography who neither exploited his invention nor sold it for the price he wanted. In 1839 the French government purchased the patent and put the rights to Daguerre's invention in the public domain. The invention was developed very fast!

   (*c*) Ramsey's pricing rule suggests price discrimination between users whose demands are inelastic and those for whom the quantity purchased is extremely price sensitive. The former class of buyers therefore will bear high prices without curtailing the quantity purchased of the goods in question, whereas the low prices offered to those in the second category (for example, scholars and university-based researchers) will spare them the burden of economic welfare reducing cutbacks in their use of the good (David 2002).

2. Granting non-exclusive licences, presumably with minimal diligence or exclusive licences with diligence, offers a partial solution to the problem of licensing knowledge produced by publicly funded research programmes in universities.

3. Cross-licensing mechanisms may be a way out of the anti-commons trap. Transactions costs can be reduced through mutual concessions and through the trading of rights (for example, within a consortium). However, this is a solution that can work only with a small number of companies. In that regard, the rapid growth of new kinds of firms does caution against overconfidence that the anti-commons problems can be surmounted. For example, the computer hardware industry had few problems with its cross-licensing arrangements until new kinds of semi-conductor companies arose.

4. There is a great deal to be done in terms of the ways in which patent offices enforce patent requirement (that is, make their assessments of utility requirement, non obviousness, patent scope). One should note, however, that hybrid and complex objects—such as genes, DNA sequences, software, databases—generate a lot of uncertainties about what IPR policy is appropriate, making the tasks of patent offices very difficult. It is difficult to provide non-ambiguous and clear answers to the question whether these new objects should be privately appropriated; and, if yes, what class of IPR should be used.

Source: Foray (2002)

A DECENTRED INNOVATION POLICY MODEL

We can now begin to outline a radically different public policy model, one that recognizes and supports the material practices and material cultures of learning in networks of communities. We have seen in this book that the dynamics of communication between communities can be approached through the principle of 'translation/enrolment' elaborated in particular by Callon and Latour. According to these authors, the innovative diffusion of ideas (for example, from the lab to the market) can be interpreted as a process of progressive contagion of communities, where each community makes efforts to 'command the attention' of other communities to convince them of the relevant interest of the knowledge it has elaborated. What they suggest is that the producer of knowledge does not face anonymous competition, but a specific structure of interaction of economic agents. The group of agents who succeed in expressing and formalizing an innovative idea is confronted by a main difficulty: not the risk of being copied (at no cost), but the risk of being misunderstood by others (including agents belonging to the same institution). It is the risk that their procedures and experience will not be reproduced by others. Inventors will thus undertake considerable efforts to alert other communities in order to convince them of the usefulness and potentials of their discovery.

Knowledge, therefore, is the product of strings of actants, and how they are powered up. Knowledge processes cannot be readily broken down into discrete chunks of tacit or codified knowledge, or human versus non-human elements, but are the sum-in-interaction of chains of varying length of mobile and immobile actants—from lists and codes to machines, skills, and experts, from huge flows of people, information, and 'immutable mobiles' to connectivity between local knowledge clusters. What matters is the integrity of the network and how the actants are aligned. These insights force recognition of the extraordinary variety of 'things' (and their dispersed geographies) that contribute to knowledge formation, they highlight the importance of the work that goes into aligning elements of a knowledge chain, and they underline the work that needs to be done to convert new knowledge into generally acceptable 'truths'.

How, then, can policy underpin this necessity of translation/enrolment? We have already seen that one tool is new usages of patents—for example, a community that has produced a new piece of knowledge using it to convince others of the value of the novelty. Patents can be viewed as a visible artefact designed to command the attention of others and become their frame of reference too.[11] But, for those communities that accept participation in an 'expanding community of interaction' that, as such, leads the innovative idea to the market, patents have a limited role to play in translation/enrolment. Other means and mechanisms are necessary, notably the construction of a cognitive weft that allows the different communities to communicate effectively.

[11] For example, Foray (2002: 4) argues that, 'traditionally, IPRs were considered one of the incentive structures society employed to elicit innovative effort. They coexisted with other incentive structures, each of which has costs and benefits as well as a degree of complementarity. We seem to be moving toward a new view, in which IPRs are the only means to commodify the intangible capital represented by knowledge and should therefore be a common currency or "ruler" for measuring the output of activities devoted to knowledge generation and the basis for markets in knowledge exchange.

Such a cognitive weft is composed of material mediaries (currency, material goods, books, articles, patents) as well as intangible mediaries (crystallized collective beliefs, negotiated and accepted conventions, internalized values). These mediaries underpin the efforts of a community to interest others in their knowledge activities, by forcing engagement, adherence, a common language, common beliefs, and alignment of interests in general (Callon 1999*a*). The procedural construction of a cognitive weft between communities makes it possible to code the experiences and the history of the network and, therefore, to give the sense, *ex post*, of the construction and stabilization of a common vision or culture assuring the global consistency of the distributed venture.

In such a perspective, how can public policies aid in the translation and alignment process? Through state-funded intermediaries? Through incentives to help build meta-narratives? Through funds to help communities sell their ideas? The answer, to a large degree, depends on the nature of the community-based projects, since each reveals its own idiosyncrasies and challenges, which can be addressed only in specific ways (as we illustrate in Box 7.2[12]). But, in general terms, policy recognition might learn to accept the inadequacy of actions centred on individual elements of a string of knowledge (for example, particular technologies or particular know-how), and appreciate the centrality of the varied and often unpredictable mediaries—human and non-human—that hold networks together, as well as the significance of enrolling others into a knowledge network to make it effective (for example, through publicity, political influence, indispensability, and cultural dominance).

Box 7.2. *Examples of community-based research projects*

Harvard School of Public Health, Boston: Helping citizens link leukemia to industrially contaminated wells. During the 1970s, parents in Woburn, Massachusetts noticed an alarming pattern of leukemia, urinary tract, respiratory disease, and miscarriages in their town, and wondered if the water supply was contaminated. State officials told them the water was safe. With the help of scientists at the Harvard School of Public Health, they initiated their own epidemiological research and identified industrial carcinogens in the town's well water. Their civil suit resulted in an $8 million out-of-court settlement (detailed in the best-selling book and forthcoming Hollywood movie, *A Civil Action*) and provided major impetus for Congressional action to reauthorize federal Superfund legislation.

Neighborhood Planning for Community Revitalization, Minneapolis: Planning to revitalize an industrial area. Residents and business owners in the South East Industrial Area (SEIA), just outside Minneapolis, were concerned that their area's

---

[12] To a degree the policy suggestions in Box 7.2 are relatively manageable, focusing as they do on communities where a public stakeholder like the local state is readily identifiable. The examples tell us less about how public policy may support the work of autonomous communities of, say, particle physicists, video-game developers, or washing-machine repair teams, where the room for public action is more restricted. We thank Gernot Grabher for this observation.

viability was threatened by increasing pollution, over-strict zoning, crime, and the lack of sidewalks, bike paths, and park space. In addition, various groups affected by the SEIA had a contentious history and had not worked together for years. The SEIA community appealed to Neighborhood Planning for Community Revitalization (NPCR) for assistance. NPCR facilitates collaborative research between universities and local community-based organizations. Researchers working jointly through NPCR and the SEIA community members conducted a research project which established that an urban area can compete with the suburbs and still retain industrial and heavy commercial business. As a result, the city, county, and state agencies formed the Southeast Economic Development Steering Committee, charging it to prepare a master development plan for the area. This project was funded by NPCR and involved 960 hours of time committed by graduate student researchers.

Center for Neighborhood Technology, Chicago: Maintaining jobs and environmental standards in the metalworking industry. In Chicago, metal finishing provides many jobs in low income neighborhoods. During the 1970s and 1980s, two waves of environmental regulation caused the immediate loss of 2,500 metal finishing jobs when non complying plants were forced to shut down. It became clear that environmental regulations threatened this key industry and thousands of related jobs. The non-profit Center for Neighborhood Technology (CNT) collaborated with industrial development organizations to conduct an in-depth study of options for bringing Chicago's remaining metal finishers into regulatory compliance. CNT helped the groups identify the problems facing metal finishers, access free environmental audits of their plants, investigate alternative technologies for compliance, determine criteria for a centralized approach that would offer economies of scale, and secure financing for implementation. This effort represented a remarkable collaboration between manufacturers and environmentalists.

Source: Sclove, Scammell, and Holland (1998)

Crucially, however, what needs attending to will vary according to the character of the network itself. In the context of supporting the creation and translation of community-based knowledge, we can consider, along with Callon (1999a), two extreme situations.

The first is a situation of 'emergent relations', corresponding to cases where the process of creation is at an embryonic stage, so that only a community (usually epistemic) has experimented and validated the creative idea. The problem here is to design incentive schemes for other communities, as well as the means of translating emergent creativity. The degree of uncertainty is so high that agents cannot anticipate the behaviour of others. Agent behaviour remains largely opportunistic. It is deliberately procedural: through processes of negotiation and continuous sets of feedback, the community initiates a process of convergence and formation of collective beliefs to reach stabilization. This period of convergence (of elimination of uncertainty) is a fertile period in the process of formation of collective beliefs. The collective beliefs are more likely to converge if a 'metacode' pre-exists between communities, helping to develop 'compromises between the need to make knowledge more explicit and the need to avoid excessive technicalities and local jargon' (OECD 2000: 27).

In the context of 'emergent relations', public policy could respond by, first, directly financing communities. The policy adopted in the 6th Framework Programme of the EU, in the domain of science and technology, is a significant example of the shift in focus of European public policy from financing individuals or institutions towards directly stimulating the functioning of communities. This programme will directly finance large communities of scientists, who will have the opportunity to decide among themselves the type of collective work to be done. Secondly, public policy could steer meta-codes and collective beliefs, in order to support a discourse of emergence through community, inter-community collaboration, and meta-code construction.[13] The development of reference standards by public bodies could also serve to simplify communication between communities and to increase compatibility of systems designed in different countries by reducing non-strategic varieties in design. Thirdly, public policy could facilitate the 'distributive power of knowledge' (David and Foray 1995) by encouraging the development of modern information infrastructures such as uniform protocols and format standards, along with providing opportunities to researchers and scientists to make a career across national systems (so that they can go back and forth without having to build up nationally based accreditation).

The second is a situation of 'consolidated relations', where the existence of shared codes and common languages allows the different communities to share their respective knowledge on a particular innovation domain, and to interact by unceasing feedbacks to improve the creative principles. Here, the degree of uncertainty is considerably reduced: the individual agents will use their past experience to act. Therefore, when interactions between communities are consolidated, agent behaviour is conditioned by history and past experience. Thus, individual behaviour converges more and more towards a pattern of substantive behaviour: through a set of tacit or casual elements translating the simplified diagrams that one develops to interpret experiences (routines, conventions, heuristics, and so on), the environment becomes consolidated. Thus, the stabilization of interactions between communities plays an important role in stabilizing the collective beliefs of the agents and in sense making.

In this context, in order to stabilize the different interactions in a community of communities, the role of public policy could be to set standards and norms of quality, to enact the efficient practices and routines by diffusing them, to recognize the outcomes of the complex process of interactions that leads to innovation. In particular, as we have seen, patents in this process play a leading role of

---

[13] An example of the implementation of meta-codes by a public body is the system of codification of cows in France, initiated by INRA in the 1950s. This system allows all the 'stakeholders' related to this domain of agriculture to exchange knowledge, and validate new ideas. This system successfully supported the debates and controversies, and facilitated the search for a solution in France, during the recent 'mad-cow' episode.

signalling devices. This can be viewed as a new way of using an instrument originally designed for its property rights characteristics. Beyond patents, though, an important question for public policy is whether, in the face of ever-increasing demand for public tools of recognition of a given competence, it is possible to think of less costly instruments than patents, and just reserve the patents for their normal use. After all, in other domains of the economy, public recognition takes diverse forms such as 'public or community utility merits' for some non-profit organizations, or *certificat d'appellation contrôlée* for wines, and so on. These measures also contribute to underpinning the work of communities and protecting them from the erosion of diversity that tends to accompany the development of market mechanisms.[14]

Perhaps the key policy task, though, lies in full public recognition that innovation is an emergent process based on gradually introducing interactions that link agents, knowledge, and goods that were previously unconnected, and that are slowly put in a relationship of interdependence: the network, in its formal dimension, is a powerful tool for making these connections and for describing the forms that they take. What produces innovation is the alchemy of combining heterogeneous ingredients within a process that cuts across institutions, forges complex and unusual relations between different spheres of activity, and draws, in turn, on interpersonal relations, the market, law, science, and technology. Given all of this, public policy has to be modest about the effectiveness of top-down interventions, and move away from detached and preconceived science and technology programmes, towards a hermeneutic approach based on providing nodal support in existing and emergent networks.

Finally, turning to firm-specific policies, perhaps a prime general principle should be the reversal of a public policy culture of market-driven or efficiency-driven restructuring programmes that have destroyed redundancy, slack, and memory in the pursuit of lean organization, maximized labour flexibility, and short-term profit. That employees—especially in the lower tiers—should enjoy each others' company, interact without utilitarian gain, be given autonomy, and be allowed to develop their creativity, has regretably come to be seen as counter-efficient and a waste of transactional efficiency. But our analysis has taken us in a different direction: that it makes perfect sense to have public incentives in support of industrial democracy, employment security, cultural development in firms, knowledge 'vacations', competence-enriching mobility, and grass-roots experimentalism—all those things that have become taboos in the contemporary rhetoric of corporate competitiveness. This is not an argument about the deficiencies of short-term obsession with 'leanness and fitness' and the virtues of a longer-term horizon. It is primarily about recognizing that a distributed system of knowledge production requires inputs from those engaged in the everyday practice of doing.

---

[14] It is, for instance, well known that the local legislations that protect brands in Germany contribute to maintain a real diversity of brand for beers in the different German regions (*Länder*).

The above examples suggest that some of the elements that are frequently found in well-governing communities might form part of a public policy aimed at enhancing the desirable aspects of community governance. As Bowles and Gintis (2000: 16) argue, there are some major shifts to be made. The first, strongly supported by experimental evidence, is that members of the community should own the fruits of their success or failure in solving the collective problems they face (this is consistent with our suggestions regarding the use of patents). Secondly, the well-functioning communities require a conducive legal and institutional environment. It is widely recognized that at times government intervention has destroyed the community governance capacities. Thirdly, it seems clear that, the capacity of communities to solve problems can be impeded by hierarchical division and economic inequality among its members. Thus, an institutional environment that complements the distinctive governance abilities of communities and underpins a distribution of property rights so that members can become the beneficiaries of community success seems to be a key aspect of policies to foster community-based problem solving.

CONCLUSION: BRIDGING 'EXPERT' AND 'LAY' KNOWLEDGE

One major implication of the approach we have developed in this book is that the production of knowledge in society is not dichotomous, marked, on the one hand, by high-tech or elite-based production of knowledge in the scientific domain, and, on the other hand, by the day-to-day or marginal production of lay knowledge at lower levels of society. On the contrary, our argument is that, in years to come, there will be both an increasing need and an opportunity to make innovations through the interactions between scientific knowledge and lay knowledge in society. As Nowotny, Scott, and Gibbons (2001) argue, 'as expertise becomes socially distributed' (p. 246) in an economy marked by the proliferation of knowledge across the social and institutional spectrum, synthesis and authority depend on the ability 'to bring together knowledge which is itself distributed, contextualized and heterogenous' (p. 247), rather than through expertise located at one specific site or through the 'views of one scientific discipline or group of highly respected researchers' (p. 247). In this regard, 'science and society have both become transgressive; that is, each has invaded the other's domain, and the lines demarcating the one from the other have all but disappeared' (p. 243).

The implication is that public policy will have to work with this tendency. Callon, Lascoumes, and Barthes (2001: 140) emphasize this potential to associate scientific (what they call 'confined' research) with lay (or 'profane') research:

The main weakness of confined research does not reside in the risk of being in a total isolation, though this risk should not be underestimated. It resides essentially in the great difficulty that this type of science faces when it has to reduce the world, and then to reconstitute it. A laboratory, even if well connected to the outside world, as well as researchers, even if fully convinced that they alone can achieve the translations that allow them to work efficiently, face insurmountable obstacles if they refuse to build and cooperate with those with profane knowledge.

Accordingly, Callon, Lascoumes, and Barthes call for *hybrid forums* (with the support of public agencies) to bring together, in innovative ways, the insight of scientific communities with that of lay communities, leading to the encapsulation of useful pieces of practised knowledge in daily practices. For instance, it is known that some disease-specific patient organizations (see Chapter 4 for the example of muscular dystrophy) often know more than their doctors do about the specific traits of a disease, and thus bring forth knowledge that complements the theoretical and practical knowledge held by the physicians. To a large extent, the establishment of hybrid forums could be at the level of society, to mirror the 'modular platforms' we have discussed in Chapter 6 at the level of organization (see Fig. 6.1). In terms of public policy, this move has important implications: hybrid forums, as well as modular platforms, do not just bring communities together with the hope that some positive outcome will result from matching active knowledge units. Their success requires building a cognitive architecture between communities, requiring time and sunk costs to be implemented. Hybrid forums have to be equipped with specific procedures, a common grammar and rules, specific interfaces between the common platform and each community. These demands require strong public policy willingness to modify the nature of the architecture of knowledge between the 'expert' and 'lay' communities of knowledge.

Lay knowledge across the ever-widening realms of society where it is developed and held—in the workplace, in associations, in interest groups—therefore needs to be recognized by public policies as one of the mainstays of a knowledge society and its innovative arenas. This imperative, plus the various new policy orientations we have outlined that follow from serious acknowledgement of the powers and potential of learning in doing through community forms of social organization, radically alters the work of government in the knowledge economy. Science, education, and technology policies will have to focus more and more on the social foundations of learning and creativity, the task of joining up and aligning distributed pieces of knowledge, and eliminating the historic hierarchy between expert and lay knowledge. They will have to accept the centrality of the democracy of the commons and of grounded practical knowledge for survival in the knowledge economy.

Epilogue

The journey we have proposed is nearly over. In the hope of developing a vision of knowledge practices in firms that bridges knowledge and knowing, we have travelled through a field of potentially irreconcilable theories of knowledge. The concept of knowledge-intensive community has played a central role in our efforts for integration, as a common thread between diverging approaches. We have highlighted practices of knowing within communities, considered as strings of hybrid knowledge inputs and as weakly cognitive learning environments. How successful we have been can only be judged by the reader, but our hope is that it may spark a new dialogue between an understanding of knowledge as a possession and that of knowledge as an embodied practice.

In some ways, we have tried to build a cognitive platform for multidisciplinary debate, one that, in turn, can enrich the research in each discipline. This is particularly necessary in *economics* and *management science*, which still suffer from excessive epistemological closure.

In *economics*, recognizing and understanding the role of practices of knowing in communities could produce valuable insights for the new economic theory of the firm, in particular the evolutionary, competence-based approach.

Firstly, acknowledging the base point that knowing occurs through the daily interactions and practices of distributed communities of actors will push economic theory towards recognizing that the very foundation of the formation of competences lies in the interplay between the knowledge that firms possess in the form of established competences or stored memory, and the knowing of communities. Departing from the well-recognized claim that routines are the building block of competences, we have highlighted that the context (or localization) in which the routines emerge is critical. Routines in different communities vary in terms of powers of replication, degree of inertia, reflexivity and coordination, and intensity of contribution to competences. In short, the complex route that leads from routine to competence cannot avoid the workings of communities. The evolutionary theory of the firm stands to gain from expanding its traditional focus on the evolution of competences to incorporate the evolution of communities, and the implications of this for knowledge dynamics.

Secondly, a broader understanding of knowledge formation in the firm sheds new light on knowledge governance challenges, which continue to remain narrowly cast in economics. We have proposed a *dual vision* of the firm, as a compromise between the transaction-costs approach and the competence-based approach. But this compromise resolves only one side of the governance challenges of firms that behave and organize themselves as knowledge-possession systems. The other side relates to how firms amplify local practices of knowing as well as make them coherent with the accumulated possessed knowledge of the firm. This dilemma suggests an in-depth reconsideration of the incentive mechanisms of the firm and of the modes of resolving conflicts. For example, analysis of the effects of cost and pricing mechanisms on knowledge formation will have to recognize the importance of irreversible fixed and sunk costs associated with building diverse and distributed cognitive platforms of knowledge.

Management science, traditionally dominated by 'organization' and overarching governance schemas, is also nudged in a new direction in this book by the distinction between knowledge and knowing, suggesting the difference between management by *design* and management by *community*. If 'organization' can be viewed as the historical locus of managing the division of work, communities can be seen as the building blocks of the division of knowledge. This distinction helps to identify a range of governance mechanisms, from those contexts in which designed forms are dominant, to those in which the interplay between autonomous or loosely coordinated communities dominates. A key question for future research is to explain how firms can benefit from the useful knowledge held by its different distributed communities at the same time as not compromising the hierarchy of the division of labour geared towards efficiency.

Management science needs to tread carefully in imagining a 'design' solution to these two governance imperatives. The differences between cognitive and non-cognitive learning, centralized and distributed learning, and coordinated and autonomous learning demand recognition of the extent to which distributed practice, cognition, and design can be thought of as reconcilable instruments in a manager's toolkit to improve organizational performance. The careful selection of adequate management tools (tools for strategic management as well as tools for managing competences of communities) will go some way towards resolving the tension between different modes of coordination. At the very least, it will open up the field of what counts as coordination, to include slack, redundancy, sociality, and emergence, in the repertoire of management tools. Management science will also have to look carefully at the governance implications of evolving communities.

Bibliography

Abramowitz, M., and David, P. (1996). 'Technological Change, Intangible Investments and Growth in the Knowledge-Based Economy: The US Historical Experience', in D. Foray and B. A. Lundvall (eds.), *Employment and Growth in the Knowledge-Based Economy*. Paris: OECD, 35–60.

Adler, E., and Haas, P. (1992). 'Conclusion: Epistemic Communities, World Order, and the Creation of a Reflective Research Programme', *International Organization*, 46/1: 367–90.

Adler, P. (2001). 'Market, Hierarchy, and Trust: The Knowledge Economy and the Future of Capitalism', *Organization Science*, 12/2: 215–34.

Akerlof, G. (1970). 'The Market for Lemons: Quality Uncertainty and the Market Mechanism', *Quarterly Journal of Economics*, 84: 485–500.

Alchian, A. (1950). 'Uncertainty, Evolution and Economic Theory', *Journal of Political Economy*, 58: 599–603.

——, and Demsetz, H. (1972). 'Production, Information Costs, and Economic Organization', *American Economic Review*, 62: 777–95.

Allen, J. (2000). 'Power/Economic Knowledges: Symbolic and Spatial Formations', in J. Bryson, P. W. Daniels, N. Henry, and J. Pollard (eds.), *Knowledge, Space, Economy*. London: Routledge, 15–33.

Amable, B. (2000). 'Institutional Complementarity and Diversity of Social Systems of Innovation and Production', *Review of International Political Economy*, 7/4: 645–87.

Amesse, F., and Cohendet, P. (2001). 'Technology Transfer Revisited, In the Perspective of the Knowledge-Based Economy', *Research Policy*, 30/9 (Dec.): 1459–79.

—— Séguin-Dulude, L., and Stanley, G. (1994). 'Vingt ans de leadership technologique, Northern Telecom à l'aube de la mondialisation', in S. Globerman (ed.), *Les Multinationales canadiennes*. Calgary: University of Calgary Press, 477–514.

Amin, A. (1999). 'The Emilian Model: Institutional Challenges', *European Planning Studies*, 7/4: 389–405.

—— and Cohendet, P. (1999). 'Learning and Adaptation in Decentralized Business Networks', *Environment and Planning D: Society and Space*, 17: 87–104.

—— —— (2001). 'Organizational Learning and Governance through Embedded Practices', *Journal of Management and Governance*, 4: 93–116.

—— and Thrift, N. (1992). 'Neo-Marshallian Nodes in Global Networks', *International Journal of Urban and Regional Research*, 16/4: 571–87.

—— —— (2002). *Cities: Reimagining the Urban*. Cambridge: Polity Press.

Ancori, B. (1992). *Apprendre, se souvenir, décider. Une nouvelle rationalité de l'organization*. Paris: CNRS Editions.

—— (1998). 'The Economics of Information: Some Comments', in P. Petit (ed.), *L'Économie de l'information. Les Enseignements des théories économiques*. Paris: La Découverte, 124–5.

—— Bureth, A., and Cohendet P. (2000). 'The Economics of Knowledge: The Debate between Codified and Tacit Knowledge', *Industrial and Corporate Change*, 9/2: 255–87.

Aoki, M. (1990). 'The Participatory Generation of Information Rents and the Theory of the Firm', in M. Aoki, B. Gustafsson, and O. E. Williamson (eds.), *The Firm as a Nexus of Treaties*. London: Sage, 26–52.

Argyris, C., and Schön, D. (1978). *Organizational Learning: A Theory of Action Perspective.* Reading, MA: Addison-Wesley.

Arrow, K. (1962*a*). 'Economic Welfare and the Allocation of Resources for Invention', in Universities National Bureau Committee for Economic Research, *The Rate and Direction of Inventive Activity.* Princeton: Princeton University Press, 609–25.

—— (1962*b*). 'The Economic Implications of Learning by Doing', *Review of Economic Studies,* 29/3: 155–73.

—— (1971). 'Political and Economic Evaluation of Social Effects and Externalities', in M. Intriligator (ed.), *Frontiers of Quantitative Economics.* Amsterdam: North Holland, 3–25.

Arthur, W. B. (1989). 'Competing Technologies, Increasing Returns and Lock-in by Small Historical Events', *Economic Journal,* 99: 116–31.

Autio, E., and Laamanen, T. (1995). 'Measurement and Evaluation of Technology Transfer: Review of Technology Transfer Mechanisms and Indicators', *International Journal of Technology Management,* 10/7–8: 643–64

Barney, J. (1986). 'Strategic Factor Markets: Expectations, Luck and Business Strategy', *Management Science,* 32/10: 1231–41.

—— (1991). 'Firm Resources and Sustained Competitive Advantage', *Journal of Management,* 17/1: 99–120.

Bateson, G. (1972). *Steps to an Ecology of Mind.* London: Penguin.

Baumard, P. (1999). *Tacit Knowledge in Organizations.* London: Sage.

Becker, M. (1999). *The Role of Routines in Organizations: An Empirical and Taxonomic Investigation.* Cambridge: Judge Institute of Management.

Bénézech, D., Lambert, G., Lanoux, B., Lerch, C., and Loos-Baroin, J. (2001). 'Completion of Knowledge Codification: An Illustration through the ISO 9000 Standards Implementation Process', *Research Policy,* 30/9: 1395–408.

Bennis, W., and Biederman, P. W. (1997). *Organizing Genius: The Secrets of Creative Collaboration.* London: Nicholas Brealey Publishing.

Bessières, H. (1999). 'Comment Alcatel digère ses acquisitions américaines', *01/Réseau,* 73 (Nov.), 52–3

Bessy, C., and Brousseau, E. (1998). 'Technological Licensing Contracts: Features and Diversity', *International Review of Law and Economics,* 18 (Dec.), 451–89.

Blackler, F. (2002). 'Knowledge, Knowledge Work, and Organizations', in C. W. Choo and N. Bontis (eds.), *The Strategic Management of Intellectual Capital and Organizational Knowledge.* New York: Oxford University Press, 47–62.

Boulding, K. (1953). *The Organizational Revolution.* New York: Harper and Brothers.

—— (1955). 'Notes on the Information Concept', *Exploration,* 6: 103–12.

Bowker, G., and Star, S. L. (1999). *Sorting Things Out: Classification and its Consequences.* Cambridge, MA: MIT Press.

Bowles, S., and Gintis, H. (1998). 'The Moral Economy of Community: Structured Populations and the Evolution of Prosocial Norms', *Evolution & Human Behavior,* 19/1: 3–25.

—— —— (1999). *Recasting Egalitarianism: New Rules for Equity and Accountability in Markets, Communities and States,* London: Verso.

—— —— (2000). 'Social Capital and Community Governance', Working Paper 01-01-003, Santa Fe Institute, www.santafe.edu/sfi/publications/Working-Papers/01-01-003.pdf.

Bozeman, B. (2000). 'Technology Transfer and Public Policy: A Review of Research and Theory', *Research Policy,* 29: 627–55.

Breschi, S., and Malerba, F. (2001). 'The Geography of Innovation and Economic Clustering: Some Introductory Notes', *Industrial and Corporate Change*, 10/4: 817–33.

Brooks, H. (1968). *The Government of Science*. Cambridge, MA: MIT Press.

Brousseau, E. (2001). 'Régulation de l'Internet: L'Autorégulation nécessite-t-elle un cadre institutionnel?', *Revue économique*, 52 (Oct.), 349–78.

Brown, J. S., and Duguid, P. (1991). 'Organizational Learning and Communities of Practice: Toward a Unified View of Working, Learning and Innovation', *Organization Science*, 2/1: 40–57.

—— —— (1998). 'Organizing Knowledge', *California Management Review*, 40/3: 90–111.

—— —— (2000). *The Social Life of Information*. Boston: Harvard Business School Press.

Burton-Jones, A. (1999). *Knowledge Capitalism*. Oxford: Oxford University Press.

Callon, M. (1994). 'Is Science a Public Good?', *Science Technology and Human Values*, 19/4: 395–425.

—— (1999*a*). 'Le Réseau comme forme émergente et comme modalité de coordination', in M. Callon, P. Cohendet, N. Curien, J.-M. Dalle, F. Eymard-Duvernay, D. Foray, and E. Schenk (eds.), *Réseau et coordination*. Paris: Economica, 13–64.

—— (1999*b*). 'The Role of Lay People in the Production and Dissemination of Scientific Knowledge', *Science, Technology and Society*, 4/1: 81–94.

—— Cohendet, P., Curien, N., Dalle, J.-M., Eymard-Duvernay, F., Foray, D., and Schenk, E. (1999) (eds.). *Réseau et coordination*. Paris: Economica.

—— Lascoumes P., and Barthes, Y. (2001). *Agir dans un monde incertain: Essai sur la démocratie technique*. Paris: Seuil.

—— and Latour, B. (1991). *La Science telle qu'elle se fait. Anthologie de la sociologie des sciences de langue anglaise*. Paris: La Découverte.

Cantwell, J., and Iammarino, S. (2001). 'EU Regions and Multinational Corporations: Change, Stability and Strengthening of Technological Advantages', *Industrial and Corporate Change*, 10/4: 1007–37.

—— and Santangelo, G. (1999). 'The Frontier of International Technology Networks: Sourcing Abroad the Most Highly Tacit Capabilities', *Information Economics and Policy*, 11: 101–23.

Cassier, M. (1995). 'Les Contrats de recherche entre l'université et l'industrie'. Doctoral thesis, École des Mines, Paris.

Casson, M. (1998). 'An Entrepreneurial Theory of the Firm'. Paper presented at the DRUID conference on 'Competencies, Governance, and Entrepreneurship'. Barnholm, June.

Castells, M. (1998). *La Société en réseaux*, i. *L'Ère de l'information*. Paris: Fayard.

Caves, R. E. (1980). 'Industrial Organization, Corporate Structure and Strategy', *Journal of Economic Literature*, 18: 64–92.

Chandler, A. D., Jr. (1962). *Strategy and Structure: Chapters in the History of Industrial Enterprise*. Cambridge, MA: MIT Press.

—— (1977). *The Visible Hand: The Managerial Revolution*. Cambridge, MA: Harvard University Press.

—— (1992). 'Corporate Strategy, Structure and Control Methods in the United States during the 20th Century', *Industrial and Corporate Change*, 1/2: 263–84.

Chesbrough, H., and Teece, D. (1996). 'When is Virtual Virtuous: Organizing for Innovation', *Harvard Business Review*, Jan.–Feb.: 65–74.

Chiesa, V., and Manzini, R. (1996). 'Managing Knowledge Transfer within Multinational Firms', *International Journal of Technology Management*, 12/4: 462–76.

Choo, C. W. (1996). 'The Knowing Organization: How Organizations Use Information to Construct Meaning, Create Knowledge, and Make Decisions', *International Journal of Information Management*, 16/5: 329–40.

—— and Bontis, N. (2002) (eds.). *The Strategic Management of Intellectual Capital and Organizational Knowledge*. New York: Oxford University Press.

Chwe, M. S. Y. (2001). *Rational Ritual: Culture, Coordination, and Common Knowledge*. Princeton: Princeton University Press.

Ciborra, C. (1996). 'The Platform Organization: Recombining Strategies, Structures and Surprises', *Organization Science*, 7/2: 103–18.

—— and Andreu, R. (2002). 'Knowledge across Boundaries: Managing Knowledge in Distributed Organizations', in C. W. Choo and N. Bontis (eds.), *The Strategic Management of Intellectual Capital and Organizational Knowledge*. New York: Oxford University Press, 575–86.

Cohen, D., and Prusak, L. (2001). *In Good Company: How Social Capital Makes Organizations Work*. Boston: Harvard Business School Press.

Cohen, M. D. (1984). 'Conflict and Complexity: Goal Diversity and Organizational Search Effectiveness', *American Political Science Review*, 78: 435–51.

—— (1991). 'Individual Learning and Organizational Routines: Emerging Connections', *Organization Science*, 2: 135–9.

—— Burkhart, R., Dosi, G., Edigi, M., Marengo, L., Warglien, M., and Winter, S. (1996). 'Routines and Other Recurring Action Patterns of Organizations: Contemporary Research Issues', *Industrial and Corporate Change*, 5/3: 653–98.

—— March, J. G., and Olsen, J. P. (1972). 'A Garbage Can Model of Organizational Choice', *Administrative Sciences Quarterly*, 17: 1–25.

Cohen, W. H., and Levinthal, D. (1989). 'Innovation and Learning: The Two Faces of R&D', *Economic Journal*, 99: 569–96.

—— —— (1990). 'Absorptive Capacity: A New Perspective on Learning and Innovation', *Administrative Science Quarterly*, 35: 128–52

Cohendet, P., Creplet, F. and Dupouët, O. (2000). 'Organizational Innovation, Communities of Practice and Epistemic Communities: The Case of Linux', in A. Kirman and J. B. Zimmermann (eds.), *Economics with Heterogeneous Interacting agents*. Berlin: Springer Verlag, 303–26.

—— —— —— and Schenk, E. (2002). 'The Economics of Linux'. Mimeo, BETA.

—— and Diani, M. (forthcoming). 'L'Organisation comme une communauté de communautés: Croyances collectives et culture d'entreprise', *Revue d'économie politique*.

—— —— and Lerch, C. (2002). 'Modularité et organization'. Working paper, BETA, Strasbourg.

—— Kern, F., Mehmanpazir, B., and Munier, F. (1999). 'Knowledge, Coordination, Competence Creation and Integrated Networks in Globalized Firms', *Cambridge Journal of Economics*, 23: 225–41.

—— Ledoux, M. J., and Zuscovitch, E. (1989). *New Advanced Materials: Economic Dynamics and European Strategy*. Berlin: Springer Verlag.

—— and Llerena P. (1999). 'La Conception de la firme comme processeur de connaissances', *Revue d'économie industrielle*, 88: 211–36.

—— —— (2003). 'Routines and Incentives: The Role of Communities in the Firm', *Industrial and Corporate Change*, 12/2: 271–97.

—— Kern, F., Mehmanpazir, B., and Munier, F. (1998). 'Routines, Governance and Creation of Knowledge', in J. Lesourne and A. Orlean (eds.), *Évolution and auto organisation*. Dordrecht: Kluwer Academic Publishers.

Cohendet, P., and Meyer-Krahmer, F. (2001). 'The Theoretical and Policy Implications of Knowledge Codification', *Research Policy*, 30/9: 1563–92.

Collins, H. (2001*a*). 'What is Tacit Knowledge?', in T. Schatzi, K. Knorr Cetina, and E. von Savigny (eds.), *The Practice Turn in Contemporary Theory*. London: Routledge, 107–19.

—— (2001*b*). 'Tacit Knowledge, Trust and the Q of Sapphire', *Social Studies of Science*, 31/1: 71–85.

Conner, K. R., and Prahalad, C. K. (2002). 'A Resource-Based Theory of the Firm', in C. W. Choo and N. Bontis (eds.), *The Strategic Management of Intellectual Capital and Organizational Knowledge*. New York: Oxford University Press, 103–31.

Cook, S. D.N, and Brown, J. S. (1999). 'Bridging Epistemologies: The Generative Dance between Organizational Knowledge and Organizational Knowing', *Organization Science*, 10/4: 381–400.

Coriat, B., and Dosi, G. (1998). 'Learning how to Govern and Learning how to Solve Problems: On the Co-evolution of Competences, Conflicts and Organizational Routines', in A. D.Chandler, P. Hagström, and Ö. Sölvell (eds.), *The Dynamic Firm: The Role of Technology, Strategy, Organization and Regions*. Oxford: Oxford University Press, 103–33.

Cowan, R. (2001). 'Expert Systems: Aspects of and Limitations to the Codifiability of Knowledge', *Research Policy*, 23/9: 1355–72.

—— David, P., and Foray D. (2000). 'The Explicit Economics of Knowledge Codification and Tacitness', *Industrial and Corporate Change*, 9/2: 212–53.

—— and Foray, D. (1997). 'The Economics of Codification and the Diffusion of Knowledge', *Industrial and Corporate Change*, 9/2: 211–53.

—— and Jonard, N. (2001). 'The Workings of Scientific Communities', MERIT-Infonomics Research Memoradum series, WP no. 2001–031.

Crémer, J. (1990). 'Common Knowledge and the Coordination of Economic Activities', in M. Aoki, B. Gustafsson, and O. E. Williamson (eds.), *The Firm as a Nexus of Treaties*. London: Sage, 53–75.

—— (1993). 'Corporate Culture and Shared Knowledge', *Industrial and Corporate Change*, 2/3: 351–86.

—— (1998). 'Information dans la théorie des organizations'. Working Paper, Institut d'Économie Industrielle, Université de Toulouse.

Cyert, R., and March, J. (1963). *A Behavioral Theory of the Firm*. Englewood Cliffs, NJ: Prentice Hall.

Daft, R. L., and Lewin, A. Y. (1993). 'Where are the Theories for the "New Organizational Forms"? An Editorial Essay', *Organization Science*, 4: i–vi.

—— and Weick, K. E. (1984). 'Toward a Model of Organizations as Interpretation Systems', *Academy of Management Review*, 9/2: 284–95.

Dang Nguyen, G., and Pénard, T. (1999). 'Don et coopération dans internet: Une nouvelle économie?', *Terminal*, 80–1 (special issue on 'Les Logiciels libres: De l'utopie au marché'): 95–116.

—— —— (2001). 'Interaction et coopération en réseau: Un modèle de gratuité', *Revue Économique*, 52: 57–76.

Dasgupta, P., and David, P. A. (1994). 'Towards a New Economics of Science', *Research Policy*, 23: 487–521.

David, P. A. (1993). 'Knowledge Property and the System Dynamics of Technical Change', in *Proceedings of the World Bank Annual Conference on Development Economics*. Washington: World Bank, 215–48.

—— (1995). 'Standardization Policies for Network Technologies: The Flux between Freedom and Order Revisited', in R. Hawkins, R. Mansell, and J. Skea (eds.), *Standards,*

Innovation and Competitiveness: The Politics and Economics of Standards in Natural and Technical Environments. Aldershot: Edward Elgar, 15–35.

—— (2001). 'Digital Technologies, Research Collaborations and the Extension of Protection for Intellectual Property in Science: Will Building "Good Fences" Really Make "Good Neighbours"?' Paper presented at the European Commission (DG Research) STRATA-ETAN Workshop on IPR Aspects of Integrated Internet Collaborations, Brussels, 22–3 January.

—— (2002). 'The Digital Technology Boomerang: New Intellectual Property Rights Threaten Global "Open Science"', in the World Bank Conference Volume: ABCDE 2002.

—— and Foray, D. (1995). 'Accessing and Expanding the Science and Technology Knowledge Base', *STI Review*, 16 (Paris: OECD), 13–68.

—— —— (1996). 'Information Distribution and the Growth of Economically Valuable Knowledge: A Rationale for Technological Infrastructure Policies', in M. Teubal et al. (eds.), *Technological Infrastructure Policy: An International Perspective*. Dordrecht and London: Kluwer Academic Publishers, 87–116.

Dewey, J. (1916/1997). 'Theories of Knowledge', in L. Menand (ed.), *Pragmatism: A Reader*. New York: Vintage Books, 205–9.

Diamond, A. M., Jr. (1996). 'The Economics of Science', *Knowledge and Policy*, 9/2–3: 6–49.

Dibiaggio, L. (1998). 'Information, Connaissance et Organization'. Doctoral thesis, Université de Nice-Sophia Antipolis.

Dosi, G. (1988). 'The Nature of the Innovative Process', in G. Dosi et al. (eds.), *Technical Change and Economic Theory*. London: Pinter, 221–38.

—— and Egidi, M. (1991). 'Substantive and Procedural Uncertainty: An Exploration of Economic Behaviours in Complex and Changing Environments', *Journal of Evolutionary Economics*, 1: 145–68.

—— and Marengo, L. (1994). 'Toward a Theory of Organizational Competencies', in R. W. England (ed.), *Evolutionary Concepts in Contemporary Economics*. Ann Arbor: Michigan University Press, 157–78.

—— —— Bassanini A., and Valente, M. (1999). 'Norms as Emergent Properties of Adaptive Learning: The Case of Economic Routines', *Journal of Evolutionary Economics*, 9: 5–26.

—— and Metcalfe, S. (1991). Substantive and Procedural Uncertainty: An Exploration of Economic Behaviours in Changing Environments', *Journal of Evolutionary Economics*, 1/2: 145–68.

Doz, Y. L. (1996). 'The Evolution of Cooperation in Strategic Alliances: Initial Conditions or Learning Processes?', *Strategic Management Journal*, 17: 55–83.

Drejer, A., and Riis, J. O. (1999). 'Competencies and Competence Development', *Technovation*, 19: 631–44.

Drucker, P. F. (1993). *Post-Capitalistic Society*. New York: Harper Collins.

Dunning, J. H. (2000) (ed.). *Regions, Globalization and the Knowledge-Based Economy*. Oxford: Oxford University Press.

Dupouët, O., and Laguécir, A. (2001). 'Elements for a New Approach of Knowledge Codification'. Paper presented at ETIC (Economics on Technological and Institutional Change), final conference, Strasburg, France, 19–20 October.

Dyer, J. H., Cho, D. S., and Chu, W. (1998). 'Strategic Supplier Segmentation: The Next Best Practice in Supply Chain Management', *California Management Review*, 42: 37–57.

Edwards, K. (2001). 'Epistemic Communities, Situated Learning and Open Source Software Development'. Working paper, Technical University of Denmark.

Eliasson, G. (1990). 'The Firm as a Competent Team', *Journal of Economic Behaviour and Organization*, 13: 275–98.

Engestrom, Y. (1993). 'Work as a Testbed of Activity Theory', in S. Chaiklin and J. Lave (eds.), *Understanding Practice: Perspective on Activity and Context*. Cambridge: Cambridge University Press, 65–103.

Ettlinger, N. (2000). 'Frontiers of Flexibility and the Importance of Place and Space'. Mimeo, Department of Geography, Ohio State University.

Farrell, J., and Saloner, G. (1987). 'Competition, Compatibility and Standards: The Economics of Horses, Penguins and Lemmings', in H. L. Gabel (ed.), *Product Standardization and Competitive Strategy*. Amsterdam: North-Holland, 1–21.

Favereau, O. (1989). 'Marchés internes, marchés externes', *Revue économique*, 2: 273–328.

—— (1993). 'Suggestions pour reconstruire la théorie du salaire sur une théorie des règles'. Working paper Laetix, Université Paris X, April.

—— (1995). 'Apprentissage collectif et coordination par les règles: Application à la théorie des salaires', in N. Lazaric and J. M. Monnier (eds.), *Coordination économique et apprentissage des firmes*. Paris: Economica, 23–38.

Florida, R. (1995). 'Calibrating the Region', in J. de la Mothe and G. Paquet (eds.), *Local and Regional Systems of Innovation*. New York: Kluwer Academic Publishers, 19–28.

Foray, D. (2002). 'Intellectual Property and Innovation in the Knowledge-Based Economy', *Isuma*, 3/1: 1–12, www.isuma.net.

Foss, N. (1998). 'Firm and Coordination of Knowledge: Some Austrian Insights'. Working paper, DRUID, Copenhagen Business School.

—— (1999). 'Understanding Leadership: A Coordination Theory'. Working paper, DRUID, Copenhagen Business School.

—— (2001). 'Bounded Rationality in the Economics of Organization: Present Use and (Some) Future Possibilities', *Journal of Management and Governance*, 5/3–4: 401–5.

Frahey, L., and Prusak, L. (1998). 'The Eleven Deadliest Sins of Knowledge Management', *California Management Review*, 40/3: 265–76.

Fransman, M. (1994). 'Information, Knowledge, Vision and Theories of the Firm', *Industrial and Corporate Change*, 3/2: 1–45.

—— (1995). 'Interpretive Ambiguity, Theory of the Firm, and the Evolution of Industries'. Paper presented for the EMOT Workshop, University of Reading, 14–16 May.

Garicano, L. (1999). 'A Theory of Knowledge-Based Hierarchies: Communication, Organization and Technological Choice'. Working paper, Graduate School of Business, University of Chicago.

Garrety, K., Robertson, P. L., and Badham, R. (2001). 'Communities of Practice, Actor Networks and Learning in Development Projects'. Paper presented at the 'Futures of Innovation Studies' Conference, Eindhoven Centre for Innovation Studies, Netherlands, 20–23 September.

Gensollen, M. (2001). 'Internet: Marchés électroniques ou réseaux commerciaux?', *Revue Économique*, 52 (Oct.), 137–64.

Gertler, M. (2001). 'Best Practice? Geography, Learning and the Institutional Limits to Strong Convergence', *Journal of Economic Geography*, 1/1: 5–26.

—— Wolfe, D., and Garkut, D. (2000). 'No Place like Home? The Embeddedness of Innovation in a Regional Economy', *Review of International Political Economy*, 7/4: 688–718.

Gibbons, M., Limoges, C., Nowotny, H., Schwartzman, S., Scott, P., and Trow, M. (1994). *The New Production of Knowledge*. London: Sage.

Girvan, M., and Newman, M.E. J. (2001). 'Community Structure in Social and Biological Networks'. Working Paper 01-12-077, Santa Fe Institute, www.santafe.edu/sfi/publications/Working-Papers/01-12-007.pdf.

Glaeser, E. (1998). 'Are Cities Dying?', *Journal of Economic Perspectives*, 12: 139–60.

Goldspink, C. (2002). 'Methodological Implications of Complex Systems Approaches to Sociality: Simulation as a Foundation for Knowledge', *Journal of Artificial Societies and Social Simulation*, 5/1: http://jasss.soc.surrey.ac.uk/5/1/3.html.

Gomez, P. Y. (1998). 'The Real Meaning of Conventions'. Seminars given at the University of Nantes, June.

Grabher, G. (2001). 'Ecologies of Creativity: The Village, the Group, and the Heterarchic Organisation of the British Advertising Industry', *Environment and Planning A*, 33: 351–74.

—— (2002). 'Cool Projects, Boring Institutions: Temporary Collaboration in Social Context', Special issue, *Regional Studies*, 36/3: 204–14.

Grandori, A., and Kogut, B. (2002). 'Dialogue on Organization and Knowledge', *Organization Science*, 13/3: 224–31.

Grant, R. M. (1996). 'Toward a Knowledge-Based Theory of the Firm', *Strategic Management Journal*, 17: 109–22.

—— (2002). 'The Knowledge-Based View of the Firm', in C. W. Choo and N. Bontis (eds.), *The Strategic Management of Intellectual Capital and Organizational Knowledge*. New York: Oxford University Press, 133–48.

Gulati, R., Nohria, N., and Zaheer, A. (2000). 'Strategic Networks', *Strategic Management Journal*, 21: 203–15.

Gupta, A., and Govindarajan, V. (2000). 'Knowledge Flows within Multinational Corporations', *Strategic Management Journal*, 21: 473–96.

Haas, P. (1992). 'Introduction: Epistemic Communities and International Policy Coordination', *International Organization*, 46/1: 1–37.

Hamel, G., and Heene, A. (1994). *Competence-Based Competition*. New York: Wiley & Sons.

—— and Prahalad, C. K. (1993). 'Strategy as a Stretch and Leverage', *Harvard Business Review*, 71/2: 75–84.

—— and Prahalad, C. K. (1994). *Competing for the Future*. Boston: Harvard Business School Press.

Hardin, G. (1968). 'The Tragedy of the Commons', *Science*, 162: 1243–8.

Hargadon, A. (1998). 'Firms as Knowledge Brokers: Lessons in Pursuing Continuous Innovation', *California Management Review*, 40/3: 209–28.

Harris, S. J. (1998). 'Long-Distance Corporations, Big Sciences, and the Geography of Knowledge', *Configurations*, 6/2: 269–304.

Hatch, M.-J. (1999). 'Exploring the Empty Spaces of Organizing: How Improvisational Jazz Helps Redescribe Organizational Structure', *Organization Studies*, 20/1: 75–100.

Hayek, F. A. von (1937). 'Economics and Knowledge', *Economica*, 4: 33–54.

—— (1945). 'The Use of Knowledge in Society', *American Economic Review*, 35/4: 519–30.

—— (1973). *Law, Legislation and Liberty*, i. *Rules and Order*. Chicago: University of Chicago Press.

Hayes, J., and Allison, C. W. (1998). 'Cognitive Style and the Theory and Practice of Individual and Collective Learning in Organizations', *Human Relations*, 51/7: 847–72.

Hicks, D. (1995). 'Published Papers, Tacit Competencies and Corporate Management of the Public/Private Character of Knowledge', *Industrial and Corporate Change*, 4/2: 401–24.

Hippel, E. von (1988). *The Sources of Innovation*. New York: Oxford University Press.

—— (1993). 'Trading in Trade Secrets', *Harvard Business Review*, Mar.–Apr.: 56–64.

Hodgson, G. M. (1996). 'Corporate Culture and the Nature of the Firm', in J. Groenewegen (ed.), *Transaction Cost Economics and Beyond*. Boston: Kluwer Academic Press, 249–69.

—— (1997). 'The Ubiquity of Habits and Rules', *Cambridge Journal of Economics*, 21/6: 663–84.

Holland, J. H. (1996). *Hidden Order: How Adaptation Builds Complexity*. Cambridge, MA: Perseus Books.

Hollingsworth, R. (2000). 'Doing Institutional Analysis: Implications for the Study of Innovations', *Review of International Political Economy*, 7/4: 595–644.

Howells, J. (2000). 'Knowledge, Innovation and Location', in J. Bryson, P. W. Daniels, N. Henry, and J. Pollard (eds.), *Knowledge, Space, Economy*. London: Routledge, 50–62.

Huberman, B. A., and Hogg, T. (1994). 'Communities of Practice: Performance and Evolution'. Working Paper, Palo Alto.

Hutchins, E. (1996). 'Organizing Work by Adaptation', in M. Cohen and L. Sproull (eds.), *Organizational Learning*. London: Sage, 20–57.

Ichigo, K, Krogh, G. von, and Nonaka, I. (1998). 'Knowledge Enablers', in G. von Krogh, J. Roos, and D. Kleine (eds.), *Knowing in Firms*. London: Sage, 173–203.

Inkpen, A. (1996). 'Creating Knowledge through Collaboration', *California Management Review*, 39/1: 123–40.

Itoh, H. (1987). 'Information Processing Capacities of the Firm', *Journal of the Japanese and International Economies*, 1: 299–326.

Jin, M. E., Girvan, M., and Newman, M.,E.,J. (2001). 'The Structure of Growing Social Networks', Working Paper 01-06-032, Santa Fe Institute, www.santafe.edu/sfi/publications/Working-Papers/01-06-032.pdf.

Johnson-Laird, P. (1983). *Mental Models: Toward a Cognitive Science of Language Inference and Consciousness*. Cambridge: Cambridge University Press.

Joly, P. B. (1997). 'Chercheurs et laboratoires dans la nouvelle économie de la science', *Revue d'économie industrielle*, 79: 77–94.

Kang, M., Waisel, L. B., and Wallace, W. A. (1998). 'Team-Soar: A Model for Team Decision Making', in M. J. Prietula, K. M. Carley, and L. Grasser (eds.), *Simulating Organizations: Computational Models of Institutions and Groups*. Cambridge, MA: MIT Press.

Killing, P. (1980). 'Technology Acquisition: Licence Agreement or Joint Venture', *Columbia Journal of World Business*, Fall: 38–46.

Kirman, A. (2000). 'La Rationalité individuelle et la rationalité collective: L'Importance des interactions entre des individus', École Thématique 'Économie Cognitive', Ile de Berder (Morbihan), 14–19 May.

Knorr Cetina, K. (1981). *The Manufacture of Knowledge*. Oxford: Pergamon Press.

—— (1999). *Epistemic Cultures: How the Sciences Make Sense*. Chicago: Chicago University Press.

Kogut, B. (2000). 'The Network as Knowledge: Generative Rules and the Emergence of Structure', *Strategic Management Journal*, 21 (Mar.), 405–25.

—— and Zander, U. (1992) 'Knowledge of the Firm, Combinative Capabilities, and the Replication of Technology', *Organization Science*, 3: 383–97.

—— —— (1996). 'What Firms Do? Coordination, Identity and Learning', *Organization Science*, 7: 502–18.

Kremer, M. (1997). 'Patents Buy-Outs: A Mechanism for Encouraging Innovation', NBER Working Paper No. 6304.

Kreps, D. (1990). 'Corporate Culture and Economic Theory', in J. Alt and K. Shepsle (eds.), *Perspectives on Positive Political Economy*. New York: Cambridge University Press, 90–143.

Krogh, G. von, and Grand, G. (2002). 'From Economic Theory towards a Knowledge-Based Theory of the Firm', in C. W. Choo and N. Bontis (eds.), *The Strategic Management of Intellectual Capital and Organizational Knowledge*. New York: Oxford University Press, 163–84.

—— and Roos, J. (1995). *Organizational Epistemology*, Basingstoke: Macmillan.

—— —— and Kleine, D. (1998) (eds.). *Knowing in Firms*. London: Sage.

Krugman, P. (1991). *Geography and Trade*. Cambridge, MA: MIT Press.

—— (1995). *Development, Geography and Economic Theory*. Cambridge, MA: MIT Press.

Kusonoki, K., Nonaka, I., and Nagata, A. (1998). 'Organizational Capabilities in Product Development of Japanese Firms: A Conceptual Framework of Empirical Findings', *Organization Science*, 9: 699–718.

Lakoff, G., and Johnson, M. (1999). *Philosophy in the Flesh*. New York: Basic Books.

Lakhani, K., and Hippel, E. von (2000). 'How Open Source Software Works: "Free" User-to-User Assistance'. Working paper, Sloan School of Management, MIT.

Langlois, R. (1993). 'Capabilities and Coherence in Firms and Markets', Working Paper 94–151, Department of Economics, University of Connecticut.

—— (1994). 'Cognition and Capabilities: Opportunities seized and Missed in the History of the Computer Industry'. Paper for the Conference on Technological Oversights and Foresights, Stern School of Business, New York University, 11–12 Mar.

—— (1998). 'Rule-Following, Expertise and Rationality: A New Behavioural Economics?', in Kenneth Dennis (ed.), *Rationality in Economics: Alternative Perspectives*. Kluwer: Dordrecht, 55–78.

—— (2002). 'Modularity in Technology and Organization', *Journal of Economic Behavior and Organization*, 49/1: 19–37.

—— and Foss, N. (1996). 'Capabilities and Governance: The Rebirth of Production in the Theory of Economic Organization'. Working Paper, DRUID, Copenhagen Business School.

—— and Robertson, P. L. (1992). 'Networks and Innovation in a Modular System: Lessons from the Microcomputer and Stereo Component Industries', *Research Policy*, 2: 297–313.

—— —— (1995). *Firms, Markets and Economic Change*. London: Routledge.

Latour, B. (1986a). 'Visualization and Cognition: Thinking with Eyes and Hands', *Knowledge and Society*, 6: 1–40.

—— (1986b). *Science in Action: How to Follow Scientists and Engineers through Society*. Cambridge, MA: Harvard University Press.

Lave, J. (1988). *Cognition in Practice*. Cambridge: Cambridge University Press.

—— and Wenger, E. (1991). *Situated Learning: Legitimate Peripheral Participation*. New York: Cambridge University Press.

Law, J., and Hetherington, K. (2000). 'Materialities, Spatialities, Globalities', in J. Bryson, P. W. Daniels, N. Henry, and J. Pollard (eds.), *Knowledge, Space, Economy*. London: Routledge, 34–49.

Lawson, C., and Lorenz, E. (1999). 'Collective Learning, Tacit Knowledge and Regional Innovative Capacity', *Regional Studies*, 33/4: 305–17.

Leadbeater, C. (1999). *Living on Thin Air*. London: Viking.

Lee, J.-H. (2002). 'Corporate Learning and Radical Change: The Case of Korean Chaebol'. Doctoral thesis, Department of Geography, University of Durham.

Leonard-Barton, D. (1995). *Wellsprings of Knowledge: Building and Sustaining the Sources of Innovation*. Boston: Harvard Business School Press.

Lerner, J., and Tirole, J. (2001). 'The Open Source Movement: Key Research Questions', *European Economic Review Papers and Proceedings*, 35: 819–26.

——— ——— (2002). 'Some Simple Economics of Open Source', *Journal of Industrial Economics*, 52: 197–234.

Lesourne, J. (1991). *Économie de l'ordre et du désordre*. Paris: Economica.

Liedtka, J. (1999). 'Linking Competitive Advantage with Communities of Practice', *Journal of Management Inquiry*, 8/1: 5–16.

Lissoni, F. (2001). 'Knowledge Codification and the Geography of Innovation: The Case of Brescia Mechanical Cluster', *Research Policy*, 30/9:1479–550.

Loasby, B. J. (1976). *Choice, Complexity and Ignorance*. Cambridge: Cambridge University Press.

—— (1983). 'Knowledge, Learning and the Enterprise', in J. Wiseman (ed.), *Beyond Positive Economics?* London: Macmillan, 104–21.

—— (1989). *The Mind and Method of the Economist*. Aldershot: Edward Elgar.

—— (1996). 'The Division of Labour', *History of Economic Ideas*, 4/1–2: 229–323.

Lorenz, E. (2001). 'Models of Cognition, the Contextualisation of Knowledge and Evolutionary Approaches to the Firm'. Paper presented at DRUID Winter Conference, Klarskovgaard, Denmark, 18–20 Jan.

Lorenzen, M., and Foss, N. J. (2002). 'Cognitive Coordination, Institutions, and Clusters: An Exploratory Discussion', in T. Brenner and D. Fornahl (eds.), *Cooperation, Networks and Institutions in Regional Innovation Systems*. Aldershot: Edward Elgar.

Lundvall, B. A., and Johnson, B. (1994). 'The Learning Economy', *Journal of Industry Studies*, 1/2: 23–41.

Lynn, L. H., Mohan Reddy, N., and Aram, J. D. (1996). 'Linking Technology and Institutions: The Innovation Community Framework', *Research Policy*, 25: 91–106.

——— ——— ——— (1997). 'Technology Communities and Innovation Communities', *Journal of Engineering and Technology Management*, 14: 129–45.

Macdonald, L. (2000). *Nortel Networks, How Innovation and Vision Created a Network Giant*. New York: John Wiley and Sons.

Machlup, F. (1980). *Knowledge, its Creation, Distribution and Economic Significance*. Princeton: Princeton University Press.

Magalhaes, R. (1998). 'Organizational Knowledge and Learning', in G. von Krogh, J. Roos, and D. Kleine (eds.), *Knowing in Firms*. London: Sage, 87–122.

Malerba, F., and Orsenigo, L. (2000). 'Knowledge, Innovative Activities, and Industry Evolution', *Industrial and Corporate Change*, 9/2: 289–314.

Malmberg, A. (2003). 'Why the Cluster is Causing Confusion – Despite Being Potentially a Core Concept in Economic Geography', in J. Peck and H. Yeung (eds.), *Global Connections: Perspectives in the Restructuring of the World Economy*. London: Sage 145–59.

March, J. G. (1988). 'Introduction: A Chronicle of Speculations about Organizational Decision-Making', in J. March (ed.), *Decisions and Organization*. Oxford: Basil Blackwell, 1–24.

—— (1991). 'Exploration and Exploitation in Organizational Learning', *Organization Science*, 2/1: 71–87.

—— and Olsen, J. (1976). *Ambiguity and Choice in Organizations*. Oslo: Universitetsforlaget.

—— and Simon, H. A. (1958). *Organizations*. New York: Blackwell, Wiley.

—— —— (1958/1993). *Organizations*. 2nd edn. Cambridge, MA, Blackwell.

—— —— (1993). 'Organizations Revisited', *Industrial and Corporate Change*, 2: 299–316.

Marengo, L. (1994). 'Knowledge Distribution and Coordination in Organizations: On Some Social Aspects of the Exploration vs. Exploitation Trade-Off', *Revue internationale de systémique*, 7: 553–71.

—— (1996). 'Structure, Competence and Learning in an Adaptive Model of the Firm', in G. Dosi and F. Malerba (eds.), *Organization and Strategy in the Evolution of the Enterprise*. London: Macmillan, 124–54.

Marmuse, C. (1999). 'Le Diagnostic stratégique: Une démarche de construction de sens', in *Actes de la VIIIème Conférence Internationale de Management Stratégique*. Paris: École Centrale.

Marshall, A. (1920). *Industry and Trade*. London: Macmillan,

Maskell, P., Eskelinen, H., Hannibalsson, I., Malmberg, A., and Vatne, E. (1998). *Competitiveness, Localised Learning and Regional Development*. London: Routledge.

Maturana, H., and Varela, F. (1980). *Autopoesis and Cognition*. Dordrecht: Reidel.

Mayo, E. (1945). *The Social Problems of an Industrial Civilization*. Boston: Division of Research, Graduate School of Business Administration, Harvard University.

Meyer-Krahmer, F. (1997). 'Public Research/Industry Linkages Revisited', in R. Barré, M. Gibbons, J. Maddox, B. Martin, and P. Papon (eds.), *Science in Tomorrow's Europe*. Paris: Economica International, 153–73.

Metcalfe, S. (1998). 'Innovation as a Policy Problem: New Perspectives and Old on the Division of Labour In the Innovation Process'. Mimeo, Centre for Research on Innovation, University of Manchester.

Milgrom, P., and Roberts, J. (1988). 'Economic Theories of the Firm: Past, Present, Future', *Canadian Journal of Economics*, 21: 444–58.

Minzberg, H. (1979). *The Structuring of Organizations: A Synthesis of the Research*. Englewood Cliffs, NJ: Prentice Hall.

Morgan, K. (2001). 'The Exaggerated Death of Geography: Localised Learning, Innovation and Uneven Development'. Paper presented to Eindhoven Centre for Innovation Studies, Technical University of Eindhoven.

Nachum, L., and Keeble, D. (1999). 'Neo-Marshallian Nodes, Global Networks and Firm Competitiveness: The Cluster of Media Firms in Central London'. Working Paper 138, ESRC Centre for Business Research, Cambridge University.

Nahapiet, J., and Ghoshal, S. (2002). 'Social Capital, Intellectual Capital, and the Organizational Advantage', in C. W. Choo and N. Bontis (eds.), *The Strategic Management of Intellectual Capital and Organizational Knowledge*. New York: Oxford University Press, 699–710.

Nelson, R. R. (1959). 'The Simple Economics of Basic Scientific Research', *Journal of Political Economy*, 67: 297–306.

—— (1991). 'Why Do Firms Differ; and How Does it Matter?' *Strategic Management Journal*, 12: 61–74.

—— (1994*a*). 'The Co-Evolution of Technology, Industrial Structure and Supporting Institutions', *Industrial and Corporate Change*, 3: 47–63.

—— (1994*b*). 'The Role of Firm Difference in an Evolutionary Theory of Technical Advance', in L. Magnusson (ed.), *Evolutionary and Neo-Schumpeterian Approaches to Economics*, Dordrecht: Kluwer, 231–40.

Nelson, R. R., and Winter, S. (1982). *An Evolutionary View of Economic Change*. Cambridge, MA: Belknap Press of Harvard University Press.

Nightingale, P. (1998). 'A Cognitive Model of Innovation', *Research Policy*, 27: 689–709.

Nohria, N., and Ghoshal, S. (1997). *The Differential Network: Organizing Multinational Corporations for Value Creation*. San Francisco: Jossey-Bass.

Nonaka, I. (1994). 'A Dynamic Theory of Organizational Knowledge Creation', *Organization Science*, 5/1: 14–37.

—— and Konno, N. (1998). 'The Concept of Ba: Building for Knowledge Creation', *California Management Review*, 40/3: 40–54.

—— and Takeuchi, H. (1995). *The Knowledge-Creating Company: How the Japanese Companies Create the Dynamic of Innovation*. New York: Oxford University Press.

—— Toyama, R., and Konno, N. (2000). 'SECI, Ba and Leadership: A Unified Model of Dynamic Knowledge Creation', *Long Range Planning*, 33: 5–34.

Nooteboom, B. (1999). *Inter-Firm Alliances*. London: Routledge.

—— (2000*a*). 'Learning by Interaction: Absorptive Capacity, Cognitive Distance and Governance'. Mimeo, Rotterdam School of Management, Erasmus University, Rotterdam.

—— (2000*b*). *Learning and Innovation in Organizations and Economies*. Oxford: Oxford University Press.

Nowotny, H., Scott, P., and Gibbons, M. (2001). *Re-Thinking Science*. Cambridge: Polity Press.

OECD (2000). Organization for Economic Cooperation and Development, *Knowledge Management in the Learning Economy: Education and Skills*. Paris: OECD.

Oinas, P. (2000). 'Distance and Learning: Does Proximity Matter?', in F. Boekema et al. (eds.), *Knowledge, Innovation and Economic Growth*. Aldershot: Edward Elgar, 57–69.

—— and Malecki, E. (2002). 'The Evolution of Technologies In Time and Space: From National and Regional to Spatial Innovation Systems', *International Regional Science Review*, 24/1: 102–31.

Orléan, A. (1994) (ed.). *Analyse économique des conventions*. Paris: Presses Universitaires de France.

Orr, J. (1990). 'Sharing Knowledge, Celebrating Identity: Community Memory in a Service Culture', in D. Middleton and D. Edwards (eds.), *Collective Remembering*. London: Sage, 169–89.

—— (1996). *Talking about Machines: An Ethnography of a Modern Job*. Ithaca, NY: Cornell University Press.

Paoli, M., and Principe, A. (2001). 'The Relationships between Individual and Organizational Memory: Exploring the Missing Links'. Mimeo, SPRU.

Patry, M. (2002). 'De la théorie de la firme à l'économie des organisations', *Cahiers de leçons inaugurales*, HEC-Montréal, 1–39.

Pavitt, K. (1984). 'Sectoral Patterns of Technological Change: Towards a Taxonomy and Theory', *Research Policy*, 13/6: 343–73.

Penrose, E. (1959). *The Theory of the Growth of the Firm*. Oxford: Oxford University Press.

Pestre, D. (1997). 'La Production des savoirs entre académies et marchés: Une relecture historique du livre "The New Production of Knowledge" ', *Revue d'économie industrielle*, 79: 163–74.

Pfeffer, J., and Sutton, R. I. (2000). *The Knowing–Doing Gap*. Boston: Harvard Business School Press.

Pine, B. J., and Gilmore, J. H. (1999). *The Experience Economy*. Boston: Harvard Business School Press.

Pinker, S. (1994). *The Language Instinct.* London: Allen Lane.

Pickering, A. (1993). 'The Mangle of Practice: Agency and Emergence in the Sociology of Science', *American Journal of Sociology*, 99: 559–89.

Polanyi, M. (1958). *Personal Knowledge.* London: Routledge and Kegan Paul.

—— (1962). *Personal Knowledge: Towards a Post-Critical Philosophy.* London: Routledge and Kegan Paul.

—— (1967). *The Tacit Dimension.* New York: Doubleday.

Popper, M., and Lipshitz, R. (1998). 'Organizational Learning Mechanisms: A Structural and Cultural Approach to Organizational Learning', *Journal of Applied Behavioural Science*, 34/2: 161–79.

Porter, M. E. (1991). 'Toward a Dynamic Theory of Strategy', *Strategic Management Journal*, Winter Special Issue, 12: 95–117.

—— (1994). 'The Role of Location in Competition', *Journal of Economics and Business*, 1: 35–9.

—— (1995). 'The Competitive Advantages of the Inner City', *Harvard Business Review*, May–June: 53–71.

Powell, W., Kogut, K. W., and Smith-Doerr, L. (1996). 'Interorganizational Collaboration and the Locus of Innovation: Networks of Learning in Biotechnology', *Administrative Science Quarterly*, 41/1: 116–46.

Power, D., and Hallencreutz, D. (2002). 'Profiting from Creativity? The Music Industry in Stockholm, Sweden and Kinsgton, Jamaica', *Environment and Planning A*, 34/10: 1833–54.

Prahalad, C. K., and Hamel, G. (1990). 'The Core Competence of the Corporation', *Harvard Business Review*, 68 (May–June), 79–91.

—— —— (1994). 'Strategy as a Field of Study: Why Search for a New Paradigm?', *Strategic Management Journal*, 15: 5–16.

Probst, G., Büchel, B., and Raub, S. (1998). 'Knowledge as a Strategic Resource', in G. von Krogh, J. Roos, and D. Kleine (eds.), *Knowing in Firms*. London: Sage, 240–52.

Quinn, J. B. (2000). 'Strategic Outsourcing of Innovations', *Sloan Management Review*, Summer: 13–28.

Rabeharisoa, V., and Callon, M. (forthcoming). 'The Involvement of Patients in Research Activities Supported by the French Muscular Dystrophy Association', in S. Jasanoff (ed.), *States of Knowledge: Science, Power and Political Culture*. Chicago: University of Chicago Press.

Rabinow, P. (1996). *Essays on the Anthropology of Reason.* Princeton: Princeton University Press.

Radner, R. (1986). 'The Internal Economy of Large Firms', *Economic Journal*, 96 (suppl.), 1–22.

Raymond, E. (1999). *The Cathedral and the Bazaar.* Sebastopol, CA: O'Reilly.

Reich, R. (1991). *The Work of Nations: Preparing Ourselves for the 21st Century Capitalism.* London: Simon and Schuster.

Reynaud, B. (1996). 'Types of Rules, Interpretation and Collective Dynamics: Reflections on the Introduction of a Salary Rule in a Maintenance Workshop', *Industrial and Corporate Change*, 5/3: 699–723.

Richardson, G. B. (1960). *Information and Investment: A Study in the Working of the Competitive Economy.* Oxford: Oxford University Press.

—— (1972). 'The Organization of Industry', *Economic Journal*, Sept.: 883–96.

Romer, P. (1993). 'Implementing a National Technology Strategy with Self-Organizing Industry Boards', *Brookings Papers Microeconomics*, 2: 345–99.

Ronstadt, R. (1977). *Research and Development Abroad by US Multinationals.* New York: Praeger Publishers.

Rothschild, M., and Stiglitz, J. (1976). 'Equilibrium in Competitive Insurance Markets: An Essay on the Economics of Imperfect Information', *Quarterly Journal of Economics,* 95: 629–49.

Rothwell, R., and Zegveld, W. (1985). *Reindustrialization and Technology.* Armonk, NY: M. E. Sharpe Inc.

Rouach, D. (1996). 'De la cession de technologie au management du transfert de l'innovation' (interview with Pascal-Marie Deschamps), *Expansion Management Review,* 115–19.

Rumelt, R. P. (1984). 'Towards a Strategic Theory of the Firm', in R. B. Lamb (ed.), *Competitive Strategic Management,* Englewood Cliffs, NJ: Prentice Hall, 556–70.

—— (1987). 'Theory, Strategy and Entrepreneurship', in D. Teece (ed.), *The Competitive Challenge: Strategy for Industrial Innovation and Renewal.* Cambridge, MA: Ballinger.

Sanchez, R., and Mahoney, J. T (1996). 'Modularity, Flexibility, and Knowledge Management in Product and Organization Design', *Strategic Management Journal,* 17 (Winter), 63–76.

Sarbrough-Thompson, M., and Feldman, M. (1998). 'Electronic Mail and Organizational Communication: Does Saying "Hi" Really Matter?', *Organization Science,* 9/6: 685–99.

Saviotti, P. (1998). 'On the Dynamic of Appropriability of Tacit and of Codified Knowledge', *Research Policy,* 26/7–8: 843–56.

Sawhney, M., and Prandelli, E. (2000). 'Communities of Creation: Managing Distributed Innovation in Turbulent Markets', *California Management Review,* 4: 24–54.

Saxenian, A. (1996). *Regional Advantage: Culture and Competition in Silicon Valley and Route 128.* Cambridge, MA: Harvard University Press.

—— and Hsu, J.-Y. (2001). 'The Silicon Valley–Hsinchu Connection: Technical Communities and Industrial Upgrading', *Industrial and Corporate Change,* 10/4: 893–920.

Schelling, T. C. (1960). *The Strategy of Conflict.* Cambridge, MA: Harvard University Press.

—— (1978). *Micromotives and Macrobehaviour.* New York: Norton.

Schoenberger, E. (1999). 'The Firm in the Region and the Region in the Firm', in T. Barnes and M. Gertler (eds.), *The New Industrial Geography.* London: Routledge, 205–16.

Sclove, R. E., Scammell, M. L., and Holland, B. (1998). Executive summary of the report 'Community-Based Research in the United States', The Loka Institute, Amherst, MA (www.loka.org).

Scotchmer, S. (1991). 'Standing on the Shoulders of Giants: Cumulative Research and the Patent Law', *Journal of Economic Perspectives,* 5/1: 29–41.

Senge, P. (1990). *The Fifth Discipline: The Art and Practice of the Learning Organization.* London: Century Business.

Shapin, S. (1995). 'Here and Everywhere: Sociology of Scientific Knowledge', *American Review of Sociology,* 21: 289–321.

Simon, H. A. (1957). *Models of Man.* New York: Wiley.

—— (1982). *Models of Bounded Rationality.* Cambridge, MA: MIT Press.

—— (1991). 'Bounded Rationality and Organizational Learning', *Organization Science,* 2/1: 125–34.

—— (1997) *Administrative Behaviour.* 4th edn. London: Free Press.

—— (1999). 'The Many Shapes of Knowledge', *Revue d'économie industrielle,* 88: 23–39.

Smith, P. G., and Reinertsen, D. G. (1998). *Developing Products in Half the Time: New Rules, New Tools.* New York: Van Nostrand Reinhold.

Spence, M. (1973). 'Job Market Signalling', *Quarterly Journal of Economics,* 87: 355–74.

Spender, J. C. (1997). 'Making Knowledge the Basis of a Dynamic Theory of the Firm', *Strategic Management Journal*, Special Issue NORDREFO, 17: 45–62.

Spinosa, C., Flores, F., and Dreyfus, J. L. (1997). *Entrepreneurship, Democratic Action and the Cultivation of Solidarity : Disclosing New Worlds*. Cambridge, MA: MIT Press.

Stalk, G., Evans, P., and Schulman, L. E. (1992). 'Competing on Capabilities: The New Rules of Corporate Strategy', *Harvard Business Review*, 70/2: 57–70.

Star, S. L., and Griesemer, J. (1989). 'Institutional Ecology, "Translations" and Boundary Objects: Animateurs, and Professionals in Berkeley's Museum of Vertebrate Zoology 1907–1939', *Social Studies of Science*, 19: 387–420.

Starkey, K. (1996) (ed.). *How Organizations Learn*. London: International Thompson Business Press.

Steinmueller, W. E. (2000). 'Will New Information and Communication Technologies Improve the Codification of Knowledge?', *Industrial and Corporate Change*, 9/2: 361–76.

Stephen, P., and Levin, S. (1997). 'The Critical Importance of Careers in Collaborative Scientific Research', *Revue d'économie industrielle*, 79: 45–61.

Stiglitz, J. E. (1987). 'Learning to Learn, Localized Learning and Technological Progress', in P. Stoneman and P. Dasgupta (eds.), *Economic Policy and Technological Performance*. Cambridge: Cambridge University Press, 124–53.

Storck, J. (2000). 'Knowledge Diffusion through "Strategic Communities"', *Sloan Management Review*, 41/2: 63–74.

Storper, M. (1997). *The Regional World*, New York: Guilford Press.

Taschler, D. R., and Chappelow, C. C. (1997). 'Intra-Company Technology Transfer in a Multinational Firm', *Journal of Technology Transfer*, 22/1: 29–34.

Teece, D. J. (1988). 'Technological Change and the Nature of the Firm', in G. Dosi et al. (eds.), *Technological Change and Economic Theory*, London: Pinter, 256–81.

—— and Pisano, G. (1994). 'The Dynamic Capabilities of Firms: An Introduction', *Industrial and Corporate Change*, 3: 537–56.

—— —— and Schuen, A. (1997). 'Dynamic Capabilities and Strategic Management', *Strategic Management Journal*, 18/7: 509–33.

—— Rumelt, R. P., Dosi, G., and Winter, S. G. (1994). 'Understanding Corporate Coherence: Theory and Evidence', *Journal of Economic Behaviour and Organization*, 23: 1–30.

Tell, F. (1997). *Knowledge and Justification—Exploring the Knowledge Based Firm*. Thesis, Department of Management and Economics, University of Linköping.

Thrift, N. (2000). 'Performing Cultures in the New Economy', *Annals of the Association of American Geographers*, 90/4: 674–92.

Toffler, A. (1990). *Powershift Knowledge, Wealth and Violence at the Edge of the 21st Century*. New York: Bantam Books.

Tracey, P., Clark, G. L., and Lawton Smith, H. (2002). 'Cognition, Learning, and European Regional Growth: An Agent-Centred Perspective on the "New" Economy'. Mimeo, School of Geography, University of Oxford.

Turner, B. (2001). 'Throwing out the Tacit Rule Book: Learning and Practices', in T. Schatzi, K. Knorr Cetina, and E. von Savigny (eds.), *The Practice Turn in Contemporary Theory*. London: Routledge, 120–30.

Tushman, M., and Nadler, D. (1996). 'Organizing for Innovation', in K. Starkey (ed.), *How Organizations Learn*. London: International Thomson Business Press, 135–55.

Vanberg, V. (1993). 'Rational Choice, Rule-Following, and Institutions: An Evolutionary Perspective', in U. Mäki, B. Gustafsson, and C. Knudsen (eds.), *Rationality, Institutions, and Economic Methodology*. London: Routledge, 11–24.

Vanberg, V. (1994). *Rules and Choice in Economics*. London: Routledge.

Varela, F. (1999). *Ethical Know-How*. Stanford, CA: Stanford University Press.

Vernon, R. (1966). 'International Investment and International Trade in the Product Cycle', *Quarterly Journal of Economics*, 80/2: 190–207.

Vicari, S., and Troilo, G. (1998). 'Errors and Learning in Organizations', in G. von Krogh, J. Roos, and D. Kleine (eds.), *Knowing in Firms*. London: Sage, 204–39.

Vygotsky, L. (1962). *Thought and Language*. Cambridge, MA: MIT Press.

Walliser, B. (1998). 'Structure et rôle de l'information et des croyances en théorie des jeux', in P. Petit (ed.), *L'Économie de l'information: Les Enseignements des théories économiques*. Paris: La Découverte, 111–22.

Weick, K. E. (1979). *The Social Psychology of Organizing*. Reading: Addison-Wesley.

—— (1995). *Sensemaking in Organizations*. London: Sage.

Wenger, E. (1998). *Communities of Practice: Learning, Meaning, and Identity*. Cambridge: Cambridge University Press.

—— and Snyder, W. M. (2000). 'Communities of Practice: The Organizational Frontier', *Harvard Business Review*, Jan.–Feb.: 139–45.

—— McDermott, W., and Snyder M. (2002). *Cultivating Communities of Practice*. Boston: Harvard Business School Press.

Wernerfelt, B. (1984). 'A Resource-Based View of the Firm', *Strategic Management Journal*, 5: 171–80.

Williamson, O. E. (1975). *Markets and Hierarchies: Analysis and Antitrust Implications*. New York: Free Press.

—— (1999). 'Strategy Research: Competence and Governance Perspective', in N. Foss and V. Mahnke (eds.), *Competence, Governance and Entrepreneurship*. Oxford: Oxford University Press, 21–54.

Winkin, Y. (1996). *Anthropologie de la communication. De la théorie au terrain*. Brussels: De Boeck Université.

Winter, S. (1987). 'Knowledge and Competence as Strategic Assets', in D. Teece (ed.), *The Competitive Challenge*. New York: Ballinger, 159–83.

Witt, U. (1994). 'Evolutionary Economics', in P. J. Boettke (ed.), *The Elgar Companion to Austrian Economics*. Aldershot: Edward Elgar: 541–8.

Wittgenstein, L. (1969). *On Certainty*. Oxford: Basil Blackwell.

Yeung, H. (2001). 'Organizational Space and the Geographical Foundations of Business Organizations: The Case of Transnational Corporations'. Mimeo, Department of Geography, University of Singapore.

Yin, R. K., Bateman, P. G., and Moore, G. B. (1993). *Case Studies and Organizational Innovation: Strengthening the Connection*. Washington: Cosmos Corp.

Young, J. S. (2001). *Cisco Unauthorized*. Roseville, CA: Forum Prima Publishing.

Zander, I. (1999). 'How do you Mean Global? A Taxonomy of Innovation Networks in the Multinational Corporation', *Research Policy*, 28: 195–213.

Zimmermann, J. B. (1999). 'L'Économie du logiciel libre', *Terminal*, 80–1 (special issue on 'Les Logiciels libres: De l'utopie au marché'): 149–66.

Zuscovitch, E. (1998). 'Networks, Specialization and Trust', in P. Cohendet, P. Llerena, H. Stahn, and G. Umbhauer (eds.), *The Economics of Networks*. Berlin: Springer Verlag, 243–64.

Index

DATE DUE
Fecha Para Retornar
